AGONISTIC POETRY

AGONISTIC POETRY

THE PINDARIC MODE IN PINDAR, HORACE, HÖLDERLIN, AND THE ENGLISH ODE

WILLIAM FITZGERALD

University of California Press

Berkeley · Los Angeles · London

University of California Press
Berkeley and Los Angeles, California

University of California Press, Ltd.
London, England

© 1987 by
The Regents of the University of California

Library of Congress Cataloging-in-Publication Data

Fitzgerald, William, 1952–
  Agonistic poetry.

  Bibliography: p.
    1. Pindar—Criticism and interpretation.   2. Pindar—Influence.   3. Odes—History and criticism.
4. Hölderlin, Friedrich, 1770–1843—Criticism and interpretation.   5. English poetry—Early modern, 1500–1700—History and criticism.   6. Horace—Criticism and interpretation.   7. Contests in literature.
I. Title.
  PA4276.F57   1988   884'.01   86–30923
  ISBN 0–520–05765–1 (alk. paper)

Printed in the United States of America

1   2   3   4   5   6   7   8   9

To my father,
Carrol Fitzgerald

Contents

Preface   ix

1.   Poetry and *Agōn*   1

2.   The Poetry of Reception   19

3.   Vertical and Horizontal: Pindar's *Olympian* 3
and Hölderlin's "Patmos"   48

4.   Progress and Fall   73

5.   The Hero's Extension:
Pindar's *Olympian* 10, Dryden's "Alexander's
Feast," and Hölderlin's "Der Rhein"   110

6.   Order and Violence:
Pythian 1, Horace's "Cleopatra Ode," and
Marvell's "Horatian Ode"   139

7.   Form and Force   170

Conclusion   191

Appendix: The Text of *Olympians* 3 and 10
and *Pythian* 1   193

Notes   203
Bibliography   229
Index   239

Preface

Pindar is probably the least read of the great classical poets. Even among classicists he is something of a specialist interest, for to approach his poetry requires engagement with the real, though perhaps exaggerated, difficulties of his language and his often bewildering train of thought and narrative style.[1] The *epinikion* is an unfamiliar, rather marginal genre, of which Pindar is practically the only extant exemplar.[2] Before we commit ourselves to the task of reading Pindar, we may well ask, "Why should we care about this hired praiser of aristocratic athletes?" Even hardy minds prepared to swallow the values of Homer's warrior aristocrats or the Spartan ethos of Plato's *Republic* for the sake of higher things, even these balk at Pindar.[3]

The history of Pindar's reception is one of controversy, but in spite of dissenting voices he has been steadily recognized as a major author, even if this recognition has not always proceeded from acquaintance.[4] Pindar has been seen as the inspired but wanton genius par excellence, an image that seems to conflict with that of the craven flatterer, but somehow the two have coexisted. As the ancient precedent for a poetry dictated by inspiration rather than rules, he has—along with Isaiah, to whom he is often compared[5]—provided the modern poet with a model and authority for breaking the "classical" mold.[6] Unfortunately, most of the poetry that claims him as its direct model is bad, or worse.[7] Some might say that the myth of Pindar receives more attention than the poetry of Pindar, though in recent years scholars have done much to debunk the image of a wayward and incomprehensible poet and to make him available to the nonspecialist and the general reader.[8] While my book does not assume that the reader has any prior knowledge of Pindar, neither do I offer a rounded picture of Pindar in the light of recent scholarship; this can be found in succinct and convenient form in the introduction to Nisetich's translation of Pindar (1980). My intention is to show that Pindar crystallized a certain nexus of problems and a poetic mode in which to contain them that have had a significant life in modern poetry.

Pindar's name is often raised in discussions of the lyric to advert to the fact that not all "lyric" poetry is subjective, inward, and asocial.[9] The name serves to indicate a blind spot in our understanding of poetry that will have to remain blind, because of our ignorance of the peculiar unity of words, dance, and music that constituted the Greek *mousikē* and because of our remoteness from the cultural events that it served.[10] But in spite of these problems the name Pindar can and should mean more to us than an uncharted region on our cultural map. W. R. Johnson has recently made a case for extending the idea of choral poetry beyond its original context of performance in archaic Greece. Johnson argues that the conditions under which we may speak of modern choral poetry are "that the agent and object of choral mimesis be present: the universal representative of the community singing for and to the community about the hopes and passion for order, survival and continuity that they all share."[11] My approach will differ from his in that I am less sanguine about the possibility of finding "the universal representative of the community singing for and to the community" in lyric poetry, even the odes of Pindar. I will argue that the community to and for which a poet speaks is not given in advance, but that the poem constitutes community, or its possibility, by a resistance to certain forms of closure and enclosure, and that community, insofar as it can be the concern of a poem, is a matter of forces rather than masses. Since the Pindaric is my subject, I shall take as my model for community the *agōn*, or contest, and will begin with an interpretation of this *agōn* and of Pindar's role in relation to it in order to frame an agonistic model for the poetic text.[12]

My title may recall Harold Bloom's book *Agon*,[13] but my understanding of this concept is the opposite of his, and I hope to provide a new context within which to consider characteristics of lyric poetry that have been interpreted through models focusing, like Bloom's, on the poet's struggle to possess voice against the threat of dispossession. Although these poets are, like Bloom's, also engaged in a struggle with "anteriority," the aim of this struggle is not supremacy for the contesting spirit but, rather, the dissolving of anteriority itself in order to open up a communal dimension. Another critical mode concerned with the possession and dispossession of voice from which I intend to adopt a certain distance is deconstruction. If many of my readings might have taken a more deconstructive turn, the reason that they do not is that these poets are not yearning for a presence or closure that is, in turn, subverted by the workings of language as writing. What others might take as signs of the tragic dispossession of voice I take as intimations of choral voice.

My study of the Pindaric mode will include several representatives of the English ode, a genre that has been treated in a different context by Kurt Schlüter (1964) and Paul Fry (1980). Both these authors took the ancient hymn as the classical prototype of the ode,[14] and my Pindaric perspective will result in a shift of emphasis. Fry's book is by far the most significant on the subject and it has been a constant source of inspiration; however, my approach to these poems will involve rejecting his emphasis on the hermetic role of the literary priest and on the exclusionary, monotheistic tendency of these poems' formal order, as I will explain at more length in Chapter 1.

In addition to the English ode and some poems of Horace, I will be taking the later poetry of Hölderlin as an example of the Pindaric mode.[15] Both Hölderlin and his influential forebear in the German ode, Klopstock, were heavily influenced by Pindar. The subject of Pindar's influence on Hölderlin is not new but, unlike previous studies, mine will focus on the common problematic with which these poets are concerned rather than on the specific Pindaric provenance of particular passages, poems, and general ideas (although naturally these questions will be addressed on occasion).[16]

I will not be saying much about the French Pindaric. Ronsard's Pindaric *Odes*, whatever their historical importance, are not very good. However, the very fine odes of Claudel and other twentieth-century poets such as Saint-John Perse and Pierre-Jean Jouve might well be considered within my framework, as I will indicate.

As for my comparative method, I am well aware of the dangers involved in making texts from different periods and cultural contexts speak to each other in a single conversation and have tried to respect these differences; my readings of Pindar himself are intended as a contribution to Pindaric studies, and I hope to keep open the channels of communication with classical scholarship which is, of course, also a language other than that of its object. Comparative literature is not the only viable form of literary criticism, but surely part of this enterprise must be to speak from the perspective of the *reader* of poetry as collected in a *library*.

Although most of the writers that I will be discussing were to some degree influenced by Pindar, and influence will occasionally be my subject, I do not claim that the Pindaric poems I analyze were necessarily sources for the modern poems with which they are compared. I will be concerned with affinities that derive from a common problematic which may not be explicitly connected with what is usually thought of as the Pindaric tradition. In fact, an exclusive focus on the superficial stylistic traits that are traditionally associated with "pindarizing" has been largely responsible for the marginalization of this poet in the discussion of the European lyric, and I aim to show that the practice of certain poets reveals a more vital Pindaric presence than the programmatic statements of pindarizers.

Most of this book consists of close readings, and I have quoted as much of the texts concerned as possible in the course of my analyses, but readers not familiar with a particular poem may find it helpful to read it in its entirety before turning to my analysis. I have provided the original and a translation of the passages from Hölderlin in the text; the translation is that of Michael Hamburger's bilingual edition (1980). The Pindar is quoted in C. M. Bowra's translations (1969) and the original Greek for the three odes that are treated in their entirety is printed in the Appendix. I have chosen these translations mainly for their closeness to the original text, preferring in general to work with translations from readily available editions of these poets rather than to provide my own, so that readers can have a complete text before them while reading my analyses. In some places I have indicated what a more literal translation would be, where this is important for the point I am making.

This book is an attempt to explore one side of a distinction between odic and lyric poetry that I touched on in a dissertation submitted at Princeton in 1980. There I treated Pindar in the context of lyric temporality and in relation mainly to poets of the more private lyric: Horace, Keats, and Rilke. I am very grateful to the supervisors of that dissertation, Froma Zeitlin and Robert Fagles, as well as to the readers, Sandra Berman and Glenn Most, whose criticisms made me realize that I needed to ask some different questions about Pindar and to place him in the context of some different poets or, in some cases, different poems of the same poets.

Perhaps the most profound debt I owe in the writing of this book is to J. K. Newman, my teacher at Downside School, whose inspiration brought me to the classics and taught me the importance of a comparative approach to the ancient texts. If I possessed his learning this would be a different book, but without his example it could not have been written.

My colleagues at the University of California, San Diego, provided the intellectual climate necessary for the writing of a book such as this; they have been the audience I have had in mind while writing this book. I would like to thank especially Page duBois, whose friendship, encouragement, and example have meant so much to me, as to so many classicists. The ideas for this book were formed in two courses I gave at San Diego, and my students in those courses, especially Rick

Swartz and Karen Shabetai, provided welcome stimulation in those early stages.

Finally, I would like to thank Paul Fry and William Mullen, whose generous, painstaking, and acute reading of my first draft gave me just the guidance I needed in preparing the final draft, and Doris Kretschmar of the University of California Press, who provided help and encouragement at all stages of my work. Pat Fox prepared the manuscript with her customary care and professionalism.

—La Jolla, June 1986

1

Poetry and *Agōn*

The root meaning of the word *agōn* is "gathering"; even Pindar can use it in this sense while celebrating a victory in an athletic contest, or *agōn* in the more common sense.[1] As the Newmans have recently reminded us, to lose the social dimension in this word is to fail to understand Pindar.[2] In the most influential modern appropriation of the word, that of Harold Bloom, it has come to signify precisely the struggle against social determination: Bloom's poetic spirit "portrays itself as agonistic, as contesting for supremacy, with other spirits, with anteriority, and finally with every earlier version of the self."[3] Bloom's *agōn* is motivated by the desire for a radical creativity, an usurping power, that seems for him to be synonymous with poetry itself: in his post-Miltonic tradition, *agōn* is "the struggle between adverting subject or subjectivity and the mediation that consciousness hopelessly wills language to constitute."[4] The poetic mode that I will be describing here is also engaged in a struggle with anteriority, but this anteriority is not experienced as a threat to the adverting subject—it is not a position that the subject seeks to usurp. Pindar's victor stands under the ray of divinity as Bloom's poet is transfigured by gnosis, but Pindar, unlike Bloom's reader, seeks not to locate himself in the same light but, rather, to create a path back from this isolation to the gathering that has produced it. But to what purpose does the *agōn* as gathering produce the separation that results from *agōn* as contest?

To answer this question, we can start by reexamining a famous passage in Homer. In the speech of Sarpedon to Glaukos in the twelfth book of the *Iliad*, Homer provides us with a rationale of the *agōn* in its most basic form: war.[5] Sarpedon reminds Glaukos that their right to the "choice meats and filled wine cups" and to a status comparable to the gods depends on the fact that they stand in the forefront of the Lykians in battle, where all may confirm that they continue to deserve their inherited social position. But he goes on to derive their need to fight from a different necessity:

> Man, supposing you and I, escaping this battle,
> would be able to live on forever, ageless, immortal,
> so neither would I go on fighting in the foremost
> nor would I urge you into the fighting where men win glory.
> But now, seeing that the spirits of death stand close about us
> in their thousands, no man can turn aside nor escape them,
> let us go on and win glory for ourselves, or yield it to others.
>
> (12.322–28, trans. Lattimore 1951)

Sarpedon and Glaukos are mortal, yet they are looked upon by their society as if they were immortals (312). They have acquired this quasi-immortality by turning the very place where the spirits of death stand close about them into the arena where *kydos* is won. Life, for them, is not an absolute value sui generis, but a chip with which one may play for *kydos*. The crucial part of Sarpedon's speech is the last two lines, where he says not "let us go on and win glory or die in the attempt" but (literally) "either we will hand (*orexomen*) the boast/prayer (*eukhos*) to someone else, or he to us." Faced with the sinister society of the spirits of death, in whose presence the warriors are passive and helpless, they construct a society based on reciprocity and exchange. The very *eukhos* that might confirm the individual's "being for self," as Hegel put it in a similar context,[6] becomes an object of exchange; the inescapable spirits of death see to it that this boast cannot be the inalienable property of any individual; instead, it becomes the shared property of the society constituted by the *agōn*, within which it circulates.[7]

The spirits of death standing about the warriors make war an action that is performed in the presence of the "ageless, immortal" gods, so that the community among mortals determined by the fact that they are not gods also creates a community with the gods determined by the polarity between mortals and gods. Homer's warriors, quasi-immortal in the context of the very *agōn* that proves their mortality, are the predecessors of Pindar's athletes, whose ephemerality is alternately raised and erased in his *epinikia*. At the beginning of the sixth *Nemean*, Pindar describes the relation between gods and mortals in a typical paradox:

> Single is the race, single
> Of men and of gods;
> From a single mother we both draw breath.
> But a difference of power in everything
> Keeps us apart;
> For the one is as Nothing, but the brazen sky
> Stays a fixed habitation for ever.
> Yet we can in greatness of mind
> Or of body be like the Immortals,
> Tho' we know not to what goal
> By day or in the nights
> Fate has written that we shall run.
>
> (1–7)

There is an absolute separation between the two forms of being, and yet gods and mortals both draw breath from the same mother, Earth, and, by virtue of the polarity that distinguishes them, they both participate in the cosmos that is formed by this distinction. I will consider this passage more fully in Chapter 7, below, but for the moment I would like to point out the similarity between this passage and the words of Sarpedon, which is that both passages present mortality as participating communally in something by virtue of a polarity through which it is individually excluded from possession of that thing: mortals participate in immortality by being its opposite pole, and the bronze sky remains a fixed habitation *with respect to* their nothingness; the warriors who cannot be what they want to be agree to create the possibility of a fulfilled *eukhos* by dividing themselves into winners and losers, killers and killed.

There is a myth that tells the story of this mechanism: the myth of Kastor and Polydeukes, tutelary deities of the Olympic Games (*O.* 3.34–38). This myth is told in full in *Nemean* 10, where its terminal position gives it special prominence.[8] Kastor and Polydeukes were the twin sons of Leda, but the father of Polydeukes was Zeus himself, while Kastor's father was Leda's husband, the mortal Tyndareos. In a fight with the brothers Lynkeus and Idas the twins triumph, but Kastor is mortally wounded. As his brother lies dying, Polydeukes calls on his father and begs for death:

> "Father Kronion, what release [*lysis*] shall there be from
>   sorrows?
> Give death to me also, Master, with him.
> Honour goes from one who has lost his friends,
> And in trouble few among men may be trusted
> To share in suffering." . . .

(N. 10.76–79)

Zeus reminds Polydeukes that he is immortal but gives him a choice: if he would escape death and hated old age, living on Olympus with Zeus and the other gods, he may, but if he stands by his brother and would share everything alike, then he will live half below earth (in Hades) and half in the sky, and his brother likewise. The ode ends with these words:

> He [Zeus] spoke, and Polydeukes set
> No double [*ou diploan*] counsel in his heart,
> But freed [loosed, *ana d'elysen*] the eye, and then the voice
> Of bronze-belted Kastor.

(89–90)

The loosening of Kastor's eye and voice brings the release (*lysis*) for which Polydeukes prayed, but whether this loosening signifies life or death is left ambiguous, for the twins will live alternately in Hades and Olympus.[9] Polydeukes' dilemma is that without Kastor, his mortal half, he is deprived of "honor" (*tima*, 78), for honor has died (*oikhetai*, 78) for one deprived of friends, but with him he is deprived of his "lot" (*lakhos*, 85) of immortality. Pindar calls the unhesitating choice of Polydeukes "no double counsel," but the passage abounds in a duality that seems to be the only mode in which Polydeukes can recover his single state of man. As a unit, the Dioscuri represent the divided status of agonistic man in the precarious moment when the human touches the divine.[10]

Ben Jonson uses the figure of the Dioscuri to similar effect in his great Pindaric "To the Immortal Memory and Friendship of That Noble Pair, Sir Lucius Cary and Sir H. Morison," an ode celebrating the moral victory of Morison's life. The death of Morison makes of the immortal pair a unit that is both single and double, and this paradox is projected onto the status of the poem that celebrates their friendship. Jonson describes his poem as an "asterisme" (line 89), which is a mark of punctuation that focuses the reader's attention on a particular passage (though the word also refers to the fact that the Dioscuri were identified with the constellation Gemini). But this single asterism of immortal fame is immediately complicated: in a remarkably dense wordplay, Jonson refers to Cary and Morison as "these twi- / Lights, the Dioscuri" (lines 92–93); the separated prefix, *twi-*, makes the lights both bright (double, twin) and obscure (twilight), and the word *twilight* is played against the translingually parallel *Di-oscuri* (double-dark),[11] once again linking light and dark. Unlike Pindar, Jonson follows the version of the story according to which the twins were separated in their alternation between Hades and Olympus: "But fate doth so alternate the design / Whilst that in heaven, this light on earth must shine" (lines 95–96). The punctual and punctuating asterism is here replaced by a temporally alternating design, controlled by a fate that is both providential and tragic. This substitution corresponds to the choice of Polydeukes, though naturally the specific rationale of the substitution is not the same as the reason for Polydeukes' choice. Polydeukes complains to Zeus that "Honor goes from one who has lost his friends" (line 78); he knows that honor exists only in a social and mortal context. Jonson replaces his asterism with an alternating pattern because, as I will show in Chapter 2, mere wonder at the "immortal pair" would isolate them from any significance they might have for the wonderers.

The Dioscuri become mediators between heaven and earth by virtue of their split fate, which is ambivalent in effect: the release or loosing with which Pindar's ode ends signifies both death and life, and Jonson's "fate" functions both as the negative or limiting force of the ancient Greeks and as the Christian providence. Hölderlin, in characteristic fashion syncretizing the story of the Dioscuri with Jacob's ladder, uses the Dioscuri to figure the simultaneous accessibility and inaccessibility of the divine to the human:

> und othembringend steigen
> Die Dioskuren ab und auf,
> An unzugänglichen Treppen,[12]

And bringing breath the Dioscuri climb up and down on unapproachable steps.

Corresponding to the ambivalent nature of the steps, which both link and, by virtue of their inaccessibility, separate, is the medium in which the Dioscuri appear: only at night are they visible, and in Hölderlin night is the historical epoch of the absence of the gods. The prophetic mediators between heaven and earth, who bring us "breath," perform their function by reminding us that we are related to the gods by virtue of our separation from them.

I would like to cite one final example of the "Dioscuri syndrome," as one might call it, in which the mythical figures are not mentioned, though the similarity to Pindar's myth is remarkable. In Keats's "Ode to a Nightingale" the immortal bird and the poet part company at the very moment that they become twins:

> Now more than ever seems it rich to die,
> To cease upon the midnight with no pain,
> While thou art pouring forth thy soul abroad
> In such an ecstasy.
> Still wouldst thou sing, and I have ears in vain—
> To thy high requiem become a sod.[13]

The bird's song gradually fades away and Keats concludes, "Fled is that music. . . . Do I wake or sleep?" putting into question form the ambiguity that attends the "loosing" of Kastor's eye and voice. After the uneasy experience of union with the nightingale, Keats undergoes the ambiguous release into a world whose status as reality will always be polarized with respect to the "drowsy numbness" caused by the nightingale's song. Like the "boast" that is possessed by the Homeric warrior only in the either-or of the *agōn*, reality for Keats will be one pole (but which?) of the pendulum swing that begins with the ambiguous moment of release.

With the passage from Keats we may seem to have strayed far from the realities of the athletic *agōn*. But if we take the *agōn* as a structure for containing and articulating the ambiguous status of beings who may experience, but not possess, divinity, then it will accommodate all of these examples. To enter the *agōn* is to have made the choice of Polydeukes, relinquishing the Absolute in order to reinstate it in the alternating design of community.

For all its concern with the meeting of gods and men, this mode is emphatically worldly. It does not conceive of the divine realm as parallel to the human or as a higher transfiguration of it; rather, it presents the two as mutually dependent and united in a single action. This is clearly the case for Hölderlin, who states that the gods *need* "heroes and humans and other mortals":

> Denn weil
> Die Seeligsten nichts fühlen von selbst,
> Muss wohl, wenn solches zu sagen
> Erlaubt ist, in der Götter Nahmen
> Theilnehmend fühlen ein Andrer,
> Den brauchen sie. . . .
> ("Der Rhein," lines 109–14)

For since / The most blessed in themselves feel nothing / Another, if to say such a thing is / Permitted, must, I suppose, / Vicariously feel in the name of the gods, / And him they need. . . .

Elsewhere Hölderlin specifies the need of the gods for a path, a need that is supplied by humans.[14] The idea sounds distinctly modern, and we may associate it with Hölderlin's more famous schoolmate, Hegel.[15] However, there can be few readers of Homer's *Iliad* who have not felt that Homer's gods need the warriors, perhaps even need them to feel vicariously in their name.

Turning to Pindar, we find this relationship between the gods and humans expressed by the story of Peleus and Thetis in *Isthmian* 8, a story that lies behind the passage I have just quoted from "Der Rhein." Elsewhere Pindar refers to the wedding of the mortal Peleus to the immortal nymph as the occasion on which mortals attained the limits of felicity, for it was at this wedding that they heard the song of the Muses.[16] The circumstances that led up to this wedding are recounted in *Isthmian* 8: Poseidon and Zeus are rivals for the hand of Thetis, but they finally agree to relinquish their claims when Themis (Right) prophesies that the son of Thetis will be greater than his father. She suggests an alternative:

> Let her have a mortal wedlock
> And see dead in war her son
> With hands like the hands of Ares
> And feet like the lightning-flashes.
>
> (39–41)

Peleus is her candidate for the bed of Thetis; the daughter of Neleus should not twice be allowed to let the "petals of strife" (47) fall near the gods. This is no sooner said than done. But here Pindar passes over the wedding itself, and also the song of the Muses, to focus on the birth of their son Achilles, and the slaughter he caused in the Trojan war. The wedding, elided in the narrative, is a transitional moment of joy and harmony through which strife passes from gods to mortals. As the gods agree to Themis's solution, the wine of the wedding is already turning to blood:

> They say that the two Masters [Zeus and Poseidon]
> Took thought for the common good and the wedding of
>   Thetis.
> The mouths of the wise revealed
> To them that knew not the young valour of Achilles;
> Who watered and stained the vines of the Mysian plain
> With the black blood of Telephos,
>
> (51–55)

Even the sexual aspect of the wedding is related to slaughter, for while the gods declare that "in evenings of full moon / She [Thetis] will unloose [*lyoi*] the lovely girdle of her virginity / To [*hyph'*] the hero" (48–49), the hero's son, Achilles, "set Helen free [*elysato*]. With his spear / He hamstrung Troy's sinews; for they hampered him / As he ordered his task on the plain / Of slaying men in battle" (57–59).[17] It is for mortals to play out the darker side of passion that will not ruffle the calm of Olympus, yet this grim role is allotted as a gracious gift from the gods and in turn provides the means by which mortals become godlike. Achilles dies in war as Themis had prophesied, and here Pindar supplies the one element in this myth that his audience will have missed, the song of the Muses, displaced from the wedding of Peleus and Thetis to the funeral of their son:

> Not even in death did songs forsake him,
> But by his pyre and his tomb
> The Maidens of Helikon stood and with many voices
> Let flow a lament.
> Even the Immortals thought fit to give
> A brave man, though he was dead,
> To Goddesses to chant in hymns.
>
> (62–66)

The circle is complete, for the son of the hero to whom the immortal Thetis was given is now "given" to the hymns of the Muses, and in the cycle of transitions the full round of experience has been run: mortals have provided the gods with a "path" back to themselves.

The relevance of Pindar's myth of the wedding of Peleus and Thetis to the passage from Hölderlin's "Der Rhein" that I quoted earlier is proven by the fact that later in this poem Hölderlin speaks of evening as a "Brautfest" (wedding) celebrated by gods and men while the sun is setting (lines 18off.).[18] In this brief period fate is "balanced" (*ausgeglichen*), but once it has passed, human experience is polarized into a day when "all that lives seems febrile and fettered" and a night in which "primeval confusion" returns (lines 217–22). As in Pindar's myth, the wedding is a pivotal point between two forms of conflict.

The pivotal moment within confusion that presents a grasp-able configuration of events is the form in which both Pindar and Hölderlin cast the human approach to divinity. For Pindar, this configuration is called *kairos*, and it is the human agent's apprehension of *kairos* that heals the rift between divine and human power.[19] Without the ability to apprehend and re-spond to *kairos*, human agency is shiftless (*amēkhanos*), ex-posed to the random fluctuations of terrestrial circumstance that make us ephemerals, that is, creatures who live from day to day.[20] But *kairos* is to be understood not only as the means by which the agent can escape the limitations of human power, but also as a principle of limitation by which that agent avoids exposing himself to divine, and human, envy (*phthonos*). The opposite of *kairos* is *koros*, which is that behavior which re-fuses to recognize the provisional nature of human achieve-ment and seeks to make permanent what can only be tempo-rary for humans.[21] So *kairos* defines the human approach to, and separation from, divine power as a mode of apprehend-ing the fluctuations of human temporality.

Hölderlin's affinity to this kind of thinking is best expressed in one of his theoretical works: "For the world of all worlds, the All in All, which eternally *is*, *presents* itself only in the whole of time—or in decay, or more genetically in the becom-ing of the moment and the beginning of time and world, and the decay and beginning is like language expression, sign, representation of a living but particular totality."[22] Here it is the apprehension of the "All" that depends on the rhythm of growth and decay. Hölderlin's study of the Presocratics is manifested in this passage: the cosmogony of Anaximander begins with an *apeiron* (unlimited) from which the cosmos is created by a separating (*krisis*) of opposites. This separation creates an order that is stable only in the rhythm of conflict between the opposites separated out of the original *apeiron*, a conflict that Anaximander described with a legal metaphor: one side commits "injustice" on the other, against which the injured party reacts with a corresponding injustice that not only rights the balance but produces a further inequality, and so on.[23] What is unsusceptible to the delimiting of perception, lacking a *peirar,* undergoes a separation that allows the judgment expressed in the legal metaphor. The birth of cosmos here is equivalent to Hölderlin's progression from being to self-presentation.

Hölderlin's phenomenological appropriation of this thought may be compared to Pindar's practical injunction to the victor to become what he is. The language of Anaximander's cosmogony is deeply embedded in Pindar's rationale of the *agōn.* Pindar sees the athletic *agōn* as a *peira* (test, trial) or *krisis* (separating, judgment) by which the contestant escapes the helpless silence to which the untested individual is relegated.[24] Pindar's "untried" (*apeiratos, I.* 4.32) aristocrat is equivalent to Anaximander's *apeiron,* and both of them must undergo a *krisis.* After the victory, Anaximander's pattern of action and reaction comes into play, for the victory causes an imbalance that must be righted by the encomium itself, which Pindar describes as a debt; furthermore, poetry *heals* the violence of competition.[25] But should the encomium exceed its own bounds and fall into *koros* (satiety), it will incur the envy of the victor's community.[26] As a result, the movement of Pindar's odes is distinguished by a persistent oscillation that is reflected by the structure of the triad. Each triad is divided into strophe (turn), antistrophe (counterturn), and epode (aftersong), and this sequence of movement and countermovement is usually played against the sense unit so that the encomium never stagnates in *koros.*[27] This kind of movement is common in Hölderlin, whose *kosmos* depends on a precariously maintained boundary between human and divine initiative in which the former is always in danger of transgression.

In the preceding I have been describing aspects of the mode that one might call, in a broad sense, choral aspects of the mode's agonistic straining to constitute a communal sphere. Sarpedon's description of the *agōn* shows us how the *agōn* itself depends on this choric perspective. One of the great gaps in our knowledge is our almost entire ignorance of the nature of the choral performance of a Pindaric ode,

though Pindar's treatment of the triad has left us with much
material for speculation.[28] Clearly, the fact that the odes were
sung and danced by a choir affects the notion of voice appro-
priate to this poetry and renders the identity of the speaking
"I" particularly problematic.[29] But before we seek a notion of
this "I" appropriate to the *performance* of the odes, we should
remember that Pindar refers in his odes to the various stages
of their being (composition, delivery, training of the choir,
etc.) and that he does not refer to these from the perspective
of the final *product,* the performance.[30] In other words, an ode
is conceived of as a process involving various agents rather
than as a score to be performed.[31] There is something para-
doxical in the relation between the voice of Pindar and that of
the choir that performs the ode, for the choir, executing the
dance movements that they have been taught by Pindar or his
agent, speak in the first person of the poet's *intention* to write
an ode and of the continuing process of writing an ode, with
its attendant difficulties. From the poet's perspective, the
composition of the ode is presented as a journey in the course
of which he may find himself going astray or may decide to
take a short cut,[32] but at the same time the audience is witness-
ing a formalized dance whose movements are regulated by
and, in turn, foreground the highly formal and recurrent met-
rical pattern of the triad. I will show, in Chapter 7, that the
verbal texture of the odes is distinguished by a conflict be-
tween subjective and objective moments of language that cor-
responds to this ambiguity.

Drawing attention to the choral nature of the Pindaric ode,
then, need not involve us in reconstructing the inaccessible
experience of the original audience which, in the poverty of
our knowledge, we have replaced by an experience oriented
about the more familiar poetic subject of the isolated written
text. Clearly the original audience must have been aware of
the multiple aspects of the voice and of the various levels or
stages of the ode's reality. The choral nature of this lyric is
complex and dialectical, and not to be compared to the simple
hymnic voice of a congregation lifting its heart as one. I would

prefer to associate the choral nature of the ode's voice with what I have described as the "Dioscuri syndrome," in which unity and identity are split and distributed over a process. We find that writers in this mode tend to represent their poems as open, rather than as the products of a fixed authority or as uniquely isolated worlds.[33] Just as Pindar often speaks in the future tense of his praise of the victor,[34] so Hölderlin represents his poetry as a *prelude* to the song (*Gesang*) that will eventually characterize our existence in the presence of the returning gods,[35] and both poets are capable of ending poems with a look toward future works or by deferring to another voice. Naturally, the utopian flavor of Hölderlin's historical vision is alien to Pindar; what they have in common is a sense that the voice is transpersonal (not *im*personal) and that its authority is not to be located outside the temporality of the process in which it is involved. We may include in this context the shifting of tenses in Milton's "On the Morning of Christ's Nativity," which distributes the voice between the Christian community celebrating the archetypal, and ritually recurring, event and the individual writer producing the first *true* account of this event.[36] As I will show later, there is some tension between these two aspects of the voice in Milton's poem, a form of tension that manifests itself increasingly in later exemplars of this mode, becoming almost tragic in certain odes of Keats.

In order to situate what I mean by the "Pindaric mode," and the sense that I want to give to *choral* in this connection, it will help to examine Paul Fry's interpretation of the ode. The classical precedent of the ode as Fry sees it, and here he follows Schlüter, is the hymn. The classical hymn, of the *kletic* ("calling") variety, invokes the presence of a deity. But in its literary form the hymn is not the voice of a congregation deferring to an external and transcendent being, but the exercise of a hermetic rather than a pastoral priestly role, and as such it seeks to *usurp* the voice of the deity. However, this enterprise is doomed to failure, since the distance and separation presupposed by invocation subvert the attempt to appropriate the power of what is invoked; the poet is, in Keats's words, tolled back to his "sole self" and exchanges the closure of poetic form for the ecstasy of participation.[37]

This model of the mechanics of invocation does not fit the invocations that frequently open the *epinikia* of Pindar.[38] Where the writer of the ode, in search of originary strength, must condense what he invokes, "banish[ing] all rival powers from its [the ode's] fane or triumphal setting," the agonistic poet diffuses, through the oscillations of human experience, the deity he invokes:[39]

> Lady Youth, herald
> Of Aphrodita's celestial affections [loves, *philotatōn*],
> Seated on the eyelids of girls and boys,
> One you lift with gentle hands of compulsion,
> Another with different touch.
> In every action the heart
> Desires not to stray from the right moment [*kairos*]
> But to have power to win the nobler loves [*erōtōn*],
> Such as waited upon the bed of Zeus and Aigina,
> (*N.* 8.1–6a)

The name of the deity, which Bowra translates "Youth," is *Hōra*, and the quality that Pindar here hypostatizes is a slippery one. Bowra was right to pick out the sense "bloom" (youth, beauty, etc.) for the content of the first line, but by the end of the first strophe the meaning has shifted to "season" ("any period, fixed by natural laws and revolutions," *LSJ*) and *Hōra* is replaced by *kairos*.[40] Pindar's invocation does not establish a confrontation across an intervening gap between two orders of being; as the bloom that is the herald of Aphrodite, *Hōra* may come upon us with gentleness or violence, but as the season or *kairos* that we may observe in our own action it is an instrument we may use to control.[41] *Hōra* is conjured out of an action rather than called down from some higher realm, and it is the experience of action that lends the invoked divinity its ambiguous status, both internal and external.

Fry's "representative anecdote" of invocation presents "the man standing at the gate," where the possible openness of the gate is a source of anxiety to the liminal figure who feels himself "exposed, edgeless, undefined."[42] This solitary confrontation provokes the poet to usurp the voice of what lies beyond the gate or, failing this, to close the gate in order to discover "the formal consolation of a whole in which to dwell."[43] We might take as our equivalent "anecdote" the passage in *Olympian* 1 where Pelops stands alone in the dark by the sea and calls out to Poseidon. Whatever edgelessness Pelops feels, as former lover of Poseidon and participant in divine life, he projects it into the *agōn* that confronts him, the chariot race undertaken to win a mortal bride: "For me this ordeal waits: and you, / Give me the issue I desire" (*O.* 1.84–85). Where the Pindaric experiences the edgelessness of the mortal, it finds a communal action that will contain both sides of Fry's spatial distinction, avoiding the anxiety that attends the definition of identity in terms of spatial boundaries.

Fry's solitary invoker has as his counterpart a single deity. Conflating Scaliger's six types of literary hymn (theurgic, valedictory, celebratory, genealogical, mythic, and inventive), Fry remarks: "Any ode necessarily takes for its occasion the happy coming to birth, through its own presentation, of the invoked power; hence it is 'celebratory.' But since a celebration is weakened if it has more than a single object, every ode is, in effect, monotheistic, and part of its business is to banish all rival powers from its fane or triumphal setting: hence an ode is celebratory and 'valedictory.'"[44] But the deities that Pindar invokes are not to be situated in an exclusive fane: they are woven into the fabric of human action and implicated in a continuum of divinities. In the opening of *Nemean* 8, for instance, *Hōra* is the herald of Aphrodite or, rather, of her "celestial affections" (*philotatōn*, 2), and these affections become the Loves (*Erōtes*, Cupids) that attended the bed of Zeus and Aigina. Pindar is more concerned with the ramifications of his deity than with its location. Where there are rival powers, the Pindaric tends to incorporate them, not to banish them, as I will show in connection with *Pythian* 1.

The example of Hölderlin shows the anti-monotheistic tendencies of this mode even in a Christian age. In "Der Einzige" ("The Only One") Hölderlin represents himself at first as "enslaved" to the polytheistic world of ancient Greece, where Apollo and Zeus came down to beget sons and daughters among humans. And yet, although he has seen "much that is lovely," the poet still seeks "the last of your [the gods'] race, the gem of the household" (lines 34–35), that is, Christ. But it is his own restless desire to possess this gem that he would banish, not the other gods. Overwhelmed with sadness because it seems that if he serves one god the other will be lacking, he confesses that he is himself at fault because he is too greatly attached to Christ ("Denn zu sehr / O Christus! Häng ich an dir," lines 50–51). The monotheistic urge is a poetic fault, a symptom of excessive subjectivity incompatible with the priestly role of the poet;[45] it is to be rectified by undoing the poem's own closure and uniqueness:

> Es hänget aber an Einem
> Die Liebe. Diesesmal
> Ist nemlich vom eigenen Herzen
> Zu sehr gegangen der Gesang,
> Gut machen will ich den Fehl
> Wenn ich noch andere singe.
>   (lines 67–72)

To One alone, however, / Love clings. For this time too much / From my own heart the song / Has come; if other songs follow / I'll make amends for the fault.

There were to be two more versions of "Der Einzige," and most of Hölderlin's later poems exist in several versions, which suggests anything but a "fane or triumphal setting." Hölderlin's undertaking to make good the fault when he sings other songs is surely modeled on Pindar's *Olympian* 10, a poem to which I will return in Chapter 5.[46] Recalling the public, professional stance of the encomiastic poet Pindar, Hölderlin commits himself to serving *all* the gods, relinquishing his private search for the "gem of the house"; he adopts a priestly role in which the poet must avoid letting the song proceed "too much from [his] own heart." The Pindaric, then, is to be distinguished from Fry's version of the ode, which "longs for participation in the divine, but it never participates communally, never willingly supplies a congregation with common prayer because it is bent on recovering a role that is not pastoral but hermetic."[47] Hermes is the god of treasure-trove, but Hölderlin would abandon his search for the gem that commands his love insofar as it interferes with the historical determination of divinity that his syncretistic vision supposes. Hölderlin's will to participate historically in the divine is also a will to participate communally, for it is threatened by the loving search for the "only one" that causes the song to proceed too much from his own heart.

Pindar and Hölderlin, the two greatest exemplars of this mode, both wrote during a period of social upheaval, a turning point in the history of their world. Hölderlin's relation to the French Revolution has for some time now been an important, and controversial, subject in the scholarship.[48] The ubiquitous storms and torrential rivers in the historical landscapes of the poems, the concern with the poet's relation to the "voice of the people," the utopian associations of "Gesang," all testify to Hölderlin's engagement with the historical developments to which he was a witness. Pindar, on the contrary, is habitually described as unconcerned with the changes that were tearing his world apart: his easy confidence with aristocratic values is contrasted with Theognis's tortured despair at the irruption of the *kakoi* (base) into the world of the *agathoi* (nobles) and at the confusion of values this had caused.[49] The *agōn* between the classes that Theognis sees all about him ostensibly has no relation to the *agōn* that in Pindar is the exclusive concern of the *agathoi* as a group; Pindar hardly mentions the *kakoi* as a social class. But Pindar's internalization of the social *agōn* within the athletes of the aristocracy is also a reaction to the challenge of the times, as we might deduce from the speech of Sarpedon: one has only to substitute for the ineluctable spirits of death that, standing about in their thousands, motivate the *agōn* of war, the Lykian masses who, observing their masters fighting in the forefront, confirm the masters' right to their privilege. Furthermore, while Theognis retreats into the bastion of friendship as the last, unassailable stronghold of aristocratic values, Pindar reaches out toward a Panhellenic aristocratic community transcending the individual cities and absorbing the social *agōn* within it.[50] In their very different ways, both Pindar and Hölderlin react to their historical circumstances by envisaging a community that embraces, or is constituted by, the *agōn*, the itinerant guest of an embattled aristocracy no less than the herald of the new, revolutionary age. Pindar was indeed a reactionary, but his strategy was more generous than Theognis's entrenchment, and the poetic mode that he instituted offered possibilities to poets of a very different political stripe.

2

The Poetry of Reception

THE IMPORTANCE OF THE LATECOMER

The first thing to be said about Pindar's *epinikia* is that they are poems of praise. We feel that we are perfectly familiar with this notion and, since praise is not an activity we rate very highly, Pindar is often written off as a mercenary flatterer. But the image of servility that this word calls to mind is contradicted by his insistence on his own presence, importance, and ability, reiterated at every turn. Is Pindar as much a rival as a servant of his patrons? Perhaps the dichotomy is misconceived in his case. If we forget the modern associations of praise and examine what it is that Pindar is doing to or for the victor in these poems, we will find that it is more appropriate to begin with those characteristics that tempt us to see him as a rival of his patron, the victor. A proper understanding of the encomiastic nature of his poems will allow us to see their importance for modern poetry that we would not call eulogy, and will also give us a context in which to understand the dangers of presumption that always concern the writer in this mode.

Pindar describes his poems as *engkōmia*. The word has entered the English language as encomium, where it means little more than eulogy. But the root of the word is *kōmos*, "revel," which refers to the gathering that escorted the victor after his victory;[1] the poem, then, is to be thought of as a kind of reception. Pindar's odes were performed on the return of the victor from the Games.[2] Sung by a choir, they received the victor into his social, genealogical, and historical community. The victor, who had been separated from his fellows in the trial of competition, isolated under the "god-given ray" (*P.* 8.96) at the

19

moment of crowning immediately after the event, was now assimilated into the community, which was reassembled and transformed by his presence.[3] At the Games his name and homeland had been announced, his family and city received into the history of the Games and of the Panhellenic community that they celebrated; returning home, he brings back a name and citizenship enriched by absence and the risk that he has undergone.[4] The plight of the loser emphasizes by opposition the importance of the victor's reception: "For them no such happy *return* was granted . . . nor did a sweet smile delight them as they came to a mother's side. But they cower in the byways, out of the way of their enemies, gnawed by their misfortune" (*P.* 8.83–87; my translation). It is this exclusion from his own community that the victor has risked, and Pindar speaks of the lack of the garlands of victory as an orphanhood (*orphaniai . . . stephanōn, I.* 8.7) against which the song of victory is "sweetly popular" (*glyky ti damōsometha, I.* 8.9).

If the poet receives the victor on behalf of his community and solicits a favorable reception from the relevant divinity, the victor himself quite literally receives the poet, who was not usually a countryman of the victor nor a resident of the city of the relevant Games; though he had his own city—and Pindar was a proud citizen of Thebes—he was also an itinerant professional who depended on the gracious reception of the host/patron, and this reception too was part of the epinician event. On a more significant level, we find the poet concerned to vindicate his own organic role in the victory and to present his undertaking as a continuation of that of the victor, in other words, to ensure his own reception into the world of the *agōn*. This is reflected in Pindar's frequent use of athletic and martial metaphors for his art, particularly significant in view of the almost complete absence of description of the athletic event.[5] Both poet and victor must have their undertakings received, and if I emphasize this rather than the notion of praise as being central to the epinician event, it is because praise in the ancient world was essentially an act of completion. We are told that in one of his lost hymns Pindar described the origin of the Muses as follows: at the celebration of his wedding, Zeus asked the other gods if they lacked anything (*ei tou deointo*), to which they replied that he should create deities that would put these great events and preparations into order (*katakosmēsousi*) with words and music (fr. 12). The event itself is incomplete, lacking, until it has been fitted into its *kosmos*.

For Pindar the victory opens up a path or, rather, a whole network of paths, that must be traveled if its significance is to be realized.[6] The victory reveals a chain of debt, from the victor's debt to his *phya* (nature) and ancestors to the poet's debt of song to the victor. The reason for this is that the Greeks were intensely conscious of the possibility that the victory might isolate the victor from his human context and that the fulfillment of a man's highest aspirations might remove him from humanity altogether.[7] The winner, as well as the loser, might never be received home. This danger that the victory may become an isolated absolute is a generating force of the poem itself. One of Pindar's finest odes thrusts off with a powerful negation of this possibility:

> I am no maker of statues
> Who fashions figures to stand unmoved
> On the self-same pedestal.
> On every merchantman, in every skiff
> Go, sweet song, from Aigina,
> And spread the news. . . .
>
> (*N.* 5.1–3)

The pedestal which merely calls attention to its self-sameness (*ep' autas bathmidos*, 1) isolates the victory, but Pindar's song refuses to become a static emphasis or even to characterize itself as an artifact; instead it undertakes a journey in which it announces that the young son of Lampon, Pythias, has won a Nemean victory "though his cheeks show not yet the summer, / Mother of the grape's soft down" (6a–b). Time and space are opened by the victory.

Perhaps the best commentary on this opening is that of a poem written some two thousand years later and influenced directly, I believe, by this poem. But it is not so much influ-

ence with which I am concerned here as with a poetic mode
and a problematic shared by the two poets. Ben Jonson's great
Pindaric, "To the Immortal Memory and Friendship of that
Immortal Pair, Sir Lucius Cary and Sir H. Morison," was writ-
ten on the occasion of the premature death of Sir Henry
Morison.[8] Although Morison died young, his life had been
perfect; like Pythias in *Nemean* 5, he had anticipated his matu-
rity in his achievement.[9] But the praise of this perfection
threatens the significance of the lives of those who survive
him. Jonson opens with a truly Pindaric "digression":

> Brave infant of Saguntum, clear
> Thy coming forth in that great year,
> When the prodigious Hannibal did crown
> His rage, with razing your immortal town.
> Thou looking then about,
> Ere thou wert half got out,
> Wise child, didst hastily return,
> And mad'st thy mother's womb thine urn.
> How summed a circle didst thou leave mankind
> Of deepest lore, could we the centre find.
>
> (lines 1–10)

The prodigy, reported by Pliny, of the infant who refused to
stay in the wretched world into which he was born presents a
partial analog for Morison, partial in the sense that it empha-
sizes the negative reflection of Morison's short but perfect life
on the imperfection of the lives of those who survive him and
are shut out of his "summed circle." It also raises the disturb-
ing possibility that the circle's perfection is empty, or at any
rate that its center is unavailable to those who live in a world
against which its perfection stands out; it offers us no comfort.[10]
The polarization of perfection and nothingness appears also
in the figure of the victorious Hannibal, who "did *crown* /
His rage with *razing* your immortal town." Pindar's ode began
with a negative version of the *epinikion* as a closed form that
merely underlines its own, and the victor's, identity. It was set
in motion by the negation of this possibility expressed by the
very first word of the Greek text (*ouk*). Jonson begins by con-

sidering whether the object of praise is in fact complete in it-
self, preempting praise by making its perfection depend on
the exclusion of its imperfect survivors. The summed circle,
like the "self-same pedestal," is the threat against which the
poem establishes itself.

Jonson's task is finished before it is even begun if the perfect
life of Morison isolates him from his community. But in the
third triad of this ode Jonson breaks the circle of perfection
with a famous enjambement that makes of Morison's tran-
scendence the prologue to a new community, linking public
and private, living and dead, and this world and the next:

> He leaped the present age,
> Possessed with holy rage,
> To see that bright eternal day:
> Of which we priests and poets say
> Such truths, as we expect for happy men,
> And there he lives with memory: and Ben
>
> Jonson! Who sung this of him, ere he went
> Himself to rest,
> Or taste a part of that full joy he meant
> To have expressed,
> In this bright asterisme:
>
> (lines 79–89)

The rage that separates Morison from what he leaves behind is
not like the rage of Hannibal that crowns itself by razing our
town. His leap may be followed by the inspired leap of the
poet, filled himself with the "holy rage" that Plato attributed
to poets. It is the example of "happy men" such as Morison
that allows the poets to imagine a "full joy" which, in express-
ing here, they hope to share after death. The separation im-
plied by Morison's transcendence is no longer exclusive; quite
the contrary, for it links the two aspects of the identity of the
poet, "Ben / Jonson." Morison's life continues both in "that
bright eternal day" and in the memory of his friend Ben, but
the persistence of Morison's life as remembered by his friend
depends on the immortality of the poet Jonson, whose pres-
ent song is an act of integration of the public and private, mor-

tal and immortal identities of Ben Jonson.[11] The rage with which Morison is possessed is a gift from the poets, which he returns by inspiring them to make a leap similar to his.

Jonson's enjambement is itself a leap, which opens the circular perfection of the epigram that haunts the form of the stanza in this ode: each stanza is made up of rhymed couplets of which the final one often has the effect of an independent epigram. The threat of a closed perfection is answered by a perfection that inspires. Pindar's odes are famous for their leaps of thought, and to write a Pindaric always involves some kind of challenge to formal regularity and propriety. In the fifth *Nemean* Pindar himself relates his leaping transition to the inspiration provided by his subject, in lines that clearly influenced Jonson:

> If my purpose is set to praise
> Wealth or strength of hands or iron-clad war,
> Dig a long pit for my jump from here;
> I have a light spring in my knees.
> Eagles swoop even across the sea.
>
> (*N.* 5.19–20)

The passage recalls the powerful insistence on motion at the beginning of the ode, with the ships on which the poem set out replaced now by the swooping eagle. A closed formal perfection is rejected by both poets in the interests of an opening out that will receive the victor (athletic or moral) into his community.

The tension between stasis and movement, or the open and the closed, in these two odes is but one manifestation of a tension that is intrinsic to the mode, insofar as the poet as celebrator finds himself in a secondary and possibly excluded position.[12] We find that the poet is as much a vindicator of the importance of his own role as a magnifier of what has already been, and this is because his calling is to act as a mediator between the intrinsic, divine, or vertically punctual and the contingent, human, or horizontally temporal. On the significance and success of his achievement depends the wholeness of human experience.

Pindar, who has been seen both as a groveling flatterer and a willful egomaniac,[13] regards himself as fully the equal of the patrons, though he acknowledges his dependence on them. It is with his own preeminence that he ends the first *Olympian*, although it is his association with victors that has made it possible:

> I pray you may walk exalted
> All these days of your life,
> And may I so long keep company with victors,
> A beacon-light of song
> Among the Hellenes everywhere.
>
> (*O.* 1.116–17)

As I have suggested above, this is more than just an expression of pride: if the encomium does not share in the victory itself, then humanity is shut out of its own highest moments. But Pindar's reception of the victory is a continuation of what the victor has done for his own *phya*, or inherited nobility. The primary meaning of *phya* is "growth"; it therefore combines a static with a dynamic sense, and this is reflected in the fact that the intrinsic, inherited status of the aristocrat must be confirmed in the test (*peira*) and risk of the *agōn*.[14] Pindar speaks of the victory and encomium as awakening the past of the victor's family and its ancient fame, which would otherwise slumber buried beneath the weight of time.[15] Through the victory the victor "becomes what he is."[16] The poet, too, brings about the conditions under which we can inherit what already is, but only on condition that his own activity be accepted as continuous with that of the victor.

The need for a continuity between the activities of praiser and praised operates also in poems that are not directly Pindaric in inspiration. There is probably no direct Pindaric influence on Keats, who knew no Greek,[17] but as a praiser Keats confronts a similar problematic in his odes. When he speaks of "things semireal" that require a "greeting of the spirit to make them wholly exist," he is taking a position similar to the ancient encomiast who sees praise as a form of completing reception.[18] At the beginning of the "Ode on a Grecian Urn," he addresses one of these "things semireal":

> Thou still unravished bride of quietness,
>   Thou foster-child of silence and slow time,
> Sylvan historian, who canst thus express
>   A flowery tale more sweetly than our rhyme!
>
> (lines 1–4)

More clearly even than in Pindar, there is a competitive tension here between the praiser and the praised, and a need for the former to vindicate his position, against the suggestion that he is superfluous. Pindar often speaks of himself as an athlete who completes the victory; here the situation is reversed, and Keats confronts a "sylvan historian" who can tell a tale *more* sweetly than he can, threatening to preempt the secondary poet. The urn is as round as Jonson's "summed circle" and as self-contained as the statue standing on its "self-same pedestal" that Pindar refused to take as a model for his ode. The marriage of the urn to quietness seems to exclude the would-be interloper, Keats, and yet the marriage has not been consummated, for the bride is not only "still," she is "still unravished"; her very stillness provokes the poet to see her as incomplete. It is this incompleteness that justifies the interference of the poet, which results in the urn's becoming "a friend to man," to whom it is eventually brought to speak in the much-discussed ending. Keats's "greeting of the spirit," like Pindar's praise, opens a path from a perfection and completion that would exclude us to the community that receives and is transformed by this perfection.

An analog to Keats's opening may be found in the most famous of Pindar's beginnings, chosen by his Alexandrian editor to stand at the head of the *epinikia:*[19]

> Water is the best thing of all, and gold
> Shines like flaming fire at night,
> More than all a great man's wealth.
> But if, my heart, you would speak
> Of prizes won in the Games,
> Look no more for another bright star
> By day in the empty sky
> More warming than the sun,

> Nor shall we name any gathering
> Greater than the Olympian.
>
> (*O.* 1.1–7)

Pindar begins with an absolute that, refusing any context, seems to speak for itself: water is best. We are tempted to ask "Best of what?" but clearly what makes water best in this case is its lack of all quality except its own, or the impossibility of comparison. Like the urn, to whose tale Keats can only point ("Who canst *thus* express"), water is indescribable.[20] The items that follow are all *comparatively* preeminent, and they lead, with a progressive encrusting of context, to the contingencies of the present undertaking: "But *if*, my heart, you would speak."[21] Water's absolute primacy, its lack of a defining context, is what sets the poem in motion, as does the silence of Keats's urn and the summed circle of the life of the infant of Saguntum. All of these represent the challenge of the complete to the completing poet.

In *Olympian* 1, water is a leitmotif whose transformations represent the transition from unmediated to mediated relations between the divine and the human in the myth, a movement prepared by the progression from the absolute to the contingent in the opening.[22] The myth tells the tale of Pelops, snatched by the amorous Poseidon and transported to Olympus, but returned to the short-lived race of mortals (66) when his father, Tantalos, abused the favor shown to him by the gods. It is on his return to mortality that he undertakes the famous chariot race in order to win as his bride the daughter of Oinomaos. Water features at the two crucial moments of Pelops's story. First, when the enamored Poseidon removes him from the mortal sphere:

> [Pelops], with whom the mighty Earth-Shaker Poseidon fell
>   in love,
> When Klotho lifted him out of the cleansing cauldron,
> With his shoulder of ivory, white and fine.
>
> (*O.* 1.25–27)

The "cleansing cauldron" from which Klotho lifts him suggests the bath in which the newborn baby was washed, which would make Pelops one who, like Jonson's infant, passes out of mortality the moment he enters it.[23] Water is here connected with a transcendence of the mortal realm. But Pelops is returned to this realm as a result of the transgression of his father, and there it is that he calls on his divine lover as he stands alone in the darkness beside Poseidon's own element, the grey salt-water (71).[24] Pelops asks for a divine completion to the race that he now undertakes to gain a human bride, and he substitutes a cooperative relation with the god, mediated by toil and risk, for the immediacy of the original appearance: "For me this ordeal waits: and you, / Give me the issue I desire" (84–85). In the world of mortality, Pelops must undertake the risk of the *agōn* or he will "sit in darkness / And cherish [literally, "boil"] to no end / An old age without a name" (82–83), and it is the threat of a nameless old age that brings him to the grey/hoary (*polias*, 71) sea. The theme of water, then, links the undertakings of Pelops the victor and Pindar the encomiast. Pure water stands for the Absolute, or the divine immediacy that is removed from human time or context. Pindar's opening generates from this Absolute a sequence of superlatives whose context progressively widens and leads to the contingencies of the present situation; water remains both distinct from and linked with the other contextualized superlatives. In the story of Pelops, the immediate and the mediate relations with the god are joined by the theme of water. Both the fallen Pelops and the secondary encomiast receive into the contingent world of mortality the absolutes represented by water, much as Keats finally receives the silent urn as a "friend to man."

We may detect in Keats's address to the "still unravished bride of quietness" an element of rivalry with the bridegroom, and this rivalry is connected with the urn's ability to tell a tale "more sweetly than our rhyme." Such aggression against the object of praise is not uncommon in this mode of poetry, in which the secondary or dependent poet must claim the importance of his own contribution if the object of praise is to have any significance.[25] Pindar suggests that the victor himself only has access to the significance of his victory through the encomium. This means that the poet does more than merely repay a debt owed to patron and victor. The beginning of *Olympian* 10 plays with the notion of debt as the poet announces, probably much to the victor's surprise, that he has forgotten his debt:

> Read me the name of the Olympian victor,
> Archestratos' son—
> Where in my heart is it written?
> I had forgotten I owe him
> A sweet song. . . .
>
> (*O.* 10.1–3)

By "forgetting" what is already there, inscribed in his heart, Pindar is able to reapproach and re-cognize (*anagnōte:* "read" or, literally, "know again") the victor, whose achievement has put him under an obligation.[26] To have paid the debt exactly as it had been inscribed would have been like making a statue to "stand unmoved / On the self-same pedestal." As in *Nemean* 5, Pindar here exchanges a static, timeless image of his relation to the victory (inscription) for a more dynamic conception of debt:

> From far away the future
> Has come upon me and made me ashamed
> Of my deep debt.
> Yet interest has power
> To deliver me from wounding complaints.
> See how the flowing wave
> Now drowns the rolling shingle
> And how we shall carry out our contract
> To his dear delight.
>
> (7–12)

The playful use of the notion of interest demonstrates that it is the poet who defines his relationship to the victor, however "inscribed" it might appear to be. Pindar's forgetting gives him room for maneuver, opening up the field of the future, whose demand on him he answers and appropriates in the metaphor of the ebb and flow of the tide.[27] The victory that claimed and marked him, prescribing what he owed it, now projects the poet into the future rather than tying him to the past, in relation to which he is always inadequate and secondary. Forgetting and re-cognizing the victory, he becomes part of it: the debt it imposes on him will be fulfilled through interest, and the victory will be released from its "self-same" nature as inscription.

Whether the victory is received into its true afterlife depends on the poet's ability to redefine the nature of his indebtedness, and this is made clear at the end of the ode. Here Pindar compares the relation between victory and ode to that between an aged father and his heir,[28] recalling the notion of interest with the word *tokos*, which means both "interest" and, literally, "child":

> Late indeed have they [the sounds of the ode] appeared
> By glorious Dirka;
> But as the son of his wife, long desired,
> Is to a father come to youth's opposite,
> And warms his heart exceedingly with love;
> (For wealth that gets for shepherd
> A stranger from an alien house
> Is most hateful to a dying man),
>
> So when a man has done well unsung,
> Hagesidamos, and comes to death's threshold [steading,
>   *stathmon*],
> He has breathed to no purpose. . . .
>   (85–93)

The late song refers back to the beginning of this ode and to the forgotten debt that will be repaid with interest. Here the song is a child or heir, whose late arrival warms the father's heart because his wealth will not now fall into alien hands. The *tokos* of the first triad figured Pindar's recasting of the debt owed to the victor so as to make the encomium the true inheritor of the victory, thus releasing the victory from confinement to its "self-same" nature as inscription. In the final triad, the father without a *tokos* comes to death's steading having breathed to no purpose. This static confinement is contrasted with the continuity that would be provided by a child of his blood, and it also refers us back to the original debt, for *stathmon* (root *sta*, "stand") means not only "steading" but also "fixed measure" (produced by balancing, *histēmi*). In other words, the simple repayment of the debt, a static balance between primary victor and secondary poet, would confine the victor as much as the steading of Hades confines the unsung hero. In the child/song-as-interest (*tokos*) both victor and victory find their true continuation, but this depends on the poet's establishing himself as one whose secondariness is his independence, his freedom to re-cognize.

Paradoxically, then, the poet as receiver of what he celebrates may appear as its adversary, insofar as its potentially absolute nature would relegate him to a radically secondary position. There is a playful aggression in Pindar's "forgetting," though it works out to the victor's advantage. This aggressive element in the encomium is even more striking in the religious context of Milton's "On the Morning of Christ's Nativity," a poem which was in part the fruit of his early studies of Pindar.[29] The Nativity fits well into a Pindaric context: although it has happened once and for all, its significance is annually renewed by the Christian community that *receives* Christ again into the human world. But, for Milton, the Nativity has not only already occurred, it has already been celebrated:

> See how from far upon the Eastern road
> The Star-led Wizards haste with odors sweet:
> Oh run, prevent them with thy humble ode,
> And lay it lowly at his blessed feet;
> Have thou the honor first, thy Lord to greet,
>   And join thy voice unto the Angel Choir
> From out his secret Altar toucht with hallow'd fire.[30]

Milton's "humble ode" is in competition with the "odors sweet" of the three wise men who celebrated the original event. The combination of humble zeal to greet the savior and ambition to be the first, or as that is no longer possible, the *true* welcomer of the divine child, is reflected in the double meaning of the word *prevent*, whose Latin meaning ("come before") only partially softens its more aggressive vernacular sense.[31] Like Pindar's forgetting, Milton's prevention claims to be true to the relationship it appears to violate: paradoxically,

by having the honor "*first* [his] Lord to greet," Milton will
"*join* [his] voice unto the Angel Choir." Suppression or fore-
stallment of the original greeting will institute the true con-
tinuity between this earthly voice and the angel choir, as
Pindar's forgetting of the original debt will allow the victory
an afterlife.[32]

The exotic "Star-led Wizards," with their "odors sweet,"
have no access to the real significance of the event they wit-
ness, which begins to receive its true context with Milton's in-
terpretation of the season in which it occurred:

> It was the Winter wild
> While the Heav'n-born child,
>   All meanly wrapt in the rude manger lies;
> Nature in awe to him
> Had doff't her gaudy trim
> With her great Master so to sympathize:
> It was no season then for her
> To wanton with the Sun, her lusty Paramour.
>   (lines 29–36)

This is the first stanza of the "Hymn," which follows imme-
diately on the passage just quoted from the last of the four
introductory stanzas. The earth's doffing of her "gaudy trim"
is a gesture that accuses the wizards with their "odors sweet."
Like the shepherds in the eighth stanza, whose unsuspecting
ears are ravished by heavenly music, the wizards are part of
the old world that is about to be renewed. It is Milton himself
who will forge a continuity between the colorful eroticism of
the pagan world and the strenuous militancy of the new era,
with the wonderful image of Christ as the rising sun/baby
Herakles (stanzas 25 and 26), an image that derives partly
from a passage in *Nemean* 1 describing the first victory of the
baby Herakles over the snakes sent by Hera to kill him.[33] As in
Pindar's *Olympian* 10, the poet who would continue the event
he is celebrating must first turn his own lateness to advan-
tage. Milton's use of the word *prevent* perfectly conveys the pe-
culiar nature of the Christian event, for in this poem the
Nativity is seen from a double perspective: both as an irrup-
tion of the eternal or ahistorical into the temporal world,

which receives its creator (who truly "comes before"), and as an historical event which involves the suspension (or prevention) of the pagan world, as we learn from the negatives that describe the *Pax Augusta* in the fourth stanza of the "Hymn."

Milton's paradoxical "prevention" of what has already happened links these two perspectives. Like Pindar's forgetting, Milton's prevention is benign, preserving in the "humble ode" the "*od*ors sweet" that it prevents, just as the figure of Christ, as the new sun and the baby Herakles, preserves the pagan world that has been suppressed. From the *timeless* perspective of the Christian worshiper ("This is the day and this the happy morn") the original celebrants of the Nativity can be reintegrated into the event from which the poet's later *historical* perspective must "prevent" them.[34] Milton's aggression against that which would put him in a secondary position is, like Pindar's, in the interests of a true reception of the primary event. For Milton, the dual temporality of Christmas, as single historical event and repeated ceremonial affirmation, makes it possible for him to "come before" the wise men. What is distinctly Pindaric here is the refusal of any absolute status to what has already been. As Pindar puts it, "the wisest witness of all / Are the days to come" (*O.* 1.33–34); the onward march of time is continually reassembling the past and receiving it into new contexts.[35]

THE DANGERS OF PRESUMPTION

In Milton's "Hymn," the poet appears in two antithetical guises: Milton associates his own calling with that of Isaiah, the humble mouthpiece of God ("From out his secret Altar toucht with hallow'd fire") at the same time that he ambitiously claims the honor "first [his] Lord to greet."[36] The fluctuation between active and passive is typical of this mode.[37] At the beginning of *Olympian* 3 Pindar uses a single metaphor, appropriated from the chariot victory he is celebrating, to express both his replacement of the victor and his dependence on him:

> the Muse has taken her stand at my side,
> And I have found a new and glittering way
> To fit to a Dorian sandal the voice

Of the choir's praises. For garlands
Bound on the hair exact from me
This holy debt,

(*O.* 3.4–7)

Between the strophes there is a shift in the force of the imagery,
which at first carries the poet's claim to an active originality and
then conveys the compulsion of the debt that derives from
garlands already bound (literally "yoked," *zeukhthentes*, 6) to
the victor's head. The very act of initiating speech is a pre-
sumption that must be compensated by a recognition of the
poet's subsumption in a context to which he is a latecomer.

The above examples show the anxiety of the poet who
must be both active and passive in relation to what he re-
ceives; should the poet presume too much, he will cease to be
a receiver. When the poet is a receiver of divinity, a mediator
between god and human, as he so often is in this mode, there
will be a danger of presumption in the poet's too active appro-
priation of divinity. The tragic fates of Coronis and Semele,
lovers of Apollo and Zeus respectively, attest that a direct con-
tact with the gods is fraught with danger. I will end this chap-
ter by looking at two poems in which these myths are impli-
cated in the poet's examination of his calling. The complexity
of the poet's anxious sense of his own activity is well ex-
pressed in Pindar's wavering at the beginning of *Pythian* 3:

I could wish
That Cheiron, Philyra's son,
(If with my lips I should utter all men's prayer)
Were alive, who is departed,

(*P.* 3.1–3)

Hieron of Syracuse, who commissioned this ode, is ill, and
Pindar expresses the wish that the great healer Asclepios,
foster-child of Cheiron, were still alive.[38] In these lines the
poet asserts his own desire, mutes it (*ēthelon . . . ke*, 1) out of
the suspicion that it may be an impious desire, and then re-
describes it as a common prayer. By the time it has been fully
expressed, there is considerable tension between the volition
emphasized by the first word and the caution in which this

extravagant desire is clothed. Pindar does not actually get as far as explaining why he could wish that Asclepios were still alive, for the wish shades into a long mythical digression from which it only emerges some sixty lines later to be applied to Hieron. But when Pindar readdresses his wish, it is modified by the warning: "Dear soul of mine, for immortal days / Trouble not: the help that is to be had / Drain to the last" (61–62). In the digression Pindar describes the circumstances that brought the child Asclepios to his tutor, Cheiron. It is a story of human presumption in the face of divine favor that spans two generations. Asclepios's mother, Coronis, pregnant with the child of Apollo, did not wait to have the semi-divine child before mingling the seed of Apollo with that of the mortal, Iskhys. Coronis is described as one of those:

> Who disdain home things and cast their glance afar,
> Chasing the empty air, with hopes
> Which they cannot attain.
>
> (*P.* 3.21–23)

Apollo sends Artemis to kill the guilty couple, but saves his child from Coronis's corpse as it is being burnt on a pyre and hands him over to the tutor, Cheiron. Under the watchful eye of this great educator, Asclepios becomes a famous healer. One day, however, he repeats his mother's presumption by raising a man from the dead, and suffers the same fate as she. Here Pindar returns to his opening wish with the words:

> —We must ask from the Gods
> Things suited to hearts that shall die,
> Knowing the path we are in, the nature of our doom.
>
> (59–60)

Pindar's own wish has been redescribed as "all men's prayer" (literally, "a common word," *koinon epos*) (2), and in its very formulation it uncovers a cautionary tale to whose authority it defers; looking into the future for the possibility of a cure for Hieron, it reveals a past that warns the poet against casting the glance too far. This tension between active and passive, assertion and humility, priority and dependence, is intrinsic to the *epinikion:* the competitor must claim his victory but rec-

ognize his limitations, the encomiast must glorify the victor
but avoid exposing him to envy (*phthonos*), he must assert the
importance of his own role in spite of his dependence (not
only financial) on the victor.

But if Pindar must abandon his potential wish before it has
been fully expressed, if he cannot bring health to Hieron in
any primary or literal sense, he still has a metaphorical heal-
ing to offer Hieron. Reflections on the limits of human hap-
piness and aspirations apropos of his restated wish brings
Pindar to the example of Peleus and Kadmos, who attained
the heights of mortal happiness:

> Untroubled life.
> Neither Peleus had, the son of Aiakos,
> Nor godlike Kadmos.
> These two, they say, had the utmost bliss of men:
> They heard the Muses
> Singing, with gold in their hair,
> On that mountain and in seven-gated Thebes
>
>   (86–91)

Peleus and Kadmos heard the singing of the Muses at their
weddings, for their brides were goddesses. Pindar uses a
medical metaphor for the solace this singing brought to their
former troubles, recalling the words used of Asclepios's heal-
ing: it healed their hearts (*estasan orthan kardian*, 96; cf. *tous
de tomais estasan orthous*, 53).[39] At the end of the ode, Pindar
makes the traditional claim that his poetry gives extended life
to those it celebrates, and, to stress the fact that this is his sub-
stitute for the aborted wish with which he began, he describes
poets as wise craftsmen (*tektones . . . sophoi*, 113), reminding
us of the earlier description of Asclepios as a craftsman of
painlessness (*tektona nōdunias*, 6).

The strictures on moderating one's aspirations (61–62) that
Pindar addresses to himself are probably meant to apply to
Hieron as well, urging him to accept the true longevity that
his poet can offer him rather than straining against his mortal
condition. If what Pindar has to offer is secondary and springs
from the recoil of his primary wish, it is no second best, being
truly rooted in the past and the conditions that attend mor-

tality. It is the poet who ensures that divinity comes to humanity as the Muses did to Peleus and Kadmos and not as Artemis did to Coronis.

The problems and nature of the poet's calling are nowhere more deeply probed than in the poetry of Friedrich Hölderlin, Pindar's greatest successor. In his unfinished poem, "As on a Holiday. . ." ("Wie wenn am Feiertage. . ."), Hölderlin treats the relation between god and mediating poet, which is for him the central problem of the poetic calling.[40] The poem revolves around the myth of Semele, like Coronis a mortal whose presumptuous behavior toward her divine lover (Zeus) led to her own destruction. Urged by a jealous Hera, she asked Zeus to appear to her in his full glory and was consumed in the lightning. Zeus rescued her unborn son, Dionysus, as Apollo had rescued Coronis's son, Asclepios. As one of the daughters of Kadmos and Harmonia, Semele is mentioned by Pindar in *Pythian* 3 (98–99), though her relationship is there described as an honor to the family, perhaps with intentional irony. Another Coronis figure, her mere mention in Pindar's poem reminds us that the presumption which had supposedly been exorcised is always ready to rear its head in human affairs. Hölderlin's poem breaks down completely under the strain of the contradictions implicit in the poet's calling. As Hölderlin presents it, the poet's task is to mediate the reception of divinity into the human world and, as often in his poetry, it is the gift of the wine-god Bacchus that affords an analogy to the gift of the poet-priest: because of the vine, "the sons of earth drink heavenly fire now without danger" ("As on a Holiday . . . ," lines 54–55).[41] But Bacchus is the son of Semele, and the possibility of a safe experience of divinity on the part of the "sons of earth" seems to presuppose the presumption of Semele, who demanded to see her divine lover in person and was destroyed by this experience. From the prose sketch of Hölderlin's ending, we learn that he fears that his own desire and need to approach the gods may vitiate the passive receptivity to the divine that is demanded of the true poet and priest of the gods: "Woe to me . . . when unrest and lack drive me toward the luxury / excess (*überfluss*) of the

gods' banqueting table."[42] Hölderlin here casts himself as
Tantalos, whose abuse of his privilege of dining with the gods
led, in Pindar's first *Olympian*, not only to his own punish-
ment but also to the fall of his son Pelops to the short-lived
race of men. It is to the fate of Pelops that Hölderlin refers
when he declares that he, the false priest, is cast down "far
among / below [*unter*] the living." At the end of the poem
Hölderlin becomes a composite of a number of Pindaric char-
acters: Tantalos,[43] Coronis / Semele, and Ixion (*P.* 2.21ff.),[44] all
of whom have in common their abuse of divine favor and their
ignorance of how to receive from the gods.

Although the myth of Semele holds the poem together, it is
implied but not narrated. The poem celebrates a daybreak that
is both natural and historical, for the forces that are recognized
in the awakening of nature represent the violence of the French
Revolution and the *Koalitionskrieg*. But the daybreak has been
preceded by a stormy night in which the trees have been ex-
posed to a lightning that comes to represent the unmediated
presence of divinity. Standing between the daybreak of the
historical manifestation of "the powers of the gods" and the
night of divine immediacy, the poet reflects on the role and
perils of the mediating poet. But this description of the poem
belies its complex shifting of perspective. The poem begins
with an extended simile starting, in true Pindaric fashion,
with the *comparatum:*[45]

> Wie wenn am Feiertage, das Feld zu sehn
> Ein Landmann geht, des Morgens, wenn
> Aus heisser Nacht die kühlenden Blize fielen
> Die ganze Zeit und fern noch tönet der Donner,
> In sein Gestade wieder tritt der Strom,
> Und frisch der Boden grünt
> Und von des Himmels erfreuendem Reegen
> Der Weinstok trauft und glänzend
> In stiller Sonne stehn die Bäume des Haines:
> (lines 1–9)

As on a holiday, to see the field / A countryman goes out, at
morning, when / Out of hot night the cooling flashes had
fallen / For hours on end, and thunder still rumbles afar, / The
river enters its banks once more, / New verdure sprouts from
the soil, / And with the gladdening rain of heaven / The grape-

vine drips, and gleaming / In tranquil sunlight stand the trees
of the grove:

Hölderlin's holiday (*Feiertag*) is the same combination of cele-
bration (*Feier*) and release from toil or danger that Pindar saw
in the athletic victory.[46] The focus of the simile seems to be the
countryman whose fear for his vineyard, which has been ex-
posed to a storm all night, is set to rest when, on going out in
the morning, he finds it gleaming and refreshed. The danger-
ous immediacy of the divine, of Zeus's thunderbolts, has
passed away, and the countryman experiences it only in its
aftermath, the mediate brilliance of the trees dripping in the
sun. The final line of the stanza, surely one of the most beau-
tiful Hölderlin ever wrote, describes the vibrant presence of
the trees under the countryman's thankful gaze. Now that his
fears have been dispelled, he sees the grove as though for the
first time, and everywhere he finds signs of a divine fury con-
verted to beneficence. This conversion is something for which
he can only give thanks; it has not been an object of direct
experience. In a sense, the mode in which the poem begins
("*As* on a holiday") casts the poet in much the same situation
of distance from the immediate or primary as the content of
the simile does the relieved countryman.

But the shift to the *comparandum* of the simile at the begin-
ning of the second stanza initiates the approach to immediacy
that is the main movement of the poem. Here Hölderlin makes
a radical, but characteristically Pindaric, change in the focus
of the simile from the countryman to the trees:[47]

> So stehn sie unter günstiger Witterung
> Sie die kein Meister allein, die wunderbar
> Allgegenwärtig erzieht in leichtem Umfangen
> Die mächtige, die göttlichschöne Natur.
> (lines 10–13)

> So now in favourable weather they stand / Whom no master
> teaches, but in / A light embrace, miraculously omnipresent, /
> God-like in power and beauty, Nature brings up.

The trees are the poets, who link the night of divine imme-
diacy that they have survived to the day in which the divine
gifts are received. Hölderlin adapts Pindar's favorite distinc-

tion between poets who are taught and poets, like himself, who know by nature to make the more humble point that the poets/trees are brought up by a Nature that is "godlike in power and beauty." With this emphasis on nature/Nature both poets are pointing to that from which their poetry derives its authentic being, the solid base without which their words have no weight.[48] As Hölderlin moves closer to the divine storm by shifting the focus from countryman to trees, he strikes deeper roots in Nature's "light embrace." The trees' standing acquires a more dynamic sense as it is carried from one strophe to the next: no longer simply a glorious apparition for the countryman, it is now an act of endurance through time. The trees stand "unter günstiger Witterung," both under the favorable weather (*Witterung*) described in the first strophe and in the keen-scented apprehension (*Wittern*) of the next:

> Drum wenn zu schlafen sie scheint zu Zeiten des Jahrs
> Am Himmel oder unter den Pflanzen oder den Völkern
> So trauert der Dichter Angesicht auch,
> Sie scheinen allein zu seyn, doch ahnen sie immer.
> Den ahnend ruhet sie selbst auch.
>
> (lines 14–19)

So when she seems to be sleeping at times of the year / Up in the sky or among plants or the peoples, / The poets' faces likewise are sad, / They seem to be alone, but are always divining, / For divining too she herself is at rest.

The poem begins with a day of rest that puts a distance between the fearful night of divinity and the day in which the countryman visits his grove. But this rest is now interpreted as divining (*ahnen*) on the part of the trees (or poets), who have experienced at first hand the storm that is now only a distant rumbling for the countryman.[49]

Beginning experimentally at a safe distance from divine immediacy, the poem circles around the opening situation to realize the conditions under which it can reintroduce the divine storm as an immediate experience of the poets. This movement toward a confrontation with divinity, or a moment of origin that is prior to the secondary moment of celebration, is typical of Pindar's odes.[50] For Hölderlin, the firm rooting of the poet in Nature and his patient participation in its divining are the conditions of his having the pure hands necessary to receive the Father's ray (line 58) without being destroyed. The poem returns several times to its own beginning as it creates the context in which the dangerous night which that beginning had *survived* can be *experienced*.

At the beginning of the third stanza (or first epode), the poet who has stood in the embrace of Nature's divining sleep declares, "But now day breaks" (line 19). His waiting is rewarded by the experience of a wakening of Nature amid the clang of arms and of a new emergence from chaos (lines 23–35). This eruption in Nature now *coincides* with the break of a new day, rather than ending with it, and at the beginning of the second triad the countryman is replaced:

> Und wie im Aug' ein Feuer dem Manne glänzt,
> Wenn hohes er entwarf; so ist
> Von neuem an den Zeichen, den Thaten der Welt jezt
> Ein Feuer angezündet in Seelen der Dichter.
> (lines 28–31)

And as a fire gleams in the eye of that man / Who has conceived a lofty design, / Once more by the tokens, the deeds of the world now / A fire has been lit in the souls of the poets.

There is no holiday release from a threatening past here, but instead the igniting of a conception that has been deeply meditated. It is a moment of recognition of that which happened before but hardly was felt (line 32).

But this introduces another circling movement in which the poet's roots in Nature, his long familiarity with the thoughts of the communal spirit as they manifest themselves in the storms that drift between heaven and earth and amid the people (lines 42–43), all this prepares for a new approach to the unmediated confrontation with divinity that preceded the "holiday" with which the poem began. It is here, at the beginning of the second triad, that Hölderlin introduces the myth of Semele. The thoughts of the communal spirit come to rest in the poet's soul:

Dass schnellbetroffen sie, Unendlichem
Bekannt seit langer Zeit, von Erinnerung
Erbebt, und ihr, von heilgem Stral entzündet,
Die Frucht in Liebe geboren, der Götter und Menschen Werk
Der Gesang, damit er beiden zeuge, glükt.
So fiel, wie Dichter sagen, da sie sichtbar
Den Gott zu sehen begehrte, sein Bliz auf Semeles Haus
Und die göttlichgetroffne gebar,
Die Frucht des Gewitters, den heiligen Bacchus.

(lines 45–53)

So that quickly struck and long familiar / To infinite powers, it shakes / With recollection and kindled by / The holy ray, that fruit conceived in love, the work of gods and men, / To bear witness to both, the song succeeds. / So once, the poets tell, when she desired to see / The god in person, visible, did his lightning fall / On Semele's house, and the divinely struck gave birth to / The thunderstorm's fruit, to holy Bacchus.

The song is conceived as the divine ray of lightning quickens recollection; it bears witness to the union of mortal and divinity. But the myth of Semele reminds us that divine self-revelation may be prompted by the foolish desire of a mortal for an immediacy that the mortal may not survive. For the moment, Hölderlin suppresses the fate of Semele to foreground the birth of Bacchus, an important figure in his poetry for reasons that are expressed at the beginning of the third triad:

Und daher trinken himmlisches Feuer jezt
Die Erdensöhne ohne Gefahr.
Doch uns gebührt es, unter Gottes Gewittern,
Ihr Dichter! mit entblösstem Haupte zu stehen,
Des Vaters Strahl, ihn selbst, mit eigner Hand
Zu fassen und dem Volk ins Lied
Gehüllt die himmlische Gaabe zu reichen.

(lines 54–60)

And hence it is that without danger now / The sons of earth drink heavenly fire. / Yet, fellow poets, us it behoves to stand / Bare-headed beneath God's thunderstorms, / To grasp the Father's ray, no less, with our own two hands / And, wrapping in song the heavenly gift, / To offer it to the people.

The first triad began with a simile depicting the vineyard's survival of the divine storm; the third begins with a reference to the myth that accounts for the mediate availability of divine fire in the fruit of the vine. From a myth told by the poets, Hölderlin turns to address the poets themselves, recapitulating the movement from the countryman's viewing of the trees to the situation of the trees themselves in the first triad. The duty of the poets is to stand "bare-headed beneath God's thunderstorms" and to receive the "Father's ray" in their own hands without the protective distance of myth; that protection is for the people, to whom the poets offer the heavenly gift wrapped in song.[51] But, conversely, the poet only keeps his hands pure enough to receive the divine ray if he is rooted in the life of the "communal spirit." Abandoning the protection of myth, Hölderlin finally reaches the moment that could not be represented at the beginning of the poem *as* its starting point any more than could the wish that Pindar presents in conditional form at the beginning of the third *Pythian*. In this immediacy the poet must keep his heart pure if he is not to suffer the fate of Semele:

> Denn sind nur reinen Herzens,
> Wie Kinder, wir, sind schuldlos unsere Hände,
>
> Des Vaters Stral, der reine versengt es nicht
> Und tieferschüttert, die Leiden des Stärkeren
> Mitleidend, bleibt in den hochherstürzenden Stürmen
> Des Gottes, wenn er nahet, das Herz doch fest.
>
> (lines 61–66)

For only if we are pure in heart / Like children, and our hands are guiltless, / The Father's ray, the pure, will not sear our hearts / And, deeply convulsed, and sharing his sufferings / Who is stronger than we are, yet in the far-flung, down-rushing storms of / The God, when he draws near, will the heart stand fast.

Here the poem breaks off and we have only fragments, beginning "But woe is me! When with (a self-inflicted wound my heart is bleeding, and peace is deeply lost to me, and freely chosen modest self-contentment, and when unrest and lack drive me toward the luxury of the gods' banqueting table)." Szondi's work on the manuscript of this poem has demonstrated that what Hölderlin fears is that his own approach to divine immediacy may be motivated, like Semele's, by personal desires and sufferings that preempt the passive receptivity that is demanded of the poet-priest.[52] The poem collapses under a form of the tension between primary and secondary that is experienced by all the poets who work in this mode. In this case it is not a matter of the secondary, or receiving, poet rescuing the primary event from its potential isolation but, rather, the converse: the poet fears that his own dissatisfaction with his secondary condition ("unrest and lack") will draw him toward a confrontation with the gods that he will not survive because he will have no context into which to receive the gods.

Hölderlin's "Wie wenn am Feiertage . . . ," his first, and in many ways most thoroughgoing, attempt at the Pindaric style that will dominate the late hymns, marks a turning point in his career: it is, as Szondi has shown, the beginning of his late style. The importance of Pindar's example for the late Hölderlin is confirmed by the Pindar fragments of 1803 in which the translation and commentary develop some of the thoughts most characteristic of Hölderlin's late period.[53] The fragment "Von der Wahrheit" is particularly germane to "Wie Wenn am Feiertage. . . ." The other modern poems I have considered in this chapter play a similar role in their respective poets' careers. Milton's "On the Morning of Christ's Nativity" is deliberately presented as the debut of a new poet.[54] Keats's ode, written in the mode though not the style of Pindar, is of course one of the four written in the great spring of 1817, when his thinking took on new dimensions. Jonson's Cary-Morison ode finds the fifty-six-year-old poet testing his moral and aesthetic norms as they had been defined in his earlier epigrams and dramas. To these examples we might add those of Horace, Ronsard, Cowley, and Hopkins, for all of whom the example of Pindar plays a vital role at crucial testing-points of their poetic careers.[55]

In this chapter I have stressed the problematical relationship between the primary and the secondary as it has been typified by Pindar's conception of his role as encomiast. On the poet's reception of the Absolute or Immediate depends the wholeness of our existence. Pindar's statue, Jonson's "summed circle," and Keats's urn represent the threat of discontinuity between our godlike and our ephemeral aspects. It is against this threat that the poet asserts himself to vindicate the poetic calling, but in so doing he receives the Absolute into the context or community in which it alone can have meaning. The dialectic of threat and vindication accounts for the often contradictory stance of the poet, the combination of aggressive rivalry and humble dependence that permeates this mode. As Hölderlin approaches the moment when he must himself adopt the role of the presumptuous Semele, he humbly spreads his roots wider in the embrace of Nature/the communal spirit, so that his hand and heart will be pure enough to receive the "Father's ray."

Hölderlin's conception of history, which is described in its basic form in the elegy "Bread and Wine," is at the root of his conception of the poet's task in "As on a Holiday . . ." as well as in other poems. According to Hölderlin, we come after the day of divine revelation, which occurred in ancient Greece, and we live in a night in which it is the poet's task to bring about the conditions that will allow for the return of the gods:

> Aber Freund! wir kommen zu spät. Zwar leben die Götter,
> Aber über dem Haupt droben in anderer Welt.
> Endlos wirken sie da und scheinens wenig zu achten,
> Ob wir leben, so sehr schonen die Himmlischen uns.
> Denn nicht immer vermag ein schwaches Gefäss sie zu
> fassen,
> Nur zu Zeiten erträgt göttliche Fülle der Mensch.
> Traum von ihnen ist drauf das Leben. Aber das Irrsal
> Hilft, wie Schlummer und stark machet die Not und die
> Nacht,
> Bis dass Helden genug in der ehernen Wiege gewachsen,
> Herzen an Kraft, wie sonst, ähnlich den Himmlischen
> sind.
> Donnernd kommen sie drauf. Indessen dünket mir öfters.
> Besser zu schlafen, wie so ohne Genossen zu sein,
> So zu harren und was zu thun indess und zu sagen,
> Weiss ich nicht und wozu Dichter in dürftiger Zeit?
> Aber sie sind, sagst du, wie des Weingotts heilige Priester,
> Welche von Lande zu Land zogen in heiliger Nacht.
> (lines 135–45)

But my friend, we have come too late. Though the gods are living, / Over our heads they live, up in a different world. /

Endlessly there they act and, such is their kind wish to spare us, / Little they seem to care whether we live or do not. / For not always a frail, a delicate vessel can hold them. / Only at times can our kind bear the full impact of gods. / Ever after our life is dream about them. But frenzy, / Wandering, helps, like sleep; night and distress makes us strong / Till in the cradle of steel heroes enough have been fostered, / Hearts in strength can match heavenly strength as before. / Thundering then they come. / But meanwhile too often I think it's / Better to sleep than to be friendless as we are, alone, / Always waiting, and what to do or say in the meantime / I don't know, and who wants poets at all in lean years? / But they are, you say, like the holy ones, priests of the wine-god / Who in holy Night roamed from one place to the next.

The new appearance of the gods is one that the poets of the night of divine absence must consciously earn, unlike the original appearance, which occurred without notice (*unempfunden*, line 113). The poet of "As on a Holiday . . ." inhabits the intermediate period after the spontaneous thunderstorm and before the return of the "Father's ray," though he offers little hope that we are ready for that return. Although Pindar has no such historical vision as Hölderlin, we may take the story of Pelops in the first *Olympian* as a mythical description of the situation of both encomiast and agonist; the ode is very much programmatic for the *epinikia*.[56] What the story tells is the exchanging of an immediate for a mediate relation with the divine. The fallen Pelops speaks to his divine lover from the darkness of mortality and asks that Poseidon give a prosperous issue to the test that Pelops will himself undertake; the god will not appear spontaneously, as he did when Pelops emerged from the "pure cauldron"; instead, he is to become an aspect of the *agōn* that Pelops, standing alone by the gray, hoary sea, announces he will undertake. The *agōn* must be undertaken by the mortal Pelops lest he should "sit in darkness and cherish [*hepsoi*, 83] to no end an old age without a name."[57] We are reminded that the reason for Pelops's return to mortality was the inability of his father, Tantalos, to digest (*katapepsai*, 55) a mighty fortune, that is, his feasting with the gods. The human failure to assimilate divine presence casts humanity into a darkness in which time does not assimilate anything but merely attenuates identity. Against this situation the *agōn* provides as remedy a form of action that avoids both Tantalos's *hybris* and the namelessness of a god-forsaken old age.

Hölderlin, whose poem begins in the aftermath of a divine presence that he must reapproach, abandons his poem as he finds himself becoming another Tantalos as well as another Semele. Yet both Hölderlin's poet and Pindar's agonist (Pelops) are figures whose action mediates, or attempts to mediate, between the divine and the human in an historical moment that is situated between a primary and a secondary appearance of divinity.

3

Vertical and Horizontal

Pindar's Olympian 3 *and Hölderlin's "Patmos"*

In this chapter I will consider more closely the nature of the
mediation between the divine and the human sphere that is
such a prominent part of the poet's calling in this mode. The
word *mediation* suggests that the poet inhabits a midpoint be-
tween the two spheres that are to be reconciled with each
other and between which he makes possible a two-way traffic.
Unfortunately there is no such place, and the poet's mediation
is more accurately to be described as his ability to relate two
opposite experiences of meaning on the human level. These
two experiences of meaning I shall call vertical and horizon-
tal, because it is in terms of this spatial opposition that the two
poems involved cast the problem of mediation.

In Pindar's *Olympian 3* and Hölderlin's "Patmos," the event
that begins the poet's era, or brings about the set of condi-
tions in which the poet finds himself, is described in the
same terms.[1] When Herakles founds the Olympic Games in
Olympian 3, he transports the olive tree from the banks of
the Ister to protect the racetrack at Olympos from "the sun's
sharp rays" (24).[2] Hölderlin's "Patmos" centers on the death
of Christ, which introduces the era of the gods' absence in
which it is the poet's task to prepare the conditions for their
return; Christ's death is described as the extinguishing of the
sun. For both poets the precondition of present human en-
deavor is that the human sphere be *protected* from the vertical
glare and immediate brilliance of divine presence. Although
there is no evidence of a conscious reference to *Olympian 3* in
Hölderlin's "Patmos," there is such a reference in "Der Ister,"
whose title is the Greek name for the Danube used by Pindar

in that poem.³ As Hölderlin tells us, it was to the Ister that Herakles came to seek the trees that would provide shade for the Olympic track ("Ister," lines 26–35). A passage immediately before this contains a contrast between the trees burning in the midday sun and the "roof" provided by the jutting rocks of the mountains ("Ister," lines 22–26), a clear example of the vertical/horizontal thematic shared by "Patmos" and *Olympian* 3.

Before the protecting olives have been planted around the racetrack at Olympos it is "naked" (*O.* 3.24), and in this exposure it is at the mercy of (literally, "obeys"; *hypakouemen*, 24) the rays of the sun. In other words, the glare of divinity takes over the site, stripping the human realm of its selfhood, which it recovers when Herakles founds the Games. The story of Pelops in *Olympian* 1 presents the *agōn* as a similar stage in the evolution of a distinctively human realm, for when Pelops undertakes the chariot race with Oinomaos he exchanges an immediate and passive relation with Poseidon for one that is mediated by his own action: he will face the danger and Poseidon will crown his courage with success.

Hölderlin must be thinking of Pindar when, in a letter to his friend Böhlendorff, he writes:

The athletic character of the Southern peoples, in the ruins of the ancient spirit, made me more familiar with the true character of the Greeks; I came to understand their nature and their wisdom and the rule they used to preserve their exuberant genius from the violence of the element.⁴

The connection of the Athletic with *protection* from the sun's violent immediacy links this passage with *Olympian* 3. In the fragment of a revised version of "Patmos," the "island of light" is described as "More athletic / In ruin" ("Athletischer / Im Ruin") when "kingdoms, the youthful land of eyes, are perished" ("Reiche, das Jugendland der Augen, sind vergangen").⁵ Here, as in *Olympian* 1, the Athletic is a stage of development in the relation between god and human marked by the loss of immediate experience (seeing).

But if human self-consciousness and meaning can only

come about when the human realm is protected from the invading brilliance of divinity, it is also the case that meaning ultimately depends on the vertical intersection of the temporal or historical axis by the light of immediate revelation. Accordingly human endeavor, as represented in both poets by the Athletic, involves a return of the vertical in a mitigated form. The olive in *Olympian* 3 is described as both a "shady plant" and a "crown for prowess" in the same line (18): one aspect of it protects from the rays of divinity, and the other summons them. In "Patmos" the Athletic, or history, maintains and interprets the presence of the very thing from which it protects us:

> Denn noch lebt Christus.
> Es sind aber die Helden, seine Söhne
> Gekommen all und die heilige Schriften
> Von ihm und den *Bliz* erklären
> Die Thaten der Erde bis izt,
> Ein *Wettlauf* unaufhaltsam.
>   (lines 205–10, my italics)

For Christ lives yet. / But all the heroes, his sons, / Have come and holy scriptures / About him, and *lightning* is explained by / The deeds of the world until now, / A *race* that cannot be stopped.

The problem confronted by the mediating poet is to reconcile the punctual immediacy of the divine vertical with the open temporality of the horizontal axis, along which human work takes place. In these two poems we find this problem dominating not only the story that is recounted but also the situation of the speaker himself, who is torn between these two modes of experience.

"Patmos" begins with the poet imaginatively situated on the mountaintop traditionally associated with divine revelation;[6] from there he experiences both the vertical pull toward God and the horizontal pull of an historical and social community. The threat that one poses to the other is clear:

> Nah ist
> Und schwer zu fassen der Gott.
> Wo aber Gefahr ist, wächst

Das Rettende auch.
Im Finstern wohnen
Die Adler und furchtlos gehen
Die Söhne der Alpen über den Abgrund weg
Auf leichtgebaueten Brüken.
Drum, da gehäuft sind rings
Die Gipfel der Zeit, und die Liebsten
Nah wohnen, ermattend auf
Getrenntesten Bergen,
So gieb unschuldig Wasser,
O Fittige gieb uns, treuesten Sinns
Hinüberzugehen und wiederzukehren.

(lines 1–15)

Near is / And difficult to grasp, the God. / But where danger threatens / That which saves from it also grows. / In gloomy places dwell / The eagles, and fearless over / The chasm walk the sons of the Alps / On bridges lightly built. / Therefore, since round about / are heaped the summits of Time / And the most loved live near, growing faint / On mountains most separate, / Give us innocent water, / O pinions give us, with minds most faithful / To cross over and to return.

The "summits of Time" are the solidified verticals of a race that has been stopped, unlike the "race which cannot be stopped" (line 209) that "explains" the lightning.[7] On the mountains are the "most loved," the persons whom Hölderlin is tempted to identify as those who have *achieved* the grasping of God.[8] For the individual, the proximity of God is a temptation to reach for an immediate experience of divinity that is not only dangerous (witness Semele), but also alienates him from the temporal and social context in which God should be grasped; the fragmentary second version of "Patmos" has "But nobody on his own can grasp God" ("Keiner aber fasset / Allein Gott," lines 1–2).[9] In the face of the experience of proximity appropriate to the beginning of any poem, Hölderlin formulates the project "to cross over and to return" (line 15), relinquishing one sense of *grasp* (take hold of) for another (comprehend). It is this more limited *grasp*, realized in the crossing and returning of these two poems' narrative structure, that preserves the integrity of the horizontal axis in the face of the divine vertical.

The opening of Pindar's *Olympian* 3 shares with that of

Hölderlin's "Patmos" a certain tension within the experience of beginning, roughly equivalent to that between the two senses of *grasp*. The gods appear in two different relations to the poetic project within the first strophe:

> To please Tyndareos' sons, the friends of strangers,
> And lovely-haired Helen is my prayer,
> And to honour famous Akragas,
> While I set up for Theron
> An Olympian victory-song, the choicest honour
> For his horses whose hooves never weary.
> For this the Muse has taken her stand at my side,
> And I have found a new and glittering way
> To fit to a Dorian sandal the voice
>
> (1–5)

In the first sentence, the Dioscuri (Tyndareos's sons, Kastor and Polydeukes) are the senior members of a hierarchy (Dioscuri, Helen, Akragos, Theron, his horses) in which Pindar himself as encomiast is enmeshed by his obligations. The Greek separates the infinitive *to please* (*hadein*, 1) from the main verb *I claim/pray* (*eukhomai*, 1) with the phrase to "honour famous Akragas," which contributes to the impression of an initiative that is hidden under a network of obligations. By contrast, the Muse who takes her stand by Pindar's side concentrates the experience of beginning into an immediacy that is expressed by the "new and glittering way" he fits voice to Dorian sandal. The finding of this new way is the vertical aspect of the beginning, which contrasts with the horizontal sense of being implicated in a network of obligations. The order in which horizontal and vertical appear is the reverse of Hölderlin's. The modern poet begins with the proximity of God to a grasp that is both prompted and frustrated by the poet's isolation. Pindar, however, seems to wrest an image of his own initiative out of the achievement of the victor who has commissioned him, by making the Muse his charioteer and appropriating in the expression "new and glittering" (*neosigalon*, 4) a Homeric adjective (*sigaloeis*) usually applied to reins.

The beginning of the first antistrophe reclaims Pindar's appropriations, by using the chariot metaphor as a means of describing the power of the debt under whose compulsion he writes:

> To fit to a Dorian sandal the voice
>
> Ant. 1 Of the choir's praises. For garlands
> Bound on the hair exact from me
> This holy debt,
> To mingle in honour fit for Ainesidamos' sons
> The harp's many notes,
> The flute's cry, and the patterned words,
> And Pisa makes me cry his name aloud.
> Thence by God's will songs come to men
>
>   (5–10)

The passive *bound* or, literally, *yoked* (*zeukhhentes*, 6) of the garlands that themselves exact a song seems to oppose Pindar's *act* of fitting in the strophe, and the complex mingling that is entailed by composition recalls the ramified action of the poem's opening sentence. But at the end of this description of composition as a mingling of *other* voices, tacked onto a long and grammatically complex clause, are the simple words "and Pisa makes me cry his name aloud." Here again, the poet's conception of his own activity is double, with his spontaneous cry pitted against the almost impersonal mingling of other sounds. But if the inspiration of Pisa, site of the Games, brings the poet into the vertical light of the instantaneous, the statement that songs come to men *from* Pisa (9–10) seems to remove him from the picture altogether.

The extraordinarily concentrated oscillation between two different conceptions of his own activity is typical of Pindar's representation of agency in general, and in the first epode the context widens to include the victor in this complex determination of human activity. Like the poet's, the victor's moment of vertical glory is inscribed in a horizontal tradition that stretches back into the mythical past:

>   songs come to men
>
> Ep. 1 In honour of him on whose hair
> The strict Aetolian arbiter,
> Fulfilling the ancient orders of Herakles,

> Sets the olive's pale-skinned ornament,
> Which once Amphitryon's son
> Brought from Ister's shadowy springs
> To be the finest remembrance
> Of the Games at Olympia.
>
> (10–15)

As the songs coming from Pisa and the end of the anti-strophe reach their destination at the beginning of the epode, the victor stands to be crowned by the umpire who casts the crown from above (*hypsothen . . . balei*, 12–13). Here is the vertical moment that lies behind the horizontal debt that the "crowns yoked to the hair" exacted from Pindar in the antistrophe. The shadowy background to Pindar's situation is beginning to emerge into the light. But the crowning of the victor is itself a response to the past, for the umpire is "fulfilling the ancient orders of Herakles" (11), and these orders concern the olive that Herakles found when he was himself fulfilling orders, as we shall see. Both poet and victor are agents whose highest moments are linked to a chain of obligation receding into a distant past. With Herakles we come to the agent with whom the chain begins.

The introduction of the olive at the end of the first triad begins the myth section of this ode, which will end at the beginning of the third and final triad. Herakles obtained the olive from the Hyperboreans, who lived, as their name tells us, "beyond the north wind." This mythical location Pindar had used in his earliest ode as a symbol of what is beyond the limits of legitimate human expectation:

> But not in ships or on foot
> Will you find the marvellous road
> To the games of the People beyond the North.
>
> (*P.* 10.29–30)

Although in the earlier ode the victor is warned by this statement not to aspire further than his present victory, the myth tells how Perseus once dined in that perfect society where feasting and music are not threatened by mortal suffering and crime.[10] The provenance of the olive, then, reminds us both of mortal limits and of what lies beyond them. In this connection the description of the olive in the second strophe of *Olympian* 3 is particularly interesting:

> Str. 2   His words beguiled Apollo's servants,
> The People living beyond the North,
> When with candid heart
> He begged for the all-welcoming grove of Zeus
> A shady tree for men to share
> And to be the crown for prowess.
> Already the Father's altars were sanctified,
> And at the middle of the month in the evening
> The gold-charioted moon
> Kindled her round [*holon*] eye for him.
>
> (16–20)

In the first epode the olive had been the object of two different actions: as a crown it was *raised* over the victor's head, but before that it had to be *transported* from the Ister. This combination of vertical and horizontal recurs in the second strophe, for, once planted around the racetrack, the olive performs a dual function, acting both as communal shade and as a crown that singles out the winner. It defines a common humanity that it protects from the divine vertical while at the same time isolating a single member of that community whom it exposes to the god-given ray (*P.* 8.96). Another version of this combination occurs in the description of the full moon, which is described by Pindar as month-dividing (*dichomēnis*, *O.* 3.19).[11] By juxtaposing the word *dichomēnis* with the word meaning "whole" (*holon*, 19), Pindar relates the vertical presence of the *full* moon to its effect on the horizontal axis, which it articulates by *dividing* the month. Probably we are meant to relate the moon to the olive as another form of mitigation of the sun's rays, which come to us reflected off the moon; at any rate, it is clear that both entities point toward a junction of the vertical and horizontal axes. It is in the narrative of the myth that this junction, and the reconciliation of the two forms of meaning represented by these axes, will be brought about.

Pindar's narrative of Herakles and the olive is one of his most subtle and complex creations, and the interlocking of two separate planes of time means that it cannot be dealt with stanza by stanza. I quote now the second antistrophe and epode and the beginning of the third strophe:

Ant. 2   He had set up the holy trial
In the great Games
And the Feast of the Fourth Year also,
On Alpheos' holy rocks.
But in the valleys of Kronos' Hill
The acre of Pelops was not green with beautiful trees:
Naked of them, the garden seemed to him
At the mercy of the sun's sharp rays.
Then did his spirit stir him
To journey to the land

Ep. 2   Of Ister. There he came
From Arkadia's ridges and twisting valleys;
And Lato's daughter, driver of horses,
Welcomed [*dexat'*, better, "received"] him, when on
       the command of Eurystheus
A doom laid by his father
Drove him in search of the doe with golden horns,
Which once Taÿgeta offered in her own stead
Holy to the Orthian Maid.

Str. 3   In pursuit of it he saw that land
Behind the blasts of the cold north wind;
There he stood and marvelled at the trees.
Sweet desire for them seized him,
To plant them on the edge of the horses' track
Where the chariots drive twelve times round.

(21–34)

As we read this narrative, we at first take Artemis's reception of Herakles at the Ister to be continuous with the journey he made there, under his heart's own prompting, to protect Olympia from the sun's rays. We are pulled up short when we read that this welcome took place on the earlier labor of the doe, imposed on him by Eurystheus under a doom laid by his father.[12] Traditionally, the founding of the Olympic Games took place after the completion of Herakles' labors, so we are to understand that the sight of the naked garden reminds Herakles of the olives he had chanced to see and wonder at on the previous occasion, and that he then returns to the land of the Hyperboreans to bring back the doe and plant the olives around the racetrack.

The narrative is framed by two corresponding passages, both of which link, somewhat paradoxically, the experience of a vertical that overwhelms the human sphere with the forming of a desire or initiative in Herakles' mind. One thinks here of the words at the beginning of "Patmos" in reference to a similar situation: "Wo aber Gefahr ist, wächst / Das Rettende auch" ("But where danger threatens / That which saves from it also grows). In the first passage, the language itself draws attention to the paradox, for it is because the garden obeys (*hypakouemen*, 24) the sun that his own heart prompts Herakles to go to the Ister, whither he had previously gone under compulsion. The passage that closes the narrative juxtaposes Herakles' static wonder at the trees, which interrupted his pursuit of the doe, with his later desire to plant them around the racetrack; his passive relation to the trees is overlaid by his later active intention to use them. Within this frame, where human initiative asserts itself in response to a potentially overwhelming experience of the divine vertical, we have the story of Herakles' service to Eurystheus under the compulsion that came from Zeus.

The structure of the narrative overlays the temporal hierarchy of obligation that accounted for Herakles' original visit to the Ister with the internal impulse that prompts him to repeat that journey. The two layers of narrative exhibit the two different forms of agency that we found in Pindar's description of his own poetic undertaking, the spontaneous (vertical) and the indebted (horizontal). But the vertical axis is now the locus not only of a spontaneity at which the Muse assists but also of an *overwhelming* divine presence, and the narrative effects the assimilation of the two vertical incursions of divinity into the horizontal that they threaten to overwhelm. The glare of the sun strips the garden of its discrete identity as a sphere for human action, and the marvelous sight of the olives strips Herakles of his purpose as he responds with blank wonder. By linking these two verticals horizontally, Herakles absorbs them into the human sphere, finding a means of protecting the human sphere from the sun by the same stroke by which he finds a human purpose for the olive.

Pindar's narrative, then, brings about two ends: it allows Herakles to appropriate to his own purposes and desires a journey that he had performed in the past at the behest of others, and it enables him, through the same journey, to absorb the overwhelming brilliance of divinity by linking its two manifestations with a human purpose. In fact, it is the threat that the vertical presence of divinity will deprive the human realm of its own forms of significance that forces Herakles to claim the horizontal axis for his own. Pindar's rather strange statement that Olympia "obeys" the sun makes the points that the human agent is vulnerable along both axes, and that there is a more dangerous loss of self-determination than the indebtedness that characterizes the horizontal axis. Without the dependence that defines every human action or agent on the horizontal axis, we would be unable to endure the vertical presence of divinity to which we would be exposed. Herakles is the first self-determined agent in this ode, not because his actions are performed without external promptings, but because he reveals that the horizontal axis is the sphere of the *possibility* of human action, not of its limitation.

The relation between vertical immediacy and horizontal elusiveness is neatly conveyed by Pindar's use of two compounds of the adjective *gnamptos* (bent, twisted). When Herakles arrives at the Ister on his first expedition, undertaken at the order of Eurystheus under the compulsion coming from Zeus, he is received by Artemis as he comes "from Arkadia's ridges and twisting (*polygnamptōn*) valleys" (27).[13] The immediate presence of Artemis is a welcome relief from the labyrinthine relationships and obligations that have sent Herakles away from Arkadia on this labor. Pindar does not describe Herakles' reaction to the appearance of Artemis, but his reaction to divinity is transferred to his response to the sight of the olive, which is the static wonder (*thambaine statheis*, 32) appropriate to a divine epiphany.[14] When the olive later becomes the instrument of Herakles' purpose to protect the racetrack from the sun, he experiences a desire to plant the olives around the twelve-times twisted (*dodekagnamptōn*, 33) edge of the horses' track. The divine epiphany must be absorbed back into the uncertain twistings of human experience epitomized by the *agōn*, where it will be preserved and, in moments like the present victory, reawakened.

Wedged between the framing verticals of the sun's rays and the olive is a story characterized by indirect relations between the actors. With the help of Artemis, who transformed her into a doe, the Pleiad Taÿgeta eluded the amorous Zeus. In gratitude to Artemis, she dedicated a doe whose horns she had gilded, "in her own stead" (*antitheis'*, 30). Neither Zeus nor Artemis has direct contact with Taÿgeta, which is just as well, since Zeus's intentions were far from honorable and Taÿgeta's dedication of the doe was probably a substitute for human sacrifice.[15] Zeus's failed pursuit of Taÿgeta is restaged successfully by the proxies of the protagonists, Herakles and the doe, and the compulsion under which Herakles engages in this labor comes from his father (*patrothen*, 38) but is relayed by a human proxy, Eurystheus. These indirections are constitutive of the horizontal axis into which the vertical epiphanies must be assimilated.

As we return from the myth to the present celebration of victory, it appears that Pindar's conception of himself as agent has been effected by the narrative of Herakles:

> And graciously now he [Herakles] comes
> To this our feast
> With low-girdled Leda's children,
> Twins and peers of the Gods.
>
> Ant. 3 To them, when he went to Olympos,
> He entrusted the rule
> Of the splendid struggle
> In men's worth and fast chariot-driving.
>   My heart stirs me to say
> That the glory come to Theron and to the Emmenidai
> Is the gift of the horsemen, Tynadareos' sons,
> Because most of all mankind they welcome them
> At their table with entertainment,

Ep. 3   And guard with humble hearts
         The mysteries of the Blessed Ones.

(34–41)

Herakles comes to the present celebration at Akragas just as songs come to the victors from Pisa in the first antistrophe. Pindar uses the same rather unusual word for *come* in both cases (*nisont'*, 10; *nisetai*, 34). The important point about the correspondence is that in the earlier passage the advent of songs from Pisa replaced Pindar's own cry, representing the impersonal aspect of the victory-song. There Pindar was uncovering the background of his own performance, but here he is bringing Herakles into the present from that background. In the same way that Herakles claimed for his own purposes the journey that had been imposed on him in the past, Pindar appropriates through his narrative what comes from Pisa, the whole complex of debts and obligations in which his performance is embedded.

Pindar's identification of himself with Herakles is suggested when he recalls the expression used of the hero's desire to return to the Ister in the parallel situation where he returns to the subject matter of the poem's opening: "My heart stirs me to say" (*thumos otrunei*, 38; *thumos hōrma*, 25). But the most impressive association of hero, victor, and poet is reserved for the final epode:

> Even as [*ei*] water is best
> And gold the most honoured of treasures,
> So now Theron has come to the verge by his prowess
> And reaches from home
> To the Pillars of Herakles.
> What is beyond may not be trodden
> By wise or unwise.
> I shall not chase it,—

(41–45)

In these final lines, we have the highly unusual phenomenon of an ancient poet quoting himself, and what he quotes is the famous opening to his proudest commission, the ode for Hieron of Syracuse, *Olympian* 1 (written for the same Olympiad as *O*. 3):

Water is the best thing of all, and gold
Shines like flaming fire at night,
More than all a great man's wealth.
But if, my heart, you would speak
Of prizes won in the Games,
Look no more. . . .

(1–5)

Pindar's quotation from his own poem here fixes it as the same kind of limit as Herakles' pillars or Theron's victory.[16] The shift of the conditional, *ei*, from the position where it conveys human choice ("But if, my heart, you would speak," *O.* 1.3–5) to that where it marks the certainty of limitation ("Even as water is best . . . So now Theron has come to the verge," *O.* 3.42–43) emphatically circumscribes the world that has been opened up by the beginning of *Olympian 1*, just as Herakles' pillars circumscribe the world opened up by his exploration. It has been remarked that Pindar's odes begin magnificently and end unimpressively,[17] and this observation is quite valid provided we do not attribute the phenomenon to a petering-out of inspiration. The gnomic content and paratactic construction of Pindar's endings are in marked contrast to the style of the openings, but if that style reflects Pindar's situation with respect to an elusive and proliferating background, the style of the endings, with their emphasis on limits, shows that a more confident orientation has been achieved. In the ending of this poem, Pindar's achievement merges with that of Herakles, for he too has been able to articulate the labyrinthine twistings of the horizontal axis by means of the verticals that intersect it.

There is, of course, a reciprocal relationship between the two axes, for if the horizontal axis has no form without the intersecting vertical, the latter has no content without the connections made with the horizontal. When Pindar confronts the pillars of Herakles, he declares that were he to treat this vertical as anything other than the limit of the horizontal axis he would be empty (*keinos*, 45). When the garden at Olympia stands in the full glare of the sun, it is described as naked (*gymnos*, 24). If the olive that crowns the victor did not also provide the shade he shares with his fellow mortals, the victory would be deprived of human significance, for the *agōn* is itself the means by which divine presence is made available to humanity through the mediations of time and society, the only form in which we can assimilate it while retaining the horizontal axis as that of human endeavor.

The necessity of mediating the divine Absolute along the horizontal axis is stressed by Hölderlin when he declares, in the first words of the fragmentary revision of "Patmos," "Voll Gut' ist. Keiner aber fasset / Allein Gott" ("'Most good is [*sc.* God]; but no one by himself / Can grasp God").[18] He also articulates something that is implicit in Pindar's myth when he states that from the danger of the vertical grows that which saves us from it. In the first stanza of "Patmos" (quoted on pp. 50–51 above), there is an implied etymological link between danger (*Gefahr*) and the journey (*Fahrt*) that saves from danger, although *Fahrt* does not actually appear in the lines that describe the journey.

The danger that the "most loved" will be lost as they fade on the isolating "summits of Time" is to be averted by a journey that is rendered both dangerous and swift by the mountaintop situation of the isolated individuals. Journey (*Fahrt*) and danger (*Gefahr*) mutually imply one another, as do the vertical and horizontal axes, and this mutual implication ensures that "where danger threatens / That which saves from it also grows." Where Herakles had rescued the human realm from the vertical threat by linking two different experiences of divine presence through his journey in both space and time, Hölderlin would save us from the isolating need to grasp God vertically by making a journey that will allow us to comprehend God in the dimensions of society and history.[19] Hölderlin's journey into the past will take him to Patmos, where St. John wrote the Book of Revelation, and from there he will himself attempt to understand the historical significance of the departure of Christ, which has imposed on us the need to *grasp* God.

The need to relinquish a subjective and active grasping of God in favor of a more objective comprehension raises the problem of subjectivity, which is a major concern of Hölderlin's from the period of "Wie wenn am Feiertage . . . ," and it continues to concern him in the later revisions of "Patmos."[20] In fact, the conditions under which "Patmos" was written closely resemble those under which Pindar wrote his *epinikia*, for Hölderlin dedicated the poem to the Landgraf von Hessen Homburg, who had asked Klopstock to write a poem defending the biblical word against Enlightenment rationalization; Klopstock refused the commission, and it is clear that Hölderlin's poem was a response to the same request. As a result, we find in this poem a problematization of language and form, insofar as these were imbued with a kind of subjectivity that contradicts the spirit of the commission.

Pindar had been led to the mythical past in *Olympian 3* by means of the temporal hierarchy of obligation, of which he found his own activity to be a part. Beginning with the shift in the significance of the chariot metaphor between the first strophe and antistrophe, the linguistic medium cast the speaker in a passive as well as an active role. Hölderlin expresses this relationship with language in a much more direct way at the beginning of his second stanza:

> So sprach ich, da entführte
> Mich schneller den ich vermuthet
> Und weit, wohin ich nimmer
> Zu kommen gedacht, ein Genius mich
> Vom eigenen Hauss'.
>
> (lines 16–20)

So I spoke, when more swiftly / Than ever I had expected, / And far as I never thought / I should come, a Genius carried me / From my own house.)

There appears to be a gap between the intention of the subject's utterance and its result, so that even the most subjective activities of the poet are infiltrated by objective forces.[21] At the beginning of the journey on which the genius takes him, twilight falls on his homeland with its "yearning streams" (lines 20–24). Here the poet recognizes his own subjectivity in the external world in which it is, for Hölderlin, always embedded.

In the first few stanzas of *Olympian* 3, the speaking subject finds himself similarly situated in a widening context; this mutual interpenetration of subjective and objective means that the subject is never fully present to itself, which is a constitutive feature of the horizontal axis in both Pindar and Hölderlin.

Hölderlin's imaginary journey takes him to the Aegean islands—or Asia, as he calls them—a place of blinding light and broad, shadowless streets (the sea) in which it is difficult to find one's way. This is not only a geographical but also an historical location, where the light represents the presence of the (Greek) gods during a period that had to give way to the era of the gods' absence when humanity became overconfident in its "possession" of the gods.[22] From the later period of the gods' absence, the earlier period is an object of longing, but in the unmediated brilliance and undifferentiated expanses of this location there is less fulfillment than confusion. It is for this reason that Hölderlin wants to put in at Patmos, one of the poorer islands, and yet, for that very reason, more welcoming:[23]

> Gastfreundlich aber ist
> Im ärmeren Hausse
> Sie dennoch
> Und wenn vom Schiffbruch oder klagend
> Um die Heimat oder
> Den abgeschiedenen Freund
> Ihr nahet einer
> Der Fremden, hört sie es gern, und ihre Kinder
> Die Stimmen des heissen Hains,
> Und wo der Sand fällt, und sich spaltet
> Des Feldes Fläche, die Laute
> Sie hören ihn und liebend tönt
> Es wieder von den Klagen des Mannes. So pflegte
> Sie einst des gottgeliebten,
> Des Sehers. . . .
>
> (lines 61–75)

Hospitable nonetheless / In her poorer house / She is / And when, after shipwreck or lamenting for / His homeland or else for / The friend departed from him, / A stranger draws near / To her, she is glad to hear it, and her children, / The voices of the hot noonday copse, / And where the sand falls, and the field's / Flat surface cracks, the sounds— / These hear him, and lovingly all is loud / With the man's re-echoed lament. So once / She tended the God-beloved / The seer. . . .

Patmos manifests the effects of the sun's vertical blaze rather than its brilliant presence. The overpowering sights of the other islands are replaced by the sounds that result from the cracking of earth in the heat, and these sounds respond to the visitor, in contrast to the light that confuses him in the broad, shadowless "streets" of the sea between the islands. The horizontal plane is now split ("sich spaltet," 70) by the sun instead of being turned into an undifferentiated, shadowless mass that deprives the visitor of his sense of direction. On Patmos the rifts in the earth reflect sympathetically the experience of the visitor, who is suffering from the loss and separation occasioned by Christ's death. The very different effects of the sun distinguish Patmos from the other islands in terms of an historical movement from the world of the Greeks, for whom the gods were too blindingly present, to the Christian world, in which the presence of God is experienced as a separation that begins with the death of Christ and the consciousness that the human realm has been split. Although Patmos is also dominated by the sun, its effects are such that relations may, and indeed must, be established on the horizontal plane. The departure of Christ, who is the last of the gods, leaves the human world to face the painful problem of its splitting, but that world acquires its own identity in the face of the problem of unity, as well as gaining, in the realization of that identity, the opportunity to grasp God.

The situation of the disciples who live in their memories of the departed Christ presents not only an opportunity but also a temptation:

> aber sie liebten unter der Sonne
> Das Leben, und lassen wollten sie nicht
> Vom Angesichte des Herrn
> Und der Heimat. Eingetrieben war,
> Wie Feuer im Eisen, das, und ihnen gieng
> Zur Seite der Schatten des Lieben.
>
> (lines 94–99)

But under the sun they loved / This life and were loath to
part from / The visible face of the Lord / And their homeland.
Driven in, / Like fire into iron, was this, and beside them / The
loved one's shadow walked.

Unable to conceive their identity apart from the specific
presence of Christ and the vertical suffusion of divine fire, the
disciples find it difficult to project themselves into the hori-
zontal plane, where their identity will be scattered. Their
identity hardens in the memory of life under the sun. The
central portion of Hölderlin's poem consists of the poet's own
struggle to accept as an opportunity, not a deprivation, the
splitting of the horizontal plane caused by God's departure,
and to find a substitute for the vertical grasping of God in the
horizontal comprehension that is the task imposed on us by
the death of Christ. Before he dies, Christ speaks of death
and love:

> . . . denn nie genug
> Hatt'er von Güte zu sagen
> Der Worte, damals und, zu erheitern, da
> Ers sahe, das Zürnen der Welt.
> Denn Alles ist gut. Drauf starb er. Vieles wäre
> Zu sagen davon.
>
> (lines 84–89)

For never / He could find words enough / To say about kind-
ness, then, and to soothe, when / He saw it, the wrath of the
world. / For all things are good. After that he died. Much
could / Be said of it.

The death of Christ cuts off his speech on the enigmatic
revelation that "all is good," and the secret of this totality goes
with him, leaving us with *much* to say.[24] In the punctual inter-
ruption of Christ's death, divine speech ends and human
speech begins; they are separated by the paratactic rift be-
tween a mysterious totality and the "much" that is our own
task. For those who cannot emancipate themselves from a
vertical relationship with divinity, the rift becomes an abyss in
which Christ's wisdom is preserved:

> und Freude war es
> Von nun an,
> Zu wohnen in liebender Nacht, und bewahren

In einfältigen Augen, unverwandt
Abgründe der Weisheit. Und es grünen
Tief an den Bergen auch lebendige Bilder,
                    (lines 115–20)

and from now on / A joy it was / To dwell in loving Night and
in fixed, / Ingenuous eyes to preserve / Abysses of wisdom.
And low down at / The foot of mountains, too, will living im-
ages thrive.

But the limitations of this "loving Night" are revealed as the
sentence continues at the beginning of the following stanza
with a protest at the terrible scattering of "the living" (*das
Lebende,* line 122) that God's departure has caused. The eyes
that preserved abysses of wisdom were "fixed" (*unverwandt,*
literally "unrelated") in an isolation comparable to that of the
"most loved" on their mountains in the first stanza. If living
images thrive at the foot of the mountains, the living itself has
been scattered.

As though trying to gather what has been scattered, Hölder-
lin embarks on a massive sentence that seeks to comprehend
the full scope of the effect of Christ's death on the horizontal
plane. The sentence begins with a gesture of protest at the scat-
tering of the disciples, who had been a community through
which the divine spirit was made present:[25]

> Denn schon das Angesicht
> Der theuern Freunde zu lassen
> Und fernhin über die Berge zu gehen
> Allein, wo zweifach
> Erkannt, einstimmig
> War himmlischer Geist;
>   (lines 123–28)

For only to part from the sight / Of their dear friends / And far
across the mountains to go / Alone, when doubly / Perceived,
heavenly spirit before had been / Unanimous; . . .

But this potential protest is interrupted by a parenthesis on the
sudden and unprepared nature of Pentecost, which "seized
[the disciples] by the hair" (line 129); it is, paradoxically, in
this moment of intense presence that the disciples become
apostles. Under this vertical, the disciples are bound together
"calling the evil by name" ("das Böse nennend," line 135) in

order to conjure Christ to stay. Again, the temptation to cling to the vertical axis asserts itself, not only in the historical situation described but also in the poem itself as this description of the galvanizing self-revelation of divinity suspends the troubled questioning of the significance of Christ's departure for those who survive it. Although the traumatic experience of God's departure induces in the disciples a sense of community, this is wrongly conceived by them as a reaction to the evil of God's departure rather than as a forward-looking realization of the words "For all things are good." As the disciples link hands under the precarious vertical of God's sudden departure, the stanza ends.

Hölderlin now resumes his survey of the effects of the loss of the one "on whom beauty most depended" ("An dem am meisten / Die Schönheit hieng," lines 137–38). Once again, the construction is suspended on a puzzled conditional ("But when thereupon he dies," line 136) that for sixteen lines considers the chaotic situation of a world that has been severed from the vertical on which it hung/depended. The suspension is resolved at the end of the stanza by the three monosyllables "Was ist diss?" ("What is this?" line 151). Both a gesture of despair and a humble question, this is answered at the beginning of the next stanza:

> Es ist der Wurf des Saemanns, wenn er fasst
> Mit der Schaufel den Waizen,
> Und wirft, dem Klaren zu, ihn schwingend über die Tenne.
> (lines 152–54)

It is the sower's cast when he scoops up / The wheat in his shovel / And throws it, towards clear space, swinging it over the thrashing-floor.

After the suspensions and puzzles of the last two stanzas, this carries an enormous impression of release. The answer is sudden, as though another voice were speaking through Hölderlin—which is not far from the truth, since he here quotes from the New Testament and, as he does so, draws on the "abysses of wisdom" preserved in the night of God's absence. These lines conflate the parable of the sower (Mark 4:3–9) with that of the separation of the wheat from the chaff (Matthew

3 : 12), so that the same cast figures both the beginning and the end of God's harvest.[26] In fact, scattering is an intrinsic part of truth. This time the vertical depth of living images is reconciled, rather than contrasted, with the horizontal diffusion of the living. The two axes mutually interpret each other, since the parables of the sower and of the winnower are clarified by the historical situation to which they are referred, while the puzzle of this situation is solved by the parables.

But the mutual interpretation of parable and history deprives the individual of his own language, and in the next section Hölderlin entertains the possibility of drawing on his own mastery of language (*Reichtum*) to form an image of Christ:[27]

> Zwar Eisen träget der Schacht
> Und glühende Harze der Aetna,
> So hätt'ich Reichtum
> Ein Bild zu bilden, und ähnlich
> Zu schaun, wie er gewesen, den Christ,
> (lines 162–66)

The pit bears iron, though, / And glowing resins Aetna, / And so I should have wealth / With which to form an image and see / The Christ as he truly was, . . .

As an individual, Hölderlin is tempted to appropriate the vertical wealth that has been left us through God's absence and to form an immediate relation with God by imitation. Two kinds of imitation are envisaged here: that of the artist who uses the pit's ore to reproduce Christ in an image, and that of the false priest who immolates himself, like Hölderlin's own Empedokles, in the fire of divine immediacy, a perverted imitation of Christ's self-sacrifice on the cross. This subjective appropriation of *Reichtum* is a betrayal of our historical and communal task. Hölderlin rejects this temptation (lines 171–75) in the same spirit that Pindar refuses to go beyond the pillars of Herakles.

Toward the end of this poem the sun's "straight-beaming scepter," broken at the death of Christ, returns in two new guises that figure the true nature of the vertical presence of God to the horizontal axis. The first is the "wand of song":

> Wenn nemlich höher gehet himmlischer
> Triumphgang, wird genennet, der Sonne gleich
> Von Starken der frohlokende Sohn des Höchsten,
>   Ein Loosungszeichen, und hier ist der Stab
>   Des Gesanges, niederwinkend,
>   Denn nichts ist gemein.

(lines 179–84)

For when the heavenly march of triumph goes higher / The jubilant son of the Highest / Is called like the Sun by the strong / A secret token, and here is the wand / Of song, signalling downward / For nothing is common.

The wand is the focal point of a community that is assembled in the shared recognition and celebration of history as the medium of God's presence. It appears when the "son of the Highest" is named as the "secret token" that defines a community rather than appropriated to the private *Reichtum* of an individual. A striking ambiguity attends the description of the wand's vertical movement, for, depending on whether we take *gemein* (common) to mean "shared" or "vulgar/unworthy,"[28] the downward signaling of the wand fills a lack or performs a benediction. The expression "for nothing is common" recalls the words "For all is good" that preceded the death of Christ and should be understood as referring both to the loss of the speaker whose presence would constitute the totality of which he spoke (nothing is shared) and to the value that attaches to the human world by which Christ's words are preserved and interpreted (nothing is unworthy). One meaning supports the other, for it is the loss of God's focusing presence that endows everything with value as crucial elements of the totality that must be reconstituted on the horizontal axis. Because nothing is yet communal, everything must become important; the wand of song that replaces the sun's scepter is the means by which the scattered horizontal is invited to "grasp" itself actively in terms of a vertical without having recourse to the nostalgic longing for "life under the sun."

In the final lines of the poem, the sun's scepter is given another replacement, related to the wand (*Stab*) of song, and that is "the solid letter" ("Der veste Buchstab," line 225) whose care and interpretation have been entrusted us by the Father:

Wir haben gedienet der Mutter Erd'
Und haben jüngst dem Sonnenlichte gedient,
Unwissend, der Vater aber liebt,
Der über allen waltet,
Am meisten, das gepfleget werde
Der veste Buchstab, und bestehendes gut
Gedeutet. Dem folgt deutscher Gesang.

(lines 220–26)

We have served Mother Earth / And lately have served the sun-
light, / Unwittingly, but what the Father / Who reigns over
all loves most / Is that the solid letter / Be given scrupulous
care, and the existing / Be well interpreted. This German song
observes.

The letter retains the vertical in such a way as to imply the
horizontal, for though it is present to be grasped as a memory
of divine presence, it can only be comprehended through in-
terpretation, which is an historical process (cf. lines 206–10).
The mutual interpretation of the two axes was realized at the
poem's climax under the pressure of the despairing question,
"What is this?" It is the act of interpretation that prevents us
from stagnating in the attempt to hang onto the vertical rela-
tion with divinity, which in some form or other must remain if
the horizontal axis is not to lose all coherence. See the passage
(lines 205–10) quoted on p. 50, where the deeds of history are
described as "a race that cannot be stopped," which interprets
the heroes, the Scriptures, and the thunderbolt.

"Patmos" is spanned by the metamorphosis of the vertical
presence of divinity from the sunlight that confuses the trav-
eler in the Greek world to the *veste Buchstab* left us by the de-
parting Christ; the letter demands interpretation (*deuten*, liter-
ally, "pointing") and can be grasped only on the horizontal
axis along which it points.[29] It is significant that in the poem's
last words Hölderlin declares that it is German song, not his
own, that pursues this interpretation; for both Pindar and
Hölderlin, speech is rooted in a movement that transcends the
speaker. It is an interesting and not entirely fortuitous coinci-
dence that both poems end by declaring what will or will not
be pursued. Hölderlin's statement that German song will pur-
sue the interpretation of the "solid letter" is the equivalent of

Pindar's statement that he will *not* pursue what is beyond "the Pillars of Herakles," for in both cases the poet as subject is subsumed under a communal authority.

Seventy years after Hölderlin wrote "Patmos," another great Pindarist, Gerard Manley Hopkins, finds the same framework in which to cast the problem of God's presence in the human sphere. In "The Wreck of the Deutschland" Hopkins tells of a nun's vision of Christ in the storm that is about to drown her (compare Semele). This immediate vision at the point of death is not available to Hopkins, who is left to interpret the signs of God's presence in the tragedy of the Deutschland. Already in the sixth stanza, he rejects the possibility of a vertical revelation in favor of a horizontal "stress" that is in, rather than above, history:

> Not out of his bliss
>   Springs the stress felt
> Nor first from heaven (and few know this)
>   Swings the stroke dealt—
> Stroke and a stress that stars and storms deliver,
> That guilt is hushed by, hearts are flushed by and melt—
>   But it rides time like riding a river
> (And here the faithful waver, the faithless fable and miss).[30]
>   (lines 41–48)

For Hopkins, as for Hölderlin, the determination to relinquish a premature vertical revelation and to situate the experience of God in the horizontal dimension is a test of faith and of intellectual endurance. Perhaps the most Pindaric characteristic of these poets is the complete interpenetration of the poetic and the moral, as a result of which we hear so clearly in the poetry the strain of the moral will.

4

Progress and Fall

I turn now to another aspect of the Pindaric struggle with an isolated or isolating Absolute and of its concern with continuity. It is no coincidence that in the mid-eighteenth century the Pindaric comes to be associated with the Progress poem, a genre in which the period's anxiety about the relation between a glorious poetic past and a present perceived to be incapable of matching that achievement is played out in a narrative tracing the historical progression of various arts, and especially poetry. It is in England that this genre is most in evidence,[1] but in Germany poems such as Herder's "Der Genius der Zukunft" (1769) and Klopstock's "Unsere Sprache" (1767), both Pindaric in inspiration, may be seen as part of the same trend. There are signs that the German poets are understanding the Pindaric in a new way, stressing its historical dimension: Herder calls Pindar "an interpreter of the ages,"[2] and by 1820 Goethe, who had earlier been drawn to the "enthusiastic" Pindar of rushing torrents, speaks of the Pindaric's roots in the historical, political, and racial background against which the individual emerges from an element that has its own motion.[3] The poems I will be examining in this chapter confront the problem of historical continuity in the face of a potentially overwhelming past. I will begin with the germ of this problem in Pindar, move on to Horace's treatment of his relation to his great forebear Pindar in the context of the Augustan age's crisis of identity with respect to the Republican past, and then to the great Progress poems of Collins and Gray (who adopts a very Horatian strategy); finally, I will show how Hölderlin recasts a situation that has reached an impasse, returning to the spirit of Pindar.

In a sense all of Pindar's odes are Progress poems, for the intention of the Progress poet is to create a continuity between a golden, or mythical, age and the present. The Pindaric narrative is structured by ring-composition, so that we move along a path, opened up by the victory, into the mythical past to what William Mullen has called "an analogical moment of grace,"[4] at which point the narrative swiftly turns back to the present in a sweeping movement of fulfillment set in motion by the divine favor accorded to the mythical prototype of the victor.[5] Already in Pindar we can see the germ of a problem that will become paramount to later poets, for the transition between past and present is not always entirely smooth. In *Pythian* 6, the victor's respect for his father (manifested in his present victory) is compared first to that of Achilles and then to that of Antilochos, who died rescuing his father in battle. Pindar returns to the present with the words, "It was long ago: / Of men now, Thrasyboulos has come nearest / To what a father would have" (43–45). At the end of *Olympian* 3, the myth shades into the victory celebration when Herakles hands over the responsibility for the Games to the Dioscuri, whom the victor's family now worship; but if Herakles has passed to apotheosis, Theron has reached his "Pillars of Herakles" and should aspire no further. Here, the figure of Herakles both links and separates past and present.

In some cases the transition from praise of the victor to myth is made by a gnome that expresses human limitations. The reverse of the movement from myth to victory at the end of *Olympian* 3 occurs at the beginning of *Pythian* 10, where the victor is told that he has reached the summit of human happiness, for "not in ships or on foot / Will you find the marvellous road / To the games of the People beyond the North" (29–30). These words conclude the second antistrophe, but the first lines of the ensuing epode move directly into the myth, where such limitations do not hold: "Perseus the prince has been at their feasts. / He came to their houses" (31–32).[6] The transition from the myth back to the present is effected by what is known as a "break-off formula" (*Abbruchsformel*) in which Pindar compares his poem to a ship that must strike anchor to avoid a reef (51–53),[7] which reminds us that for mortals of the present day the journey to the Hyperboreans can be made neither on ship nor on foot. The narrator almost disowns his narrative; at any rate, the continuity between a golden, mythical past and the present is put into question.

In the above cases, the limitary gnomes have served a transitional function in spite of their content; we might more accurately say that there is a dialogue between past and present in which is preserved a continuity that is threatened by the different statuses of mythical hero and victor. *Olympian* 2 is perhaps the most remarkable example of this dialogue, which in this case includes the future, for here the narrative is repeatedly punctuated by gnomes. One example from this ode, which I have analyzed at length elsewhere,[8] will suffice. The myth of *Olympian* 2 follows the story of the house of Kadmos, from which the victor, Theron of Akragas, traced his descent. It begins with the daughters of Kadmos, Semele and Ino, whose sufferings in life were balanced by apotheosis after they died. After he has declared that "unperishing life has been ordained for Ino / For the whole of time" (29–30), Pindar contrasts this situation with the lot of ephemeral humanity:

> Truly no mark is set for the death of men,
> Nor when we shall close the quiet day, the Sun's child,
> With unfaltering joy.
> Many are the streams that come to men,
> Now with the heart's delight, and now with sorrow.
> (lines 30–34)

The gnome seals off the mythical age from the present, and there seems to be no path from the daughters of Kadmos back to the shifting temporality in which Theron is implicated. But the next lines, which open the ensuing epode, find a way back to the mythical forebears of Theron by discovering in the gnome a way of interpreting the story of the house of Kadmos:

> So Fate, who holds for them the friendly fortune
> That their fathers had,

> With heaven-born joy brings grief,
> Itself to turn about with time;
> Ever since his doomed son [Oedipus] encountered Laios
> And killed him. . . .
>
> (lines 35–39)

The very reflection that creates a caesura in the narrative continuity between the heroic age and the present proves to be a way of recovering the past from the standpoint of the present.

For later poets the Progress theme takes on an extra dimension, since the adoption of the Pindaric manner calls up memories of the heroic age of poetry and of a tradition that the later poet may feel himself inadequate to continue. In the eighteenth century this dimension becomes crucial; the important transitional figure is Horace, whose "Pindarics" deal with the relation between the golden age of Republican Rome and the Augustan dispensation, while at the same time exhibiting the anxiety of the imitator in the face of his inimitable model. In the so-called Roman odes, the first six of book 3, Horace speaks for and to the Augustan regime in the Pindaric style. Since Augustus's renewal of the Roman state depended to a large extent on a resuscitation of the values of the Republican past, Pindar was a natural model for more profound reasons than that he was the poet of official celebration par excellence: Pindar was also, in the words of Herder, "the interpreter of the ages." More often than not, though, Horace's use of Pindaric techniques serves to show up the difficulty, and possibly the undesirability, of realizing Pindaric continuities in the history of Rome. After all, the very qualities that had made the Republic into a heroic age had precipitated Rome into the maelstrom of civil war from which Augustus rescued it.[9]

Before turning to Horace's treatment of the problematic relation between the Republic and Augustan Rome and of the related problem of progress within the history of poetry, I would like to examine the poem that introduces the Roman odes. In this poem Horace uses Pindaric forms to convey a radical *dis*continuity in the poetic persona itself, insofar as this persona reaches back to the ancient hieratic status of the poet. The first of the Roman odes (3.1) pretends to establish the persona of the poet-prophet, or *vates*, who will address the community in this sequence.[10] It begins with the statement that Horace, the "priest of the Muses" (*Musarum sacerdos*, 3), will sing things hitherto unheard, to the boys and girls on whom, presumably, the future of Rome depends. This presentation of poetry as the vital link in a hierarchical and continuous chain (Muses—Horace's poetry—boys and girls), constituting a divine order, derives from the opening of *Pythian* 1. But what was a proem in Pindar becomes the whole poem in Horace, for the opening generates another hierarchical chain in which kings rule their subjects and Jupiter rules the kings, moving all with his mighty nod (5–8). This reversal of the chain from the divinity through Horace to the future deprives the human agent of his active role. The poem now becomes a priamel describing various kinds of human activity and endeavor which we expect to lead us back to the poet.[11] Each section of this priamel is dominated by the iron rule of *Necessitas* over a closed order in which human endeavor and ambition are rendered futile in the light of an inescapable death. By the time we reach Horace, in the last two stanzas, he has abandoned the active, public persona of the opening in favor of retirement:

> quodsi dolentem nec Phrygius lapis
> nec purpurarum sidere clarior
>   delenit usus nec Falerna
>   vitis Achaemeniumque costum,
>
> cur invidendis postibus et novo
> sublime ritu moliar atrium?
>   cur valle permutem Sabina
>   divitias operosiores?
>
> > (lines 41–48)

If neither Phrygian marbles nor purples / more lustrous than starlight / nor Falernian vines nor Persian nards / can comfort one grieving, / Why should I construct a lofty hall / in the latest style with enviable pillars; / why should I change my Sabine dale / for burdensome wealth?[12]

Horace's pronouncements as "the Muses' priest" seek to derive his persona from the order of things, but the focusing priamel that takes up most of the poem fails to claim the role that the opening stanza projects and from which the final stanza withdraws.[13] The Pindaric ring-composition here results in a *dis*continuity between the private and public, which are so closely integrated in Pindar; Horace adopts the form of the Pindaric opening, which inserts the poet's present undertaking into a dynamic hierarchy but uses it only to reveal his own uneasiness with the role of *vates*.

In the famous "Regulus Ode" (3.5), the same discontinuity arises within the Roman identity between the golden age of the Republic and the present. Again, Horace begins by positing a continuity between gods and men, and this is to be fulfilled by Augustus's military projects:

> Caelo tonantem credidimus Iovem
> regnare: praesens divus habebitur
> Augustus adiectis Britannis
> imperio gravibusque Persis.
> (lines 1–4)

His thunder confirms our belief that Jove / Is lord of heaven; Augustus shall be held / an earthly God for adding to the Empire / the Britons and the redoubtable Persians.

The purpose of Augustus's projected Parthian campaign was to recover the legions and standards that had been captured from Crassus in one of the worst military disgraces of Roman history (at Carrhae, 53 B.C.). Horace goes on to discuss the scandalous possibility that Italian legionaries had found Parthian wives and were now fighting on the side of their in-laws. Perhaps the soldiers, in their long captivity, have become barbarians and are no longer recoverable as Romans.

This plunges us into one of the great Republican myths, the story of Regulus, who was captured by the Carthaginians and sent back to Rome in order to negotiate the terms under which his soldiers would be ransomed. Horace tells how Regulus persuaded the senate *not* to bring back the legionaries, since defeat and captivity had deprived them of their "true manhood" (*vera virtus,* 29), which could no longer be recovered. The ode does not lead back, in Pindaric fashion, from the past to the present but ends with Regulus returning to the certain death that awaits him at Carthage. In an oblique way, though, the ode does end in the present, for Regulus's departure from Rome is described in a famous simile taken from contemporary Roman life:

> atqui sciebat quae sibi barbarus
> tortor pararet; non aliter tamen
>   dimovit obstantis propinquos
>   et populum reditus morantem
>
> quam si clientum longa negotia
> diiudicata lite relinqueret,
>   tendens Venafranos in agros
>   aut Lacedaemonium Tarentum.
>   (lines 49–56)

He knew very well what the alien / torturers proposed. Nevertheless, / he parted the kinsmen blocking his path / and the crowd delaying his going, / as though, some tedious law-suit settled, / he were leaving his clients' affairs / in order to travel amid Venafran fields / or perhaps to Spartan Tarentum.

The poignant asymmetry between the mythic event and the familiar image has the effect of a pathetic reaching toward a world that is lost and a tradition the present is hopelessly inadequate to uphold. Where Pindar's narratives release a force from the past that is uncovered by and reaches into the present in a sweeping circle, Horace leaves us overawed by the irrecoverable glory of a Republican *virtus* that can no more be brought back intact than can the legionaries of Crassus or Regulus. Once again, the initial project is abandoned and the Pindaric ring cannot be closed.

In the fourth book, Horace specifically tackles the problem of his own relationship to Pindar in the context of his position as the *vates* of the Augustan revolution. Horace published his fourth book of odes ten years after the publication of the collection that makes up books one through three. During that interval he had turned to another genre and written the two books of epistles. It is usually thought that his return to the ode form was stimulated by the commission he received to write an ode for the Secular Games that Augustus had celebrated, in accordance with the Sibylline books, to mark the inception of a new age (*saeculum*). The second ode of this book contains the description, which is to become canonical, of Pindar's poetry as a river in full spate, and the danger of trying to rival the inspired and lawless Pindar is connected with Horace's reluctance to become the encomiast of the Augustan age. Yet it is in the spirit of Augustanism that Horace makes his *recusatio*—in the spirit, that is, of Augustus's peace, itself predicated on a rejection of Republican *gloria*. Horace's attitude toward his poetic forebear, then, holds some resemblance to his attitude toward the Republic, which is to be admired for its fostering of an ambitious militarism that has left so many examples of *virtus*, but not to be imitated by an age that has passed through the civil wars in which the Republic culminated.

Should we look for a specific connection between Pindar and the dangerous aspects of the Republic, we will find it, I think, in the famous description of Pindar's poetry as a raging river:

> monte decurrens velut amnis, imbres
> quem super notas aluere ripas,
> fervet immensusque ruit profundo
>   Pindarus ore,
>
> laurea donandus Apollinari,
> seu par audaces nova dithyrambos
> verba devolvit numerisque fertur
>   lege solutis. . . .
>
>   (lines 5–12)

As a river swollen by the rains above its usual / banks rushes down from the mountain, / so does Pindar surge and his deep / voice rushes on, / commanding the prize of Apollo's bays / whether he rolls new words along in audacious / dithyrambs and is carried by numbers / freed from conventions; . . .

This must surely remind us of the description of the overflowing Tiber in the poem in the corresponding position of book 1 (1.2).[14] The overflowing of the Tiber is there one of the por-

tents connected with the chaos of the civil wars from which
Augustus has delivered Rome:

> vidimus flavum Tiberim retortis
> litore Etrusco violenter undis
> ire deiectum monumenta regis
>   templaque Vestae,
>
> Iliae dum se nimium querenti
> iactat ultorem, vagus et sinistra
> labitur ripa Iove non probante u-
>   xorius amnis.
>
> (lines 13–20)

We saw the tawny Tiber (his waves / flung back with fury from
the Tuscan shore) / advance to mine King Numa's palace / and
Vesta's shrine; / and boast he'd now avenge his Ilia (who pro-
tested / too much); and flow at large across / his own left bank
(uxorious river) with- / out Jove's consent.

It is worth noting that Hölderlin uses a similar image of a river
out of control to describe the suicidal "death wish" (*Todeslust*)
of nations in certain revolutionary epochs, a movement from
which he dissociates himself.

Horace approaches the imitating of Pindar in the first stanza
of this ode with the same mixture of enthusiasm and doubt
that Hölderlin brings to his consideration of the torrential
river as "the voice of the people":[15]

> Pindarum quisquis studet aemulari,
> Iule, ceratis ope Daedalea
> nititur pennis vitreo daturus
>   nomina ponto.
>
> (lines 1–4)

Whoever attempts to emulate Pindar, Julus, / depends from
wings that are fastened with wax / by Daedalian art and shall
give his name / to some glassy sea.

The story of Daedalus and Icarus exemplifies both laudable
daring and foolhardy presumption.[16] Horace suppresses the
name of Icarus beneath that of his father, proverbial for hu-
man resourcefulness, and the fall of Icarus is represented in
the most positive light, for by this fall he gives his name to a
sea. The dark side of the story is supplied by the reader. By

the final stanza of the poem, it is Julus who is associated with
the mighty Pindar, for he is to write the great poem in praise
of Augustus, while Horace will celebrate the *Princeps* from
his own private standpoint. The contrast between Julus and
Horace is drawn in their respective sacrifices on the return of
Augustus from war: Julus's sacrifice is distinguished only by
its size, whereas Horace's is described in the loving and care-
ful detail that imparts a special value to his humble offering:

> te decem tauri totidemque vaccae,
> me tener solvet vitulus, relicta
> matre qui largis iuvenescit herbis
>   in mea vota,
>
> fronte curvatos imitatus ignis
> tertium lunae referentis ortum,
> qua notam duxit, niveus videri,
>   cetera fluvus.
>
>   (lines 53–60)

Ten bulls and as many cows shall acquit / your vow: a tender
calf mine, / which has left its mother and attained its youth /
amid lush pastures, / its brow resembling the crescent curve /
of the new moon at its third rising, / snowy white where it
bears that mark, / all else pure ochre.

This ending suggests that Horace has turned his back on
the Pindaric manner and rejected the possibility of imitating
the Theban eagle brought up in the first stanza. But in the
first stanza one word stands out as linking it with the atmo-
sphere of the final stanza, and that is the curious detail *vitreo*
("glassy," 3), which draws our attention to the glitter and
color of the sea in which Icarus's tragic (or heroic) fall takes
place. The detail anticipates Horace's lingering over the colora-
tion of the single victim that will absolve his vow.

These Alexandrian touches are good examples of the style
that Horace claims for himself in the middle of the poem
where he makes the famous comparison between the swan
(Pindar) and the Matine bee:

> multa Dircaeum levat aura cycnum
> tendit, Antoni, quotiens in altos
> nubium tractos: ego apis Matinae
>   more modoque

grata carpentis thyma per laborem
plurimum circa nemus uvidique
Tiburis ripas operosa parvus
   carmina fingo.

(lines 25–32)

A mighty wind lifts the swan of Dirce, / Antonius, whenever he strives for some high tract / of clouds; but I, very much in the manner / of a Matine bee / laboriously harvesting thyme / from numerous groves and banks of the many- / streamed Tibur, inconspicuously accrete / my intricate verses.

Although the bee here represents Horace as distinct from Pindar, it is an image that Pindar himself uses in connection with his own style, which "darts from one thought to another like a bee" (*P*. 10.54).[17] The bee was traditionally regarded as an artificer comparable to Daedalus; Vergil, for instance, had described its labyrinthine hives as *Daedala tecta* (*G*. 4.179). From the bees comes the wax by which Daedalus's wings were attached (*ceratis . . . pennis*, 2–3) and to confirm this connection Horace describes his poems as *operosa* (31), recalling the words *ope Daedalea* in the first stanza. The point of Horace's comparison of himself to the bee is not to separate him from Pindar but to specify what aspect of Pindar he replicates. In the same way, the implicit connections between the bee and Daedalus emphasize the craft over the daring of that mythical figure. In Greek the verb derived from Daedalus's name, *daidallein*, means "to work cunningly," approximately equivalent to Horace's *fingo* (32). *Daidallein* and other words from the same semantic field are frequently used by Pindar,[18] and they well describe the complex and variegated surface of his poetry. Through the myth and figure of Daedalus, then, Horace not only expresses the overpowering and potentially debilitating nature of Pindar's example, but also creates the terms in which he can see himself as an independent successor of the master. As I have suggested, Horace's relation to Pindar in this poem is analogous to that between Republican and Augustan Rome, but in this case, and by contrast with the Roman odes of book 3, Horace has found a means of establishing a progression from the past to the present without playing down the dangers and undesirability of simply imitating the charismatic figures of the poetic or historical past. The shift of emphasis in the figure of Daedalus that takes place in the middle of the poem and, as it were, reinterprets the opening allows Horace to maintain a delicate balance between humility and pride in the revaluation of the last stanzas. We will see Gray's "Progress of Poesy," itself full of allusions to Horace, perform a very similar maneuver, which corresponds approximately to what Bloom called *kenosis*.[19]

Horace's use of the myth of Daedalus to find a viable path between Pindar and himself is Pindaric in its intention if not in its form; what it lacks is the narrative dimension that is so important in Pindar. The mythical narratives of Pindar are arranged as a search for some crucial point that will carry us from the mythical past to the present victory in a swift leap. What Horace has learnt from his model is that every myth contains innumerable aspects waiting to be called out by the demands of the present and to release, in turn, a potential for the future. The pressure of these demands may even enforce a radical reinterpretation or correction of the myth.[20] Horace's historical consciousness, both poetic and political, gives him a more pronounced uneasiness than Pindar about his relationship with the past, and this makes him a crucial link with the eighteenth century.

In the sixth poem of the fourth book Horace again addresses the problem of Roman history with the help of Pindar, and this time he gives us a Pindaric narrative. The poem concerns Horace's commission to write an ode to be performed at the Secular Games. Horace invokes Apollo as the source of his poetic gift and instructs the boys and girls who are to sing the *Carmen Saeculare* to hymn the god, concluding that when they have grown up and married they will proudly recall that they performed Horace's poem on the occasion of the Secular Games. But half of the poem is taken up by a mythical "digression" in which Apollo is credited with having saved Troy from the utter destruction that Achilles would have inflicted on it had he lived, and thus with enabling Rome to be founded by the survivors of Troy, led by Aeneas. Apollo is invoked as the punisher of Niobe's vaunt against Artemis ("magnae / vindicem linguae," 1–2) and of Tityos's assault on Leto, Apollo's mother, and finally as the antagonist of Achilles, "almost victor of Troy" (3); this detail sparks off in Pindaric fashion the story of Achilles at Troy in the second stanza, and the poem does not return to the suspended invocation until the beginning of the seventh. Since the poem expresses Horace's pride in the commission to write the *Carmen Saeculare,* the invocation of Apollo as the punisher of human boastfulness, presumption, and even success has the effect of reining in the personal impetus behind it.

The opening invocation is taken up in the seventh stanza in the historical context of Rome's emergence from the survivors of Troy, so that Apollo links the private and public aspects of the occasion. Horace's own acknowledgment that it is Apollo who gives him his inspiration and skill (29–30) is set against the story of Rome's derivation from the fall of the great hero Achilles, who failed to recognize the limits of his power (5–8). Here again we find an ambivalent attitude to Rome's relation with a mythical past. The fall of Achilles, a precondition of Rome's founding, is represented as the passing away of a certain type of heroism, which is replaced by a dubious expediency and guile:

> ille non inclusus equo Minervae
> sacra mentito male feriatos
> Troas et laetam Priami choreis
>   falleret aulam;
>
> sed palam captis gravis, heu nefas! heu!
> nescios fari pueros Achivis
> ureret flammis, etiam latentem
>   matris in alvo,
>
> ni tuis victus Venerisque gratae
> vocibus divum pater adnuisset
> rebus Aeneae potiore ductos
>   alite muros.
>   (lines 13–24)

Who did not hide in the horse, that spurious / offering to Minerva, to deceive the Trojans / keeping holiday and Priam's court rejoicing / in the dances, / but openly harsh to his captives—alas, alas, / the sin—would sooner have burned in Argive fires / the innocent children, even the baby concealed / in his mother's womb, / had not the Father of the Gods, won over / by your, and by pleasant Venus's pleas, vowed for / Aeneas' wierd [*sic*] that with better auspices other / walls would be raised.

There is both horror and awe in the depiction of what Achilles might have done to Troy had he lived, and the wooden horse is a device that marks the end of the heroic age. Whether the Rome that rises under the protection of Apollo (Augustus's patron deity) is really founded with a "better auspice" is questionable in view of the fact that Apollo has been invoked as the god who slaughtered the innocent children of Niobe. When Horace turns to address the children who will sing the *Carmen Saeculare,* then, these children are associated both with those spared from Achilles by Apollo and with the children of Niobe slaughtered by Apollo, for Horace may himself become another Niobe if he does not curb his boastful tongue. If Rome's founding depended on the humbling of the great Achilles by Apollo, then the implications of the Niobe story make its future depend on the humble acceptance of their lesser status by those who are to celebrate the Secular Games. With the death of Achilles, the world of the heroic individual, both monstrous and awe-inspiring, has passed away; Achilles is replaced by the deceitful strategists of the wooden horse and then by the lesser heroes of a more enlightened *pietas,* such as Aeneas. Horace's Pindaric myth grows out of the suspended invocation of Apollo that is taken up in the second half of the poem, where the poet both makes his claim to greatness and acknowledges his dependence on Apollo. Between the invocation and the personal statement comes the transition from Troy to Rome, and the ambivalent agent of this transition is the death of Achilles. Here, as in the other poems I have cited, Horace uses Pindaric forms to link the individual poet with his tradition, poetic or historical, and to work out his own relation to the past, as lesser and yet better than its towering figures.

The eighteenth century, as W. J. Bate has shown us, is "the first period in modern history to face the problem of what it means to come *immediately* after a great creative achievement."[21] During the latter half of that century, the period of Gray and Collins, Neoclassicism, which had earlier seemed a viable solution to this problem, had brought in its wake a sense of those qualities of the classical achievement which the present revival lacked.[22] The time was ripe for the Pindaric which, in the form of the Progress poem, both allowed the poets to renew their style with those very qualities that were felt to be lacking and to draw on the Horatian use of the Pindaric to define their own position in the poetic tradition. One of the primary concerns of this period was the failure to produce examples of the greater genres, such as epic and tragedy, and it was into this breach that the Pindaric ode stepped, trying to "sustain the weight of the epic on the lyre," as Quintilian had said of Pindar's precursor Stesichoros (*Inst.* 10.1.62).[23] It is the Pindaric that both supplies the lack and confronts the problem of historical continuity.

The typical plot of the Progress poem was the migration of poetic genius from its origins in classical Greece and Rome, through Italy, to England, where Shakespeare and Milton were the great figures against whom the present poet must measure himself.[24] The motivating force of this migration was usually the decline of political liberty in each civilization, and this connection of politics and poetry is very much in the spirit of Horace. The poems of Gray and Collins, however, make at the most a passing bow to this element of the genre, and the narrative aspect is almost buried under the weight of the images that are the most striking part of these poems.[25] This failure to integrate image and narrative, as Pindar had done so successfully, is a symptom of the broader problems that make these poems such magnificent failures. Gray's "Progress of Poesy" is never able to settle on the terms in which continuity is to be cast and is constantly altering the framework as it casts up a succession of brilliant images. Collins's "Ode on the Poetical Character" seems to trade the creation of sublime images for the sense of continuity to which the genre aspires.

The ending of Gray's "Progress of Poesy" performs the same kind of gambit as did Horace in 4.2 and 4.6, that is, by admitting his inferiority to the heroic figures of the tradition, he claims a moral superiority. In the final stanza, the lyre that had been ordered to "awake" in the first line of the poem is again addressed in the context of the "progress" that has been described:

> Oh! lyre divine, what daring spirit
> Wakes thee now? Though he inherit
> Nor the pride nor ample pinion,
> That the Theban eagle bear
> Sailing with supreme dominion
> Through the azure deep of air:
> Yet oft before his infant eyes would run
> Such forms as glitter in the Muse's ray
> With orient hues, unborrowed of the sun:
> Yet shall he mount and keep his distant way
> Beyond the limits of a vulgar fate,
> Beneath the Good how far—but far above the Great.[26]
>
> (lines 112–23)

This ending has been the source of much criticism, since Gray's moral claims seem to bear no relation to the issues of the poem up to this point.[27] But Gray has not abandoned the theme of poetry entirely, and he claims for himself a new form of inspiration, based not on the images of nature that have represented the poetic tradition throughout the poem but, rather, on the imagination ("unborrowed of the sun," line 120). The rejection of what is borrowed is consistent with the statement that he has not *inherited* Pindar's "ample pinion" and also with the claim to moral independence in the final lines. In fact, Gray's flight refers to two passages that appear in close succession in Horace's odes: the description, in the last poem of book 2, of Horace himself turning into a bird by virtue of his poetic fame, and the flight of *Virtus*, spurning "common crowds" (*coetus vulgaris*), in the second poem of book 3. The references to Horace suggest that Gray's ending *links* poetry and morality. But why is it that this "Progress poem" ends by claiming a moral superiority for the poet who is independent of the tradition he has described; has he simply abandoned the project of reawakening the lyre to tremble with the "mazy progress" of "Helicon's harmonious springs" (lines 3–4)?

Gray begins by conjuring up a force of nature that represents the poetic tradition in which he must himself claim a place, and this force is the river familiar from Horace's description of Pindar:

> Awake, Aeolian lyre, awake,
> And give to rapture all thy trembling strings.
> From Helicon's harmonious springs
> A thousand rills their mazy progress take:
> The laughing flowers, that round them blow,
> Drink life and fragrance as they flow.
> Now the rich stream of music winds along,
> Deep, majestic, smooth, and strong,
> Through verdant vales and Ceres' golden reign:
> Now rolling down the steep amain,
> Headlong, impetuous, see it pour:
> The rocks and nodding groves rebellow to the roar.
>   (lines 1–12)

The image of the river contains both Horace and Pindar as different moments of the same natural phenomenon.[28] This distillation of an essence out of the succession (from Pindar to Horace) that raises the question of progress for the later poet seems neatly to sidestep the anxiety that usually attends the Progress poet. By reversing the succession from Pindar to Horace in the image of a river flowing majestically and then rolling impetuously, Gray subsumes history into the variety of nature. But, as Fry has acutely observed, in this image "early lyricists . . . *are* Nature: they speak only to each other, and Gray's first attempt at capture closes him out of the net."[29] Gray must address the history of poesy if he is to harness its forces for himself. However, this history will be not a true narrative but, rather, a succession of aloof, self-sufficient natural images that will play against the temporal and geographical movement.

The progress begins in the second antistrophe with the primitive origins of poetry in a frozen landscape of the remote North:

> In climes beyond the solar road,
> Where shaggy forms o'er ice-built mountains roam,
> The Muse has broke the twilight-gloom
> To cheer the shivering native's dull abode.
>
> (lines 54–57)

The advent of the Muses cheers this scene at the expense of its sublimity, allowing Gray to absorb the image he had contemplated with awe into a movement that will lead toward his own civilized world. The Muses bring in their wake a procession of abstract human qualities (Glory, Shame, Mind, and Freedom) to replace the "shaggy forms" that roam the imagined mountains. From the extreme climates of primitive poetry the Muses migrate to Greece, but Gray does not describe the transition, and once again the stanza begins with an abrupt image of sublime nature:

> Woods that wave o'er Delphi's steep,
> Isles that crown the Aegean deep,
> Fields that cool Ilissus laves,
> Or where Maeander's amber waves
> In lingering lab'rinths creep,
>
> (lines 66–70)

This scene is not conjured up in order to be animated by the arrival of the Muses, for we soon discover that it has already been deserted by them in the "sad hour" of Greece's decline. Like the frozen climes with which we were confronted at the beginning of the previous stanza, this scene's grandeur depends on the *absence* of the Muses. The narrative continuity of the progress is disrupted by the search for sublime images that are necessarily closed off from the history of which Gray should be part; nature, then, is both the conductor of the poetic tradition on which Gray would draw and the sublime Other that exercises his imagination while excluding him.

In this stanza Gray is clearly addressing himself to Milton's Nativity ode, a poem that might well be considered in the context of the Progress poem. Milton describes the departure of the animating spirit of paganism from its landscape at the birth of Christ and focuses on the dramatic moment of departure that Gray has passed over:

From haunted spring and dale
Edg'd with poplar pale,
   The parting genius is with sighing sent;
With flow'r-inwov'n tresses torn
The Nymphs in twilight shade of tangled thickets mourn.
                                                    (lines 184–88)

Here the extraordinary beauty of the natural images is di-
rectly connected with the historical drama of the moment,
and Milton carries over this beauty into the beginning of the
Christian era, forging the continuity that Gray seems to reject:

So when the Sun in bed
Curtain'd with cloudy red,
   Pillows his chin upon an Orient wave,
The flocking shadows pale
Troop to th'infernal jail;
                                        (lines 229–33)

The historically charged natural images in Milton's poem give
way to a separation of narrative and image in Gray's, which is
starkly apparent in the movement from Greece to the next
stop of the Muses: England. At the end of the stanza on
Greece, Gray pays lip service to the traditional Progress theme
of the migration of liberty from one civilization to the next:
the Muses flee from the Greco-Roman world when it loses its
"lofty spirit" (line 81) and arrive at Albion's "sea-encircled
coast" (line 82). But the next stanza, which begins the series
of particular English poets, opens without any connection to
the theme of liberty and with another natural tableau set at
some distance from the viewer:

   Far from the sun and Summer-gale
In thy green lap was Nature's darling laid,
What time, where lucid Avon strayed,
To him the mighty mother did unveil
Her awful face. . . .
                                (lines 83–87)

Nature's self-revelation to Shakespeare occurs in a secret place
hidden from Gray's view; it is an event that is impressive be-
cause it is exclusive. Here again the relation to the model is
instructive, for in the ode of Horace by which this scene is in-

spired it is the speaker himself who describes his childhood
as protected by the Muses and Nature:

> me fabulosae Vulture in avio[30]
> nutricis extra limen Apuliae
>   ludo fatigatumque somno
>   fronde nova puerum palumbes
> texere,
>
> (*Carm.* 3.4.9–13)

On pathless Vultur, beyond the threshold / of my nurse
Apulia, when I was exhausted / with play and oppressed with
sleep, / legendary wood-doves once wove for me / new-fallen
leaves. . . .

Gray turns this autobiographical scene into an imagined tab-
leau from which he is excluded. Shakespeare is simply con-
jured up in the lap of nature and does not provoke a response,
as did Horace's wandering child, from a sympathetic nature;
in Gray it is the Avon that strays, not the child. Nature is the
initiating agent and its beneficence is gratuitous.

The daring of Horace's "animosus infans" (20), a daring
that is required of Gray if he is to claim a place for himself
in the poetic tradition represented in this tableau, is displaced
onto the next link in the progress of English poetry: Milton.
But this daring becomes not a little suspect: Milton's flight be-
yond the bounds of nature to its source is modeled on the
flight of Milton's own Satan and on that of the morally and
theologically problematic Epicurus:[31]

> Nor second he, that rode sublime
> Upon the seraph-wings of Ecstasy,
> The secrets of the abyss to spy.
> He passed the flaming bounds of place and time:
> The living throne, the sapphire-blaze,
> Where angels tremble while they gaze,
> He saw; but blasted with excess of light,
> Closed his eyes in endless night.
>
> (lines 95–102)

Compared with Nature's chaste unveiling of herself to Shake-
speare, this passage is violently sexual, and it culminates
accordingly in a post-coital fall. It has been observed that

Milton's own description of the "secrets of the abyss" that Satan spies in the fourth book of *Paradise Lost* is colored by a fascinated horror of the female body.[32] Here, Milton's penetration of regions where "angels tremble while they gaze" is presented with a similar kind of eroticism. Milton has taken up the challenge that faces Gray and has sought an active relation with the wellsprings of poetic inspiration, but the result of this necessarily bold enterprise seems to have been to preempt repetition or continuation, and it appears that the enterprise itself may have been suspect.[33]

Since immediate vision has been ruled out by the fate of Milton, the terms of the progress shift from the appropriation of poetic power from nature to the powers of the imagination. Dryden, who appears next in his "less presumptuous car" (line 103), is attended by Fancy, and this leads to the final stanza, where Gray makes his own claim to imaginative power. Although he cannot inherit the "ample pinion" of Pindar,

> Yet oft before his [Gray's] infant eyes would run
> Such forms as glitter in the Muse's ray
> With orient hues, unborrowed of the sun:
>   (lines 118–120)

Closed off from the revelation accorded the infant Shakespeare, Gray claims for his own infancy a revelation that does not depend on the nature that has contained the poetic tradition up to this point. In this he avoids the dangerous presumption of a Milton, who responded to the fact that he came after the spontaneous self-revelation of nature by forcing his way into its origin and source. Gray, too, will fly, but his flight will accuse Milton and Pindar, outbidding them by being weaker:

> Yet shall he mount and keep his distant way
> Beyond the limits of a vulgar fate,
> Beneath the Good how far—but far above the Great.
>   (lines 121–23)

Through his treatment of Milton, Gray exorcises his sense of failure at being unable to assume a position in the great tradition. To this extent Gray goes beyond Horace's ambivalent relation to the heroic past, which allows him to feel superior in being less great, for Gray's claim to be above the Great (though below the Good) rests on his independence. In the final stanza, Gray seems to have repudiated the notion of progress altogether. But just as Horace had reinterpreted the Icarus-Daedalus-Pindar complex to create his own forebears, so Gray has reconstituted the history of poetry as a succession of images that "glitter in the Muse's ray," figures of his imagination that are intrinsically unsusceptible to the notion of an historical progress. The sublime indifference of the natural tableaux, which frustrated the narrative flow of the progress, is now claimed by the poet who could not assimilate them. Nature is not the conduit of the historical flow of tradition but the stimulus to Gray's imaginative powers. The "progress" has never really left the "climes beyond the solar road" in which it began, for in Gray's eyes it has become a storehouse of images colored by "orient hues, unborrowed of the sun."

The collapse of narrative into image is even more striking in Collins's "Ode on the Poetical Character," probably written five years before Gray began work on his "Progress." Collins's ode consists of three stanzas with a typically Pindaric temporal sequence. In the first stanza, Collins compares the girdle of poetry which he would inherit to the girdle of chaste love which, in Spenser's *Faerie Queene*, could only be worn by one woman.[34] The second stanza describes the origin of this girdle in the mythical past when God created the world, and it raises the question of who is to inherit it now. The third stanza begins abruptly, with the description of a sublime landscape in which a hill "of rude access, of prospect wild" (line 56) is crowned by an Eden that turns out to be Milton's. Collins approaches the hill as Milton's successor, but concludes:

> In vain—such bliss to one alone
> Of all the sons of soul was known,
> And Heaven and Fancy, kindred powers,
> Have now o'erturned the inspiring bowers,
> Or curtained close such scene from every future view.
>
> (lines 72–76)

Like Gray, Collins casts the poetic forebear as a landscape sub-
limely aloof and shows that the imaginative process of conjur-
ing up this landscape is his own claim to the girdle of poetry in
spite of, or perhaps because of, the fact that this imaginative act
will prevent him from *inheriting* that girdle. The mighty inver-
sions and suspensions of the two outer stanzas are truly
Pindaric in representing the *process* of creating a relation to
the past. Consider the first stanza, where Collins reaches to-
ward the girdle with an act of interpretation that is fraught
with doubt:

> As once, if not with light regard
> I read aright that gifted bard,
> (Him whose school above the rest
> His loveliest Elfin Queen has blessed)
> One, only one, unrivalled fair
> Might hope the magic girdle wear,
> At solemn tourney hung on high,
> The wish of each love-darting eye;
> Lo! to each other nymph in turn applied,
>   As if, in air unseen, some hovering hand,
> Some chaste and angel-friend to virgin-fame,
>   With whispered spell had burst the starting band,
> It left unblest her loathed, dishonoured side;
>   Happier hopeless fair, if never
>   Her baffled hand with vain endeavour
> Had touched that fatal zone to her denied!
> Young Fancy thus, to me divinest name,
>   To whom, prepared and bathed in heaven,
>   The cest of amplest power is given,
>   To few the godlike gift assigns
>   To gird their blest prophetic loins,
> And gaze her vision wild, and feel unmixed her flame!
>   (lines 1–22)

The opening gesture ("As once . . .") projects a confident par-
allel between past and present, but this is immediately ques-
tioned ("If not with light regard") and is only completed
fifteen lines later after the full, and far from encouraging, con-
text of the Spenserian event has been unfolded. One thinks
of the opening of Pindar's third *Pythian,* where the wish that
Asclepios were still alive shades into the story of that mythical

character, and this story becomes a cautionary tale casting a sinister light on Pindar's opening wish. Collins's "once" suggests an easy relationship between the storyteller and the past, but its association with the conventional "once upon a time" is quickly overlaid with the implication of uniqueness, which *separates* past from present ("One, only one"). The "once" that is the first point in a continuum reaching to the now may, in fact, be an exclusive *once*. That is the conclusion reached in the last stanza, where "one alone" (line 72) has been accorded the bliss of poetic inspiration. But Collins does not draw this conclusion immediately, and when he resolves the suspended construction of the opening the "one" has become "few" (line 20).

The structure of Collins's poem deliberately avoids any continuity between Spenser and Milton, the only poets mentioned. In fact, what we have is a threefold repetition of the attempt to approach the source of poetry, and the discontinuity between these attempts is played against the Pindaric movement from the present back to a mythical origin and forward again to the present. The second stanza describes the creation of the girdle but, like the Spenserian tournament in the first stanza, this event is of an ambiguous nature, especially in its relation to time. Here is how Collins describes the creation:

> The band, as fairy legends say,
> Was wove on that creating day
> When He, who called with thought to birth
> Yon tented sky, this laughing earth,
> And dressed with springs and forests tall,
> And poured the main engirting all,
> Long by the loved Enthusiast wooed,
> Himself in some diviner mood,
> Retiring sat with her alone,
> And placed her on his sapphire throne,
> The whiles, the vaulted shrine around,
> Seraphic wires were heard to sound,
> (lines 23–34)

Creation is first presented as an instantaneous and necessary act of the sovereign mind of God, but then it is suggested that it was a contingent result of the "diviner mood" brought on by the long wooing of the Enthusiast (Fancy). Although the two descriptions can be understood as a hendiadys, the form of the expression conveys Collins's concern as to whether the creative acts of his forebears exist in a temporal continuum with his own or not; God, who calls the world "with thought to birth," is of course the original writer of odes.[35] From the first to the second stanza, Fancy has changed from the conveyer of the girdle to the wooer of God. If the one who assigns the girdle has already given herself to the original creator, then Collins must himself actively, and perhaps impiously, seek the girdle. The second stanza ends by asking who presumes to inherit the girdle:

> Where is the bard, whose soul can now
> Its high presuming hopes avow?
> Where he who thinks, with rapture blind,
> This hallowed work for him designed?
> (lines 51–54)

These lines describe a mental process that is repeated again and again in these failed Progress poems of Collins and Gray: the would-be successor formulates or imagines something that he cannot then claim as his own; he is shut out of his own imaginings. Here the bard has hopes that presume to link the past with the future but cannot "now . . . avow" these hopes. He approaches the "hallowed work" with a "rapture *blind*" that seems to preclude any understanding of how (or whether) it is *designed* for him.

Collins leaves in suspension the questions with which the second stanza ends, to begin the final stanza by conjuring up a landscape of sublime inaccessibility:

> High on some cliff to Heaven up-piled,
> Of rude access, of prospect wild,
> Where, tangled round the jealous steep,
> Strange shades o'erbrow the valleys deep,
> And holy genii guard the rock,
> Its glooms embrown, its springs unlock,
> While on its rich ambitious head,

>   An Eden, like his own, lies spread;
>   I view that oak, the fancied glades among,
>   (lines 55–63)

This magnificent description allows the landscape its own independent being, much as Gray does in some stanzas of his "Progress." But, as we read on, the lines turn out to be part of a great inversion that takes shape only when we arrive at the words "I view." Like the hendiadys of the two creations in the second stanza, this inversion serves to display Collins's problematic relation to the past. The construction is barely able to subordinate the adjectival clause to the main clause: Collins cannot "avow" his "high presuming hopes." What is more, as the mountain takes on the identity of Milton's Eden, the describing voice is assimilated to Milton's Satan, jealously admiring the world from which he has been excluded.[36] The oak that Collins sees among the "fancied glades" is the oak by which Milton lay to catch the heavenly sounds that inspired his verse (lines 64–67). Retreating from Waller's "myrtle shades" (line 69) and the Augustan mode they represent, Collins pursues Milton to his bower but, like Satan, he comes too late:

>   In vain—such bliss to one alone
>   Of all the sons of soul was known,
>   And Heaven and Fancy, kindred powers,
>   Have now o'erturned the inspiring bowers,
>   Or curtained close such scene from every future view.
>   (lines 72–76)

Although these lines clearly bring to mind the expulsion from paradise in Milton's *Paradise Lost,* just as earlier Collins himself had been cast as the excluded Satan, they also recall Guyon's destruction of the Bower of Bliss in the second book of Spenser's *Faerie Queene,* an event that has the opposite significance, since it represents the triumph of temperance over a bestial sensuality. The Spenserian parallel makes Milton into the knight that the witch Acrasie has seduced and who has hung up his arms to lie with the enchantress, their lovemaking accompanied by the most exquisite music; Guyon comes upon this couple, captures Acrasie, and overturns the

Bower. As in Gray's "Progress," Milton's unapproachable example is given an ambivalence that mutes the failure of the aspiring poet, and this is a maneuver that we have already seen in Horace.

From the first words of the poem ("As once") there has been an oscillation in the characterization of a past event between a unique occurrence and a moment in a temporal continuum. A similar ambiguity dominates the treatment of nature in Gray's "Progress," where it appears both as the conduit of poetic tradition and inspiration and as a sublimely remote and indifferent tableau. In his final stanza Collins resolves the ambiguity as Milton becomes a uniquely privileged poet who cannot, and perhaps should not, be followed. But although Collins has failed to inherit the girdle of poetry, the poem has constituted a striking exhibition of his own powers, not least in the description of Milton's inaccessible Eden and its awe-inspiring approach. When he concludes that Heaven and Fancy (the retiring lovers of the second stanza) have overturned the "inspiring bowers," we may ask whether it is the very overturning and curtaining of these bowers that turns them into a source of inspiration. It is through the mechanism of the Sublime, which this poem so well exemplifies, that the aspiring Collins can draw strength from his very weakness in relation to the great tradition.[37]

The reconstitution of the mythical past as a collection of sublime images removed from the historical flow of history is the latecomer's way of appropriating a tradition that he is inadequate to inherit. A generation after Collins and Gray, Schiller makes the same gesture in his famous poem about the Greek religious experience, "Die Götter Griechenlands." In this poem the modern poet regrets the passing of a mythological mentality that animated the nature which, for modern man, has become a mere mechanism. The major part of the poem consists of a "sentimental" description of a nature permeated by divinity now lost to our experience. But if we are no longer strong enough to experience nature in this fashion, our poetry is nevertheless enriched by the distant images of an Olympian pantheon:

> Aus der Zeitflut weggerissen, schweben
> Sie gerettet auf des Pindus' Höhn,
> Was unsterblich im Gesang soll leben,
> Muss im Leben untergehen.[38]
>
> (lines 125–28)

Torn from the flood of time, they hover / Preserved on the heights of Pindus; / What is to live immortally in song / Must die in life.

Schiller has reduced the image of the "flood of time" to one of mere impermanence, and it is left for Hölderlin to revive it and at the same time to rescue the Progress theme from the stalemate at which it has arrived.

The Progress question is one of the most important threads running through the career of Hölderlin,[39] whose later work is almost entirely concerned with the interpretation of history from the point of view of the present "night" of the gods' absence following the "day" of their presence in ancient Greece. The tyranny of Greece over the German mind during the period in which Hölderlin was writing is well known;[40] it is most powerfully conveyed by Winckelmann's description of the qualities of "noble simplicity and calm greatness" that made the achievements of Greek art so definitive.[41] Much of Hölderlin's theoretical writing is taken up by the attempt to find a way of seeing the Greeks that will allow the modern poet to overcome this tyranny without disowning them. It is interesting to note that at the same time that Hölderlin wrote his essay "The Standpoint from Which We Must Regard Antiquity" he was trying to emancipate himself from the oppressive influence of Schiller. In the essay he puts the problem as follows: "we dream of originality and independence and it is ultimately all reaction, as it were a gentle revenge against the slavery that has characterized our relation to antiquity. There really seems almost to be no other available choice than either to be oppressed by the tradition and the Positive, or, with violent presumption, to range oneself with vital power against all that has been learnt and given in positive form."[42] The key word here is *positive,* for Hölderlin's solution to this problem is to overcome the kind of static definition of Greek achievement that Winckelmann had produced. Instead, the Greeks are to be seen in terms of a project that involves two terms and that relates these terms so as to form a chiasmus with the project of modern (or "Hesperian") man: the project of the Greeks was to control their fiery nature in the "Junonian" realm of their art, which they had to *conquer,* whereas for us who are born with a nature of "Junonian sobriety" the problem is to "find a fate" ("treffen ein schicksal").[43] In this way the Greeks are brought into a dialectical relationship with us that makes history no longer an oppressive weight on the backs of the latecomers.

In his Progress poem "At the Source of the Danube" ("Am Quell der Donau"), Hölderlin reinstates the Greek world in the "flood of time" from which Schiller had removed it. He begins, like Gray, by conflating the opening of Pindar's first *Pythian* with Horace's description of Pindar in 4.2:

> Denn, wie wenn hoch von der herrlichgestimmten, der
>   Orgel,
> Im heiligen Saal,
> Reinquillend aus den unerschöpflichen Röhren,
> Das Vorspiel, wekend, des Morgens beginnt
> Und weitumher, von Halle zu Halle,
> Der erfrischende nun, der melodische Strom rinnt,
> Bis in den kalten Schatten das Haus
> Von Begeisterungen erfüllt,
> Nun aber erwacht ist, nun, aufsteigend ihr,
> Der Sonne des Fests, antwortet
> Der Chor der Gemeinde; so kam
> Das Wort aus Osten zu uns,
> Und an Parnassos Felsen und am Kithäron hör'ich
> O Asia, das Echo von dir und es bricht sich
> Am Kapitol und jählings herab von den Alpen
>
>   Kommt eine Fremdlingin sie
> Zu uns, die Erwekerin,
> Die menschenbildende Stimme.
>
>   (lines 25–42)

For as when from the gloriously voiced, the organ / Within a holy hall / Untainted welling from inexhaustible pipes, / The prelude, awakening men, rings out in the morning / And far and wide, from mansion to mansion, / Now pours the refreshing, the melodious current, / Down to the chilly shadows even filling / The house with inspirations, / But now awake and rising to it, to / The sun of celebration, responds the / Community's choir—so the word / Came down to us from the East, / And by the rocks of Parnassus and by Cithaeron, / O Asia, I hear the echo of you, and it breaks / Upon the Capitol and sudden down from the Alps / A stranger it comes / To us, that quickening word, / The voice that moulds and makes human.

Gray's river of poetry operated in a natural world that seemed to speak only to itself, but Hölderlin, typically, sees nature as the manifestation of a history of which we are part:[44] the long Pindaric simile fuses nature and culture to such an extent that we are no longer sure what is being compared to what. Hölderlin's organ recalls the lyre of Pindar's first *Pythian*, but here the choir "*answers* the organ's prelude," a deliberate modification of the Pindaric passage, where the choir obeys/ hears. These factors all contribute to the loosening of the "positive" aspect of the past. In fact, a characteristically Pindaric ring-composition indicates that the "untainted welling" (*Reinquillend*) of the word from the East is being brought within an historical process, for the gloriously voiced (*herrlichgestimmten*) organ of the first line becomes the human-molding voice (*menschenbildende Stimme*) that arrives from Greece via Rome at the beginning of the second stanza.

From Hölderlin's sketches, we know that the poem was to start with two additional stanzas, and that in its present version the poem begins with the third stanza of the first triad. These sketches explain the title of the poem, "At the Source of the Danube," for this river flows from the poet's land toward the East and carries the poet's greeting to the dormant world of the ancient cultures. The poem, then, was to have begun with the poet's greeting ("Dich, Mutter Asia, grüss'ich") and the "untainted welling" of the organ is a *reflex* of the eastward movement of the Danube and the poet's own wakening of the past. Unlike Gray, who conjures his own lyre to wake by submitting itself to the inspiration of Helicon's "harmonious springs" ("And give to rapture all thy trembling strings," line 2), Hölderlin himself provokes the westward flood and wakes the sleeping Asia; the sketch of the second stanza begins, "But now you rest, and wait, if perhaps an echo of love from a living breast should meet you."[45] Echo and reflex figure a reciprocity that revives the original Pindaric notion that the victor awakes the "slumbering" glory of family and city,[46] which both imposes on him the duty to compete and, once awakened, projects him into a divinely favored future. By reaching back to Pindar, Hölderlin overcomes that problem of a "positive" or definitive past, which haunts the Progress tradition from Horace onward.

The characteristic that all of the poems in this chapter share with Pindar is that they reread the past and its myths so as to situate the present poet in the earlier context, just as Pindar selects from, or even alters in content or focus, the myths he is to narrate, according to the demands of the present. So Horace rereads the myth of Daedalus, Gray rereads *Paradise Lost* so that Milton becomes Satan, and Collins rereads the *Faerie Queene*. Hölderlin not only read the classical poets, he translated them, and it is in connection with his translation that he formulated some of his ideas about the reciprocal relation between the Greeks and the Hesperians. It is not surprising, then, that in this poem he quotes from, or rereads, a work that he was himself in the process of translating, Sophocles' *Antigone*.[47] When the wakening voice comes from the East it is not only human-molding but also potentially overwhelming, as it had been for previous Progress poets. The inability of Western man to confront directly the divine gifts from the East, prompting the wisest to protect themselves in darkness ("Und Nacht / war über den Augen der Besten," lines 44–45), is expressed with a reference to the famous chorus on man from *Antigone*:

> Denn vieles vermag
> Und die Flut und den Fels und Feuersgewalt auch
> Bezwinget mit Kunst der Mensch
> Und achtet, der Hochgesinnte, das Schwerdt
> Nicht, aber es steht
> Vor Göttlichem der Starke niedergeschlagen,

> Und gleichet dem Wild fast; das,
> Von süsser Jugend getrieben,
> Schweift rastlos uber die Berg'
> Und fühlet die eigene Kraft
> In der Mittagshizze.
>
> (lines 46–56)

For much can our kind / Accomplish, and flood and rock and even the might of fire / With art can subdue, / Nor, noble in mind, recoils from / The sword-blade, but faced with powers divine / The strong will stand abashed / And almost are like the beast of the wilds; which / impelled by sweet youth / Roams restless over the hills / And feels its own strength in / The noonday heat.

Sophocles' chorus had wondered at human resourcefulness, which can control and dominate nature but is limited by its inability to escape death. Among the manifestations of this resourcefulness is the art of hunting. Here is Hölderlin's translation of the relevant lines:

> Und leichtträumender Vögel Welt
> Bestrickt er, und jagt sie;
> Und Wilder Tiere Zug,
> Und des Pontos salzbelebte Natur
> Mit gesponnenen Netzen,
> Der kundige Mann.
> Und fängt mit Kunsten das Wild'
> Das auf Bergen übernachtet und schweift.
>
> (lines 360–67)

And the world of light-dreaming birds he snares, and hunts it; and the flock of wild beasts, and the salt-enlivened nature of Pontos with spun nets the resourceful man [hunts]. And [he] catches with arts the deer that sleeps on the mountains and roams.[48]

In the poem the deer represents man, not the nature man controls. This reversal of the Sophoclean context is to be connected with Hölderlin's theory of the relationship between the Greeks and us, expounded in the "Comments on *Antigone*" that he appended to his translation. For the Greeks, for whom the fire from heaven was natural, the problem was "to be able to restrain themselves" ("sich fassen zu können"), and it seems likely that this is how Hölderlin understood Sophocles' description of the capturing of the wild and restless deer *with arts*. This being so, the deer that breaks out of the Sophoclean context to roam over the mountains in the poem represents modern man, whose nature is "Junonian" and who needs, therefore, "to attain something, to have a destiny" ("etwas treffen zu können, ein Geschick zu haben"). Hölderlin has also reversed the order of human action and limitation, for in *Antigone* the recital of human "wonders" is followed by the grim reminder that mortals cannot flee the realm of death, whereas in Hölderlin's translation the deer's experience of its own strength in the midday heat follows from the fact that "faced with powers divine / The strong will stand abashed." Hesperian man is released into an experience of his own strength by his very shiftlessness with respect to the divine gifts that come from the East. The translation ("carrying across") of the *Antigone* passage includes the moderns in a single dialectical process now expressed in terms of this highest, and potentially most threatening, achievement of Greek literature.

But, like the deer that had reveled in its own vitality in the midday heat, Hesperian man later succumbs to sleep when the sun descends (lines 60–61). Hölderlin describes this sleep as a waking sleep (line 60), a concept he uses elsewhere to express the protected waiting required in times when humanity is too weak a vessel to bear divine fullness.[49] This waking sleep is to be distinguished from the blinding and curtaining that in Gray and Collins ensue upon the immediate vision of their great forerunner, Milton; Hölderlin himself distinguishes those who wake in this way from those whose "vision was extinguished in the face of those God-sent gifts" (lines 38–39). The waking sleepers are part of the Greek world and at the same time distinct from it, a relationship expressed by Hölderlin's use of Sophocles' deer: their sleep preserves both the continuous context of the *Antigone* chorus and the experience of their own strength in the face of what comes from the East. This takes us beyond the sublime but ahistorical confrontations that we have seen in Gray and Collins.

The waking sleepers return to the childhood of humanity, the innocent festival represented by the Games:

> Und sie wandelten oft
> Zufrieden unter euch, ihr Bürger schöner Städte,
> Beim Kampfspiel, wo sonst unsichtbar der Heros
> Geheim bei Dichtern sass, die Ringer schaut und lächelnd
> Pries, der gepriesene, die müssigernsten Kinder.
>
> (lines 68–72)

And often, you citizens / Of beautiful towns, they walked among you contented, / At Games, where once in secret the hero / Invisible sat with poets, watched the wrestlers and smiling / Praised—he, the recipient of praise—those idly serious children.

Like the quotation from *Antigone*, this passage inserts the later into the earlier: the scene at the Games recalls Pindar, but with a crucial difference, for the hero sits "invisible" and "in secret" beside the poets, and the poet's role of celebrating the hero is transferred to the waking sleepers of the later age. As they wake from their sleep, they recapitulate the caesura that separates the ancient from the modern world and bring the self-absorbed unity of the former into a relationship of historical reciprocity with the moderns:

> Ein unaufhörlich Lieben wars und ists.
> Und wohlgeschieden, aber darum denken
> Wir aneinander doch,
>
> (lines 73–75)

An endless loving it was, and is. / And rightly severed; yet nonetheless we think / Of one another still. . . .

The waking sleepers have been inserted into the ancient *epinikion* just as Hesperian man had been inserted into the chorus from *Antigone*.

The final triad begins with an invocation of Asia and its patriarchs, who "For days were rooted on mountains / And were the first who knew / How to speak alone / To God"

("Taglang auf Bergen gewurzelt, / Zuerst es verstanden / Allein zu reden / Zu Gott," lines 84–86). This invocation recalls the greeting to "Mother Asia" that was to have opened the poem, according to Hölderlin's sketches. We can now see why the poem as we have it does not actually begin with this greeting but with the "untainted welling" of the organ's voice that represents the imperious and "positive" claim of the ancient world on the modern: only when the positive aspect of this voice has been muted, which has been the effect of the poem thus far, can the poet cast himself in an active role with respect to the past. Hölderlin now proceeds to recapitulate the beginning of the poem as it stands, this time with the Hesperians taking the initiative:

> Die [Patriarchen] ruhn nun. Aber wenn ihr
> Und diss ist zu sagen,
> Ihr Alten all, nicht sagtet, woher?
> Wir nennen dich, heiliggenöthiget, nennen,
> Natur! dich wir, und neu, wie dem Bad ensteigt
> Dir alles Göttlichgeborne.
>
> (lines 86–91)

These now rest. But if, / And this must be said, you ancients / Would never tell us whence it is that / We name you, under a holy compulsion we / Now name you Nature, and new, as from a bath / From you emerges all that's divinely born.

The opening stanza has been reversed, for where the voice from the East had awakened (*Erwekerin,* line 17) and refreshed (*erfrischende,* line 6) the Hesperians, coming as a river, now the silence of the East provokes us to name it *as* Nature itself, which emerges fresh as from a bath. Instead of the organ and responding congregation, we have a chiasmus pivoting on the "holy compulsion" of Asia's silence ("Wir nennen dich, heiliggenöthiget, nennen, / Natur! dich wir"); it is this chiastic process brought about by the absence of a "positive" answer to our calling that constitutes Nature as an historical presence enabling us to "think of one another still" (lines 74–75).

Hölderlin associates this Nature, arising from the silence of the Asian past, with the texts that the Greeks have left behind for us as they departed (lines 101–3). Their presence is like a "holy cloud" that will envelop us from time to time so that "we are amazed and do not know how to interpret it" (line 106). The presence in absence of the "kindly spirits" in this cloud answers the similar presence of the Hesperian waking sleepers at the ancient Games, but it also inverts the process by which Nature is reborn in our naming when the Asians are silent, for here the silence of the Hesperians who cannot interpret is met by the grace of the kindly spirits: "But you with nectar spice our breath" ("Ihr aber würzt mit Nectar uns den Othem," line 107). Chiasmus, inversion, and reciprocity mark both the development of this text and the relation between Asia and Hesperia, or the historical periods that they represent. But the poem ends in Pindaric manner with a personal statement that reveals the precariousness of these figures that depend ultimately on the strength of the poet:

> wenn ihr aber einen zu sehr liebt
> Er ruht nicht, bis er euer einer geworden.
> Darum, ihr Gütigen! umgebet mich leicht,
> Damit ich bleiben möge, denn noch ist manches zu singen,
> Jetzt aber endiget, seeligweinend,
> Wie eine Sage der Liebe,
> Mir der Gesang, und so auch ist er
> Mir, mit Erröthen, Erblassen,
> Von Anfang her gegangen. Doch Alles geht so.
>
> (lines 109–17)

But when too greatly you love a man / He finds no rest till he is one of you. / Therefore, benign ones, surround me lightly, / And let me stay a while, for much remains to be sung; / But now, like a legend of love, / Blissfully weeping, my song / Comes to its end, and so too, / Amid blushing and blanching, it's gone / With me from the start. But that is how all things go.

Pindar's gnomic endings, with their oscillating movement, serve to prevent victor or poet from lingering in the divine milieu of victory; Hölderlin faces the danger of a nostalgic return to the Greek world which he must resist, "for much remains to be sung." How different from the final stances of Horace, Gray, and Collins is this statement of the continuity of "song"! But this continuity depends on the poet's avoidance of the kinds of personal struggles with the past that were the main concern of those poets. The insistence of the positioning of *mir* at the beginning of two consecutive lines recognizes the circumscription of Song in the particular song that is in danger of becoming a "legend of love," a stage that Hölderlin's own poetic development had to surpass.[50] In the final line, the rhythm of Hölderlin's personal relationship with the Greeks is assimilated to the impersonal rhythm of the "All" or, rather, the abstraction of the rhythm from the subjective content of experience itself constitutes the "All."

Hölderlin manages to avoid casting the relation between the voice of the past and the voice that must now speak as a struggle for power. If the relation between Asia and Hesperia as he sees it resembles any of the types of strategic response to anxiety described by Bloom, it is the tessera, in which "the later poet provides what his imagination tells him would complete the otherwise 'truncated' precursor poem or poet."[51] But Hölderlin does not conceive of the completing of a whole as the fitting of the final piece into a puzzle, as Bloom's term suggests. The chiastic relation between the Greeks and the moderns constitutes a rhythmical whole that privileges neither the later nor the earlier.

5

The Hero's Extension

*Pindar's Olympian 10, Dryden's "Alexander's
Feast," and Hölderlin's "Der Rhein"*

One of the most frequently encountered commonplaces of
encomiastic poetry is that the man of action depends on the
poet to prevent his achievement from sinking into oblivion,
or, in more positive terms, that the poet gives a form of im-
mortality to the object of his praise.[1] So common is this claim
that we may be inclined to dismiss it as merely a conventional
advertisement of the poet's services or, at best, a feeble at-
tempt on the part of the hired flatterer to maintain some shred
of dignity. In fact, there are all too many poems where this
topos is simply part of the stock-in-trade of the genre and
where the relation between the poet and the hero, or the
poem and the achievement it celebrates, remains on the most
superficial level. In this chapter I shall be considering poems
in which this relation is itself the central focus. Here the con-
frontation between poet and hero makes the poem, rather
than its future readership, the dimension in which one form
of human agency is extended by another. In all of these poems,
there is an almost antagonistic relation between poet and hero
and, of course, in Pindar's *epinikia* there is a noticeable ele-
ment of rivalry with the victor. As I hope to show, this is not
incompatible with the poet's claim to give extension to the vic-
tor's achievement. The poem is the place where the potential
arrogance of the victor encounters the modal irony of the
poem's turns and counterturns, and what is at stake in this
encounter is the possibility of an open-ended human agency
that is extended by and toward the divine.

Before turning to more complicated versions of the relation
between poet and hero, we can observe this relation at its

simplest in Pindar's *Nemean* 1.[2] This ode tells of the first trial of Herakles who, while still an infant, strangled the snakes sent by Hera to kill him in his cradle. The prophet Teiresias, called by Herakles' father to witness this feat, foretold the career and apotheosis of the hero. The ode ends, rather untypically, with the words of Teiresias describing the marriage of Herakles to the goddess Hebe (Youth). Pindar does not modulate, as he usually does, from the myth back to the present, nor does he end with the usual gnomic utterances. The reason for this is that his own voice has merged with that of the prophet Teiresias, commenting on the hero's extraordinary feat, of which the present victory is a descendant. This merging is indicated by a parallel drawn between the situation of Pindar as encomiast and that of the onlookers in the myth by the motif of standing-on-the-threshold that opens both the second and fourth triads.[3] Of himself, Pindar says:

> I have taken my stand [*estan*] at the courtyard-gate
> Of a man who welcomes strangers,
> And sweet is my song.
>
> (19–20)

and of Herakles' father, Amphitryon, before he summons Teiresias:

> He stood [*esta*] dumbfounded in wonder
> Hard to endure but delightful.
>
> (55–56)

From his liminal position Pindar can protect the victor against envy, bringing water against the smoke of cavil (24–25). Corresponding to the spatial distance between Pindar and the victor is the temporal gap between the attack of the snakes and Amphitryon's arrival on the scene, during which time the gods had "turned [*paligglōssan . . . thesan*] the messengers' tale to falsehood" (57–58). In both these cases, the realization of truth is connected with a gap or distance that allows an intervention in the immediate report, an intervention that, in the second case, manifests the presence of the divine in human action.

When Herakles strangles the snakes, a remarkable expression seems to take the victory out of his agency:

> In two unescapable hands
> He seized the two serpents by their necks:
> He strangled them, and *Time*[4]
> Squeezed the life out of their unspeakable frames.
>
> (44–47)

Time is the dimension in which Herakles' triumph acquires its significance, and so it is Time that completes the action that he has begun, squeezing the life out of the snakes he has grasped. The victory of the baby Herakles in this ode looks forward, of course, to the career of this hero as prophesied by Teiresias: Herakles will clear the world, and even heaven, of unwanted monsters (62–69); after his life of toil, he will receive "for the whole of *time*," unending rest from his labors (69–70) with his immortal bride, Hebe.

It is the perspective of the watching Teiresias that divides this first deed of Herakles between himself and a completing time. But Teiresias is himself a prototype of Pindar, and Herakles of Khromios, the victor celebrated in the present ode. Just like Teiresias, Pindar offers the victor rest from his toils, a fact that is indicated when he opens the ode by invoking Ortygia, the victor's home on Syracuse, as "Holy breathing-place of Alpheos" (Alpheos being a river that flows past Olympia, disappearing into the sea to emerge again at Syracuse as the fountain Arethiosa).[5] Pindar turns place into time as he associates Ortygia with the victor's drawing of breath (*ampneuma*, 1) after the toil of the *agōn*. This drawing of breath is recalled in the myth when Time "takes the breath out" (*apepneusen*, 47) of the snakes. The two words, *ampneuma* and *apepneusen*, are linked in a circulation of breath that makes the toil of Herakles' *agōn* continuous with Khromios' rest after victory. There are no self-contained acts in the *epinikion*, just as there are no self-sufficient agents, and the participation of *Khronos* in the hero's victory depends on the gap between the hero absorbed in his act and the poet standing on the threshold.

It is the transition between one agent and another that produces a significant action in the world of the *epinikion*. When Dryden declares, in "Alexander's Feast," that "None but the Brave deserves the Fair," he is making a Pindaric statement about the transitional status of these values and of human agency in general. Dryden's poem introduces an ancient poet, Timotheus, whose celebration of Alexander's victory involves turning the hero from one mode of agency to another:

> War, he sung, is Toil and Trouble;
> Honour but an empty Bubble.
> Never ending, still beginning,
> Fighting still, and still destroying,
> If the World be worth thy Winning
> Think, O think, it worth Enjoying.
> Lovely *Thais* sits beside thee,
>   (lines 99–105)[6]

The martial, or heroic, mode is complemented by the amorous mode as winning is by enjoying, and without such a turn the hero is trapped in a vicious circle, an "empty Bubble." Paradoxical though it may seem, the poet gives extension to the hero's act by undermining the latter's self-identity and by resisting the centripetal force of his action. Dryden's Timotheus draws Alexander out of his identity as hero or victor through the gamut of the musical modes and their corresponding moods.[7] The turns and counterturns of Pindar's triads perform a similar function with respect to the victor, whom he draws into the windings of hymns (*hymnōn ptykhais, O.* 1.105) which weave backward and forward around the victory until it becomes a nodal point in an ever-widening pattern of forces. This confrontation between poet and hero in the turning modality of the poem gives action a transitional status in which forces that transcend the individual are realized. In Hölderlin's poetic theory, the triadic turning of the poem is linked to a theory of modes that posits a "harmonious opposition" between the Naive, the Heroic, and the Ideal, which are in a constant state of transition (*Metapher*) from one to another.[8] It is through this transition that identity is realized in the context of "the living Whole."[9] In "Der Rhein" the demigod hero (the Rhine) must be incorporated into the turning of this modality to prevent him from resolving his ambiguous identity, through which gods and humans are united in a transitional continuity:

Denn weil
Die Seeligsten nichts fühlen von selbst,
Muss wohl, wenn solches zu sagen
Erlaubt ist, in der Götter Nahmen
Theilnehmend fühlen ein Andrer,
(lines 109–13)

For since / The most Blessed in themselves feel nothing /
Another, if to say such a thing is / Permitted, must, I sup-
pose, / Vicariously feel in the name of the gods,

It is this division of the identity of action between agents
that achieves the extension traditionally promised to the hero,
but an extension that now does not *belong* to the hero. In
Olympian 10 we find Pindar describing the foundation of the
Olympic Games as a divided action in which *Khronos* again
performs the work of the poet:

To Kronos' Hill he gave a name; for before
It was nameless when Oinomaos ruled,
And drenched with many a snowstorm.
In this first birthday-rite
The Fates stood near at hand,
And he who alone proves the very truth,

Time. In his forward march
He has revealed all clearly:

(49–55)

Dryden ends "Alexander's Feast" with a division of musical
power itself between the "mighty master" Timotheus and the
new Christian musician, Cecilia, though, for reasons that I
will explain, this fails to produce the extension it claims:

Let old *Timotheus* yield the Prize,
Or both divide the Crown;
He rais'd a Mortal to the Skies;
She drew an Angel down.
(lines 167–70)

As we shall see, Dryden's poem pinpoints the difficulty for the
modern poet of realizing an agency that is open toward the
divine, for a self-conscious virtuosity has cut "practical" mu-
sic off from the metaphysical *Musica Mundana* that used to
connect us with the heavenly spheres.[10]

In *Nemean* 1 the relation between hero and poet was un-problematic, but in the three poems from which I have just quoted there is an element of struggle between the agents that arises from the conflict between the contracting force of the hero and the modal turning performed by the poet. This is immediately apparent in the transformation that Pindar's story of Herakles and the snakes undergoes in Hölderlin's "Der Rhein." The poem begins with the poet sitting, like Pindar, at the threshold of the hero's sphere, "Amid dark ivy . . . At the forest's gate" (1–2), from where he hears the Rhine thundering within the forest. But here the separation of hero and poet is more precarious, for the river is an image that in Hölderlin's poetry represents the urge of an humanity, im-patient with limitation, to take "the quickest route back to the All."[11]

This is an urge that is characteristic of Hölderlin's revolu-tionary friend, Sinclair, the addressee of this poem and a man to whose fiery temperament the poet felt dangerously suscep-tible.[12] In another poem addressed to Sinclair ("An Eduard"),[13] Hölderlin describes himself as, like Ganymede, an "easy booty" (*leichte Beute*) of his friend, who will carry him off to confront the "god of Time" (*Zeitengott*).[14] Hölderlin's fear that he will be swept away by the revolutionary fervor of his friend and take the "quickest route" is reflected in his version of Herakles and the snakes, where the Rhine plays the part of Herakles:

> Nicht liebt er, wie andere Kinder,
> In Wikelbanden zu weinen;
> Denn wo die Ufer zuerst
> An die Seit ihm schleichen, die Krummen,
> Und durstig umwindend ihn,
> Den Unbedachten, zu ziehen
> Und wohl zu behüten begehren
> Im eigenen Zähne, lachend
> Zerreisst er die schlangen und stürzt
> Mit der Beut. . . .
>
> (lines 62–71)

Nor is he fond, like other children, / Of weeping in swaddling bands; / For where the banks at first / Slink to his side, the crooked / And greedily entwining him, / Desire to educate /

> And carefully tend the feckless / Within their teeth, he laughs, / Tears up the serpents and rushes / Off with his booty. . . .

The more complicated relation between poet and hero is indicated here by the *protective* role of the snakes, which the limited perspective of the hero cannot comprehend. The banks have been placed in the Rhine's path by the god who "wishes to spare his sons a life so fleeting" (lines 76–77) and to protect the hero from his own self-destructive tendencies. But the winding of the swaddling clothes and of the "crooked" banks also represent the movement of the poem, whose triadic turning will modulate the Rhine's thoughtless onrush, provided the hero does not succeed in making the poem into the "booty" of its rampage, as Sinclair threatened to do with Hölderlin. In this poem the survival of the poet, as well as that of the hero, is at stake.

An earlier poem of Hölderlin's "Buonaparte," poses the problem of the relation between vital hero and containing poem in a simpler form:[15]

> Heilige Gefässe sind die Dichter,
>   Worinn des Lebens Wein, der Geist
>   Der Helden sich aufbewahrt,
>
> Aber der Geist dieses Jünglings
>   Der schnelle, müsst' er es nicht zersprengen
>   Wo es ihn fassen wollte, das Gefäss?
>   (lines 1–6)

> Poets are holy vessels / in which the wine of life, / The spirit of heroes is preserved; / But this young man's spirit, / The quick—would it not burst / Any vessel that tried to contain it?

The poem concludes that Bonaparte cannot "live and last" in the poem, only in the world. "Der Rhein" is not so easy with its distinctions, and that is primarily because the poem is no longer merely a vessel in which the hero is "preserved," as the much-abused *topos* of encomiastic poetry would have it. In "Der Rhein," it is the winding of the poem that allows the hero to last in the world in which he would otherwise exhaust himself.

I have already spoken of the beginning of Pindar's *Olympian* 10 in connection with the poet's "forgetting" of the debt imposed on him by the victory.[16] As in "Der Rhein," the hero (victor) threatens to appropriate the poet, on whose heart he is "inscribed." Pindar reacts by claiming that he has forgotten the inscription, but this act of aggression against the victor is as benign as that of the snakes in Hölderlin's poem, for, by diverting the original debt into an area that is controlled by the poet (interest), Pindar extends the victory into a wider human context, symbolized by the *tokos* (child/interest) that appears at the end of the poem. The encomium provides a *transition* from victor to poet rather than a surface on which the victor is inscribed.

The myth in this poem concerns Herakles' punishment of Augeas for his refusal to pay the debt incurred when Herakles cleaned the Augean stables; it clearly reflects the relation between poet and victor, though, as we shall see, in a more complex fashion than one might at first assume. Herakles first enters the ode in a short mythical exemplum, reminding the victor of his own debt (of gratitude); the passage occurs in the first epode, which effects a transition between Pindar's debt to the victor and the victor's debt to his trainer:

> we shall carry out our contract
> To his dear delight.
> For Simplicity [*Atrekeia*] rules the city
> Of the Lokrians in the West,
> And their care is for Kalliopa
> And brazen Ares.
> —Even prodigious [*hyperbion*] Herakles
> Was turned in battle with Kyknos—.
> Let Hagesidamos,
> Who has won in the boxing at Olympia,
> Thank Ilas as Patroklos thanked Achilles.
>
> (11–19)

If the care of the Lokrians for the Muse Kalliope is to be exemplified by Hagesidamos's relation to Pindar, then the victor is as much in the poet's debt as vice versa.[17] There is a pointed silence about Kalliope as the reference to Ares is developed, and one may assume that what is said about Ares is implied about Kalliope. Pindar mentions the story of Herakles' fight with Kyknos, Ares' son, to remind Hagesidamos that he cannot stand alone: Herakles was forced to retreat before Kyknos when Ares joined in against him, but he returned with Athena to defeat the monster. Hagesidamos should acknowledge his human limits by giving thanks to his trainer, Ilas, rather than testing them, as did Herakles. Similarly, Hagesidamos should recognize the extent of his dependence on Pindar. Not only is this implied by the symmetry between Ares and Kalliope, it is also more subtly suggested by the clash between the strict, *unwavering* nature of the "Simplicity" (*Atrekeia*) that demands Pindar's repayment of his debt and the *turning* of the victor's mythical counterpart in the battle with Kyknos.[18] The word *Atrekeia*, etymologically cognate with the Latin word *torqueo* (twist),[19] means "undeviating," and clearly contrasts the justice that the Lokrians might exact from Pindar with the turning (*trape*, 15) of Herakles in the fight with Kyknos. In fact, what Pindar does in the first triad is to "turn" the language of debt (see especially the metaphor of the tide, 7–10) in order to make the dependence of victor and poet mutual. The time that comes from afar and shames (*kataiskhynei*, 8) the poet's deep debt becomes a wave that sweeps away (*kataklyssei*, 10) the pebbles that compute the debt. Pindar exposes the fixed relation figured by the inscription of the debt on the poet's mind to the reciprocity that characterizes relations in the *epinikion*. At the end of the ode, Pindar will claim that this turning works out to the victor's advantage by releasing his victory from the world of contracted relationships governed by strict repayment into the expanding world of transitional relationships, where it will find an heir.

The narrative in the second triad takes us through a labyrinthine winding to the punishment of Augeas:

> The ordinances of Zeus have roused me
> To sing of the grandest of Games,
> Which by the ancient tomb of Pelops,
> With contests six in number, Herakles founded
> When he slew Poseidon's son, fine Kteatos,

And slew Eurytos, to exact
From violent Augeas,
Willing from an unwilling giver,
The wages for his serfdom [*latrion*].
In bushes under Kleonai
He trapped and broke them on the road;
For his Tirynthian army,
When it sat in the vales of Elis,
Had been slaughtered before

By the insolent Moliones;
The Epeians' king, cheater of strangers,
Soon afterwards saw his rich land in stubborn flame,
And under strokes of iron
Into a deep pit of doom
His own city sinking.

(24–38)

The narrative is constructed to emphasize the reversals that Herakles inflicts on enemies who had at first humiliated him: Augeas who had welshed on his debt, and his nephews, the Moliones, Kteatos and Eurytos, who had defeated Herakles in an ambush.[20] This follows the pattern set up by the reference to Herakles' battle with Kyknos, in which the hero was at first turned back because of Ares' aid to his adversary, but then returned for a rematch with Athena as ally and success as the outcome. Both the structure and the language of the main narrative focus on the reversibility of human relationships. The texture of the language is particularly dense with reversals and ambiguity at the beginning of the second antistrophe (28–30), where the juxtaposition "willing from an unwilling" (*aekonth' hekōn*, 29) indicates the reversal of the original relationship, in which Herakles unwillingly served Augeas. Because the verb *exact* takes a double accusative (of thing exacted and person exacted from), the adjectives *servile* (*latrion*, 28) and *violent* (*hyperbion*, 29) may grammatically apply to Augeas or to the wages that Herakles exacted, although this is not apparent in the translation, because English word order is less flexible than Greek. Herakles exacts the wages for his servility from Augeas, but since the adjective *latrion* is separated from the noun *wages* and juxtaposed with *Augeas*, with whom it shares the accusative case, we are to understand that servility is something that circulates between the cheated Herakles and the punished Augeas. The adjective *hyperbion* is also separated from its apparent noun, *Augeas,* and appears next to *wages* (*misthon,* 29). Not only is Augeas "overweening / violent" in his refusal to honor his debt to Herakles, but Herakles is also potentially guilty of the same overbearing violence when he collects his payment by destroying the whole city of Augeas. The word *hyperbion* has already been used of the Herakles who could not prevail against Kyknos and Ares (15) on his own; it describes the quality of presumption that leads a man to exceed his brief.[21] In the struggle for mastery between Augeas and Herakles, servility and overbearing violence are qualities that circulate between them. The "prodigious" (*hyperbion,* 15) Herakles is turned and returned from the moment he enters the ode in connection with Pindar's exhortation that the victor give thanks to his trainer. Neither hero nor victor can stand as a fixed locus of value, for to be "overwhelming" in this world is to be "overweening."

Clearly the myth of Herakles and Augeas reflects the relationship between Pindar and Hagesidamos, or at least the more aggressive aspects of this relationship. The question of debt is at stake in both cases. Herakles, as the punisher of one who has not respected his obligations, plunging this guest-deceiver (*xenapatas,* 34) into a "deep pit of doom" (*bathun es okheton atas,* 37), enacts the punishment of Pindar, the potential deceiver of his host (*alitoxenon,* 6) who is shamed by his "deep debt" (*bathu khreos,* 8). But there is another way of applying this myth, according to which the Herakles who served a lesser man, and turned the tables on his apparent master when the latter refused to recognize him, is Pindar himself. The victor had been urged to give thanks to his trainer, as the human representative of Ares, and (implicitly) to Pindar, as the human representative of Kalliope. In the figure of Herakles, victor and poet are combined or, rather, the claims of each on the other are represented in the same action. Both the form of the narrative, which emphasizes a reversal of relations between Augeas and Herakles, and the ambiguous application of the myth to the relation between Pindar and Hagesidamos serve to undermine the rule of un-wavering accuracy (*Atrekeia*) that would inscribe Pindar's heart with the name of his creditor. Up to this point, Pindar's pur-pose has been to escape the confinement that debt and strict repayment might impose on both himself and the victor. This first part of the ode, then, is distinguished by its sinuous turn-ing as Pindar evolves a more dynamic and flexible form of re-lationship between the agents. By contrast, the second part of the ode is much more straightforward in form and expres-sion, because a transitional relation between the agents has been achieved.

After Herakles has destroyed Augeas's city, he recognizes his dependent status by founding the precinct of Zeus at Olympia and instituting the Olympic Games. This founding act passes into the hands of Time in a way reminiscent of Herakles' first victory in *Nemean* 1:

> To Kronos' Hill he gave a name; for before
> It was nameless when Oinomaos ruled,
> And drenched with many a snowstorm.
> In this first birthday-rite
> The Fates stood near at hand,
> And he who alone proves the very truth,
>
> Time. In his forward march
> He has revealed all clearly:
>
> (49–55)

There are aspects of this founding that recall the opening of the poem. Pindar called on the Muse to read out the name in-scribed on his heart; Herakles addresses by name the Hill of Kronos, which was nameless and covered with snow in the reign of Oinomaos.[22] The forgetfulness figured by the snow-storms in which the hill is submerged is original, unlike the forgetfulness of Pindar, which intervened in the relationship between victor and poet.[23] Herakles' originary naming con-trasts with Pindar's recognition of the victor's name, but if Herakles originates the identity of the hill and founds the Olympic Games, it is the attendance of Time and the Fates (*Moirai*) that introduces these acts into the dimension of

Alatheia (truth, unforgetfulness). Pindar's forgetting and rec-
ognizing substituted a new beginning for the contracted and
contracting debt with which his heart was inscribed, and,
with the song represented as *tokos,* it linked him with the
forward-moving Time that took over from Herakles' originary
naming of the Hill of Kronos. Time now goes forward (55) to
expand the significance of the hero's act, whereas in the first
antistrophe it moved backward from the future to contract the
victor's environment into the deep debt in which he would en-
gulf it (7–8). In order to reach this representation of the origi-
nal relation between the heroic act and a fulfilling Time,
Pindar had first to modify the backward-looking relation be-
tween himself and the victor and to loosen the fixity of the
heroic identity.

The first naming of the victor in the ode's second line al-
ready implies that identity is established through time, since
Hagesidamos is referred to as the "son of Archestratos"; the
names of both father and son mean "leader of the people," so
that to read the son's name is to recognize the father's. From
the beginning, Pindar plays the role that will be given the at-
tendant Time at the end of the myth, refusing to see truth, or
un-forgetfulness, confined within fixed identities or rela-
tions. Paradoxically, *Alatheia* depends on a form of forgetting
that separates poet from victor in order to produce a continu-
ity between them. In the *epinikion,* identity is always pro-
jected across a distance.[24]

Pindar follows the founding of the Olympic Games with
an unusually bare and rather lengthy passage in which he
enumerates the victors at the first Games. Continuing the for-
ward movement of Time that "reveals all clearly" (53–55), this
passage emphasizes the direct motion of the victors to their
goal, of which the footrace's "straight stretch" (*euthun tonon,*
64) is typical. The simplicity of language and lack of detail
convey the godlike ease with which these mythical figures
made their prayer/boast (*eukhos*) in expectation and took hold
of it in action (63). This contrasts markedly with the labyrin-
thine turning to which action was subject in the first part of
the ode, in which the poet was concerned to prevent the hero
from contracting the context of his act. Now that the heroic

act is in the hands of time, it may be presented as more direct. The final triad of the ode begins with the words, "Late indeed have they [the sounds of the ode] appeared" (85). As they are enjambed from the previous triad that describes the original Olympic Games, and in turn introduce the simile of the late child that represents the present encomium, there is an ambiguity as to the referent of the "long time": is this the time elapsed since the first Olympic Games, of which the present games are indeed a late child, or is it the time elapsed since the poet "forgot" his debt to the victor? Both lapses of time are the dimension in which the poet realizes the full context of victory: the shout that greeted the victors at the first Olympic Games (72–73) still sounds in the present ode, in which the mythical event is reawakened, and the victory/debt acquires its child/interest in the gap between the poet's forgetting and the appearance of these sounds. By conflating these two lapses of time, Pindar associates his own lapse of memory with the space across which the mythical event and the present victory mutually realize one another's identity. In effect, the forgetting by which Pindar acquired a separation from the victor was a prerequisite of his provision of a "child" for the victory. There could be no better image of the transitional nature of identity in the *epinikion* than the child that prevents an alien from inheriting the aging father's wealth, a child (*tokos*) identical with the interest (*tokos*) paid by the poet on a debt he had forgotten and then recognized.

In the final lines of the ode, Hagesidamos, or the "son of Archestratos," is associated with the most fortunate of children, Ganymede, who was carried to Olympos by Zeus's eagle, to be the cupbearer of the gods. Ganymede's divine function is responsible for some of the imagery of the final stanza in which Pindar steeps (*katabrekhōn*, 99) the city of noble men with honey, praising Hagesidamos, whom he saw

> By the Olympian altar in those days,
> Beautiful in body
> And touched by [*kekramenon*] the youthfulness
> Which once kept shameful death away
> From Ganymede, with help of the Kypros-born.
> (100–105)

The mixer of the gods' drinks is himself "mixed" (the literal meaning of *kekramenon*) with youthfulness, and Pindar himself assumes Ganymede's function with respect to the victor's city, which he steeps in the honey of his song. An action of mingling that transcends the boundaries of individual agency emerges, and one through which a path is opened up toward divinity.[25]

The combative tone of the poet's relation to the hero, which is inseparable from the poet's opening up or extending of the hero's achievement, is clearly noticeable in Dryden's "Alexander's Feast." Dryden's "myth," which describes the encomium of Timotheus at the feast celebrating Alexander's victory over the Persians, is a self-conscious reflection on the question of "the power of music," which is the poem's subtitle.[26] The late seventeenth century had seen a wave of Pindarics celebrating the accomplishments of nobility and royalty, and usually associated with public occasions. It is primarily these productions that have been responsible for giving the Pindaric a bad name, since they usually amount to little more than bombastic flattery. Against this background we must see Dryden's poem itself, commissioned by the London Musical Society, which had begun celebrating the power of music in 1683, with an annual St. Cecilia's Day ode.[27] The ironic relation of the poet to the victor's arrogant, or arrogating, identity is the theme of the myth section of Dryden's "Alexander's Feast," which takes up the bulk of the poem. Here, the ability of the poet Timotheus to turn Alexander's emotions through the modes of his song corresponds to Pindar's turning of the debt and to his narrative of Herakles and Augeas, with its reversals and inversions. The main difference between these two poems is that Dryden's ironic turning becomes a confinement from which the poem cannot escape, and the relation between hero and poet is characterized by contraction rather than expansion.

"Alexander's Feast" is a disillusioned poem, disillusioned not only about the role of the hired flatterer but also about the nature of music. At the time this poem was written (1697), music had lost its symbolic significance as a link between human activity and the heavenly concord from which we have fallen. As a matter of human virtuosity, music now contracts rather than expands our horizons, reducing the connection between heaven and earth to a metaphor that flatters the human practitioner.[28] This means that the poet himself becomes a form of hero, as I am defining that notion in this chapter; that is, he is an agent whose mastery threatens a contraction of identity. Dryden recognizes that Timotheus has become another form of Alexander as this "Mighty Master" draws Alexander into the cycle of moods that he commands; it is for this reason that Cecilia confronts Timotheus at the end of the poem as Timotheus had confronted Alexander at the beginning. In an attempt to open the circle closed by Timotheus's performance, Dryden posits a *progression* from the pagan music of Timotheus to the Christian music of Cecilia, which "added length to solemn sounds." As we shall see, this attempt founders because the power of music has become a containing rather than an expanding force. Already in the "Song for Saint Cecilia's Day" of 1687, Dryden had indicated the circularity of music's power, asking, "What passion cannot music raise and quell?" In that poem the status of the passions, made and unmade by music, is that of the "universal frame" itself, conjured up by harmony from a heap of "jarring atoms," into which it will be resolved at the last trumpet when "Musick shall untune the sky."

"Alexander's Feast" concerns the power of the musician or poet to create extension of and within the human realm. Two axes, then, are involved: the vertical axis that extends earth toward heaven, and the horizontal axis along which the various passions extend each other. In fact, as we see more clearly in Pindar and Hölderlin, the two axes are interdependent, for the possibility of a vertical relationship between earth and heaven depends on the realization of an open or transitional agency on the horizontal, or human, axis. The bulk of the poem is taken up by a description of the cycle of passions through which Timotheus leads Alexander, but the beginning and end concern the possibility of raising a mortal to the skies. When Timotheus is attributed with this latter power, which is apparently trumped by Cecilia's drawing an angel down, we are inclined to read it in its debased, metaphorical sense, equivalent to praising someone to the skies. In the opening of the poem, where the stage is set for Timotheus's performance, expressions of height are similarly loaded with the debased metaphors of the encomium, even where the height also refers to a real state of affairs. Alexander, the "God-like Heroe," sits "Aloft in awful state" and opposite him is Timotheus, "placed on high." Though Timotheus is quite literally high up in the choir, the expression conveys the respect that is graciously accorded the "higher" values of art by the warrior, a generosity that, of course, redounds to the latter's benefit, for "None but the Brave deserves the Fair" (15). From his sublime position, Timotheus's notes "ascend the Sky / And Heav'nly Joys inspire" (lines 23–24), which means either that they inspire joys in heaven or "Heav'nly Joys" on earth; the possible extension of the human realm toward heaven is in fact the appropriation of heaven as metaphor by the humans who have granted Timotheus his status, and the movement upward is really a drawing-down of heaven. Timotheus repays his elevation by bringing heaven down to earth in the story he tells of Jupiter's *amour* with Olympia (lines 25–33), which produces Alexander, "a present deity," as the crowds acclaim him.[29] "The vaulted roofs rebound" (line 37) with an echo of this cry; as Fry observes, "An echo fills the space from which the god is absent."[30] The myth is then replayed with human actors when Alexander, playing Olympia to Timotheus's Zeus, hears the poet "with ravish'd ears" (line 37) and "assumes the God" (line 39). Dryden's use of *assume* indicates that behind the myth of Olympia, in which a mortal body takes *in* the god that comes from above, lies the desire of a mortal to take *on* the god as a human role. The relation between Timotheus and Alexander is not transitional but reciprocal: the poet has been placed on high in order that Alexander may assume the God, and the circular reciprocity between them ensures that heaven remain an earthly metaphor. Timotheus, "plac'd on high," is granted a sphere that metaphorizes Alexander's situation, "aloft in awful state," but he holds this position only if he uses it to repay the loan of metaphorical height by contracting heaven to earth.

Dryden's poem begins with the potentially transitional moment in which "the Brave deserves the Fair." By "the Fair" we must understand the beauty represented both by Alexander's concubine Thais and by the poet, perhaps equally meretricious. At the end of the Alexander story, it is these two agents who return Alexander to war. When Alexander has been turned to thoughts of love by Timotheus, Thais cradles the "Vanquished Victor" on her breast (line 115), but the victor's warlike spirit is vanquished, to be roused again to vengeance only by Timotheus's "lowder Strain" (line 124), and as the king seizes a torch to destroy the Persian palace it is Thais who leads him:

> *Thais* led the Way,
> To light him to his Prey,
> And, like another *Hellen* fir'd another *Troy.*
> (lines 148–50)

It would seem that the brave deserve the fair only to have the fair return them to further acts of "bravery," a circular relationship that allows for variety but not extension. Like Pindar, Timotheus inserts the hero into an ironic turning in which identity (here, the identity of the passions) is in a constant state of transition: as Alexander weeps with pity for Darius, "the Mighty Master smil'd to see / That Love was in the next Degree" (lines 93–94). The word "Degree," however, indicates the difference between Pindar and Timotheus, for the latter's mastery consists in his ability to close the circle or complete the gamut of the passions and ends by confirming the hero in his martial spirit. On the horizontal, as on the vertical, axis the relation between poet and hero is reciprocal and serves only to confine the hero; metaphor and irony, the dimensions of Timotheus's potential extension of Alexander, are merely new forms of closed mastery.

It is Cecilia who is introduced in the final stanza to break the circle and to straighten out the movement of the poem into an extending progression:

> Thus, long ago
> 'Ere heaving Bellows learn'd to blow
>   While Organs yet were mute;
> *Timotheus,* to his breathing Flute,
>   And sounding Lyre,
> Cou'd swell the Soul to rage, or kindle soft Desire.
>   At last Divine *Cecilia* came,
>   Inventress of the Vocal Frame;
> The sweet Enthusiast, from her Sacred Store,
>   Enlarg'd the former narrow Bounds;
>   And added Length to solemn Sounds,
> With Nature's Mother-Wit, and Arts unknown before.
>   (lines 155–66)

This is the equivalent of the straightening-out that Pindar's ode undergoes after Herakles founds the Olympic Games: the turning power of Timotheus, who can divert rage into desire, is subsumed into the power of Cecilia to enlarge the bounds of a circular modality.[31] But Dryden is in fact unable to break out of the poem's circularity, and the relationship between Timotheus and Cecilia fails to escape the mold; finally Cecilia plays Timotheus to Timotheus's Alexander:

> Let old *Timotheus* yield the Prize,
>   Or both divide the Crown;
> He rais'd a Mortal to the Skies;
>   She drew an Angel down.
>   (lines 166–70)

The succession from Timotheus to Cecilia is bent into the circle of the crown that they make up between them: Cecilia's achievement seems to cast an ironic light on Timotheus's, insofar as the Christian context convicts the pagan encomiast of empty presumption, but in fact the two actions are complementary aspects of a single process in which what goes up comes down, and the metaphorization of heaven is the result. Cecilia draws the angel down as Timotheus (and Olympia) drew down Jove in the second stanza, where the god stamped "an Image of himself, a Sov'raign of the World" on the breast of a mortal. As Timotheus had repaid the height lent him by the hero who placed him "on high," so Cecilia pays back

Timotheus for yielding the prize by performing an action that complements his and completes the circle of the crown that they share. Dr. Johnson pointed out that the argument of the conclusion is vicious, since Timotheus's raising of a mortal to the skies had only a metaphorical effect, whereas Cecilia really drew an angel down: "the crown, therefore, could not reasonably be divided." [32] This is true enough, but it is clear that Dryden has assimilated the by then trivialized Cecilia legend of amatory verse to the same level as the metaphorical effect of Timotheus's encomium. Furthermore, Cecilia's achievement in seducing an angel from heaven is hardly more praiseworthy than Timotheus's inflation of a mortal to divine status.

In Dryden's ode, the division of action between two agents not only fails to release a power, such as Pindar's Time, that transcends the individual and releases the hero's mastery from its confinement, it has the opposite effect, of arrogating power and extension (now a metaphorical creation) to the human agents. Music is no longer the guarantee of our extension toward heaven, but, rather, the proof of our power to bring heaven down to earth. Dryden's Cecilia myth produces a motion between heaven and earth opposite to that of the Ganymede myth with which Pindar ends *Olympian* 10; in Pindar, as René Schaerer has put it, man is only an actualizable possibility, and the act is God's. [33]

One of the main concerns of Hölderlin's later poetry is to release action from its dependence on a subjective intention, and this is connected with a theory of modes and of metaphor that takes us beyond the enclosed circularity of human agency and musical modality in Dryden. When Hölderlin speaks of *Metapher*, he foregrounds its original sense ("to carry across") and its transitional force, giving it a function quite the opposite of that which it has in Dryden's poem. For Hölderlin, the poem is a "metaphor" because it is a process of transference between the three modes: naive, heroic, and ideal. These modes are not the degrees of a circle or scale, as in Timotheus's performance, but, rather, partial states that exist in constant tension with one another. The application of the theoretical writing of Hölderlin to any particular poem is highly problematic, and, even though he left an account of the "rule" (*Gesetz*) of "Der Rhein," I shall not attempt to fit the poem into a particular scheme.[34] However, Hölderlin's description of the poem's "rule" presents the same general structure that we have seen in *Olympian* 10 and "Alexander's Feast": "The rule of this song is that the two first parts are opposed in form as progress and regress, but similar in content, while the last resolves all in a continuous *Metapher*." The oppositional turning of progress and regress in the first four triads is straightened out into a continuous transition (*Metapher*) in the final triad, a procedure Pindar follows and Dryden tries to follow. In all three cases, the turning portion of the poem serves to release action into the wider context of the final part by undermining the contracting force of the hero's act.

In general conception, Hölderlin's "Der Rhein" resembles Goethe's Pindaric "Mahomets Gesang." The life of the hero is represented as the course of the river, an idea clearly derived from Horace's presentation of Pindar in *Carm.* 4.2. But in Hölderlin's poem the presence of the poet reflecting on the fate of the river/hero and on his own problematic relation to that fate is far more emphatic than in Goethe. In fact, the poet's gradual understanding of the river's *Schicksal* accounts for the metamorphic succession of different types of heroic life that provides the analogy with the river's course. The poem presents us with a somewhat internalized version of the pair poet-hero. As de Man has observed, the pairing of a "titanic" hero with a reflective counterpart is a recurring motif in Hölderlin's work, and it points to the dual nature of the poetic act itself. The heroic or prophetic element of this act must be preserved from its self-destructive urge toward a blind confrontation with death (or immediate revelation) by the reflective element, which creates for it a temporal dimension that keeps it bound to the earth.[35] The first part of the poem focuses on the Rhine as rebellious demi-god, chafing at his alienation from the divine source; here the reflecting poet's description of the river's turbulent course serves to figure the deflection of the demi-god from the different forms of excess through which he would resolve his ambiguous status. As the poem straightens out into a more linear narrative, the *Schicksal* of the Rhine is transformed successively into that of three figures with whom Hölderlin feels a special affinity: Rousseau, Socrates, and Sinklair. The Rhine, who has been diverted from the "quickest route" in which the All would be contracted by the resolution of his status, is assimilated into a *continuous* metamorphosis of the heroic in which linear extension is reconciled with the ironic "smile of the Father" to which humanity must remain open.

The contrast between Hölderlin's *Metapher* and Dryden's metaphor has its roots in their different conceptions of the relationship between hero (demi-god), poet, and heaven. While Dryden's poet participates in the hero's contraction of heaven to earth, Hölderlin tries to prevent the Rhine from resolving its ambiguous status toward either heaven or earth. Like the god who "wishes to spare his sons a life so fleeting" (lines 76–77), the poet extends the life on earth of the heroic Rhine, alienated from its divine source and raging to escape its imprisonment. In the place of Timotheus's smile we now have the smile of the god who watches the demi-god raging in the depths (lines 76–80); it is a smile that indicates an ironic perspective on the Rhine's partial sense of its context, but not the perspective of the poet/master who will complete the circle—in Hölderlin it is never the poet who smiles.[36] In fact, the god himself needs the hero as much as the latter needs the god to extend his fleeting life (see lines 109–13, quoted on p. 114). The earth is the temporal dimension of divine Being or, rather, the place where that Being is temporalized, as the demi-god there experiences the divine source in his falling away from it.[37] Here, the human and the divine mutually extend each other. The poet, who is situated at the beginning of the poem "Amid dark ivy . . . At the forest's gate" (1–2), recalls Pindar's Teiresias; like Teiresias, the poet "perceived a destiny" ("Vernahm . . . ein Schicksaal," 10–11) from his marginal position, but Hölderlin's relation to the Rhine-as-Herakles differs from that of Teiresias to Herakles and is more comparable to the problematic relationship between poet and hero in *Olympian* 10. From his shady idyll, the poet had nostalgically projected himself to the geographical and historical locus of divine immediacy, Italy and Greece (lines 11–15), when he was recalled to the present by the "destiny" of the Rhine, a being similarly drawn to the divine "source." By following, or revealing, the destiny of the Rhine, held to the earth by the smiling god, Hölderlin will foil his own tendency to take "the quickest route," provided he resist the temptation to be drawn into the Rhine's heroic excess.[38]

The story of the poet's relation to the Rhine in this poem is the story of his survival of various forms of resolution into which the Rhine's *Schicksal* threatens to contract. The *Metapher* of the heroic is realized by Hölderlin's "carrying across" of the Rhine's excess (*Übermass*) through a succession of different forms and of different heroic figures. As the figures in which the heroic is localized become close to Hölderlin himself (Rousseau, Socrates, Sinklair), the poem's movement of "progress and regress" is straightened into the linear temporality of the day in the middle of which the poem begins. But the relation of human to divine now takes the form of the hero's recognition (*Erkennen*) of the god's smile, which depends on accepting the unfinished extension of the human realm.[39]

As a demi-god, the Rhine is a being for whom the divine is constantly present in the mode of its absence, a being that cannot forget the divine source as others do. Its impatience with the shackles of the earth lead it alternately to separate from and to rejoin its environment. The first triad, which begins with the poet sitting in the protective confinement of "dark ivy," ends with the distinction between the man and beast who know where they should build and the demi-gods in whose "inexperienced [*unerfahren*] souls" has been implanted "the defect of not knowing where?" ("Der Fehl dass sie nicht wissen wohin?"). But this bifurcation of existence on earth is reversed by the movement of the second triad, which begins by declaring that what is "of pure origin" (*Reinentsprungenes*, line 46) is a mystery that even song cannot reveal but ends with the Rhine supporting children in cities it has founded. Between these two points, the Rhine's presence threatens to draw nature into its bacchantic riot, a form of union that is prevented by the god who restrains it with the "holy Alps" until it contents itself with the founding of German cities. This taming of the mystery of what is of pure origin by overlaying a human founding on a divine origin runs the risk of *hybris*, so the third triad begins by reminding us that the dwellings and laws of man will sooner be destroyed than the Rhine forget his origin. The repose achieved at the end of the second triad is broken up in the third by warnings of the destruction inflicted on the man who attempts to be like the gods, for what they need is one who will "feel vicariously" in their name, recognizing his own difference.

In the first three triads, the Rhine is turned through a number of metamorphoses, becoming a succession of mythical heroes, each of which presents (for the poet) a form of attraction that threatens to draw him into the Rhine's heroic excess. The baby Herakles, who is not content with his earthly swaddling clothes, turns into the enchanter Orpheus, dissolving with his song the resistance of matter:

> und wie Bezauberte fliehn
> Die Wälder ihm nach und zusammensinkend die Berge.
> (lines 74–75)

and like enchanted things / The forests join his flight and, collapsing, the mountains.

But this enchantment is resisted, and the bacchantic transcendence of the earth is converted into the service of the culture hero who founds cities, perhaps another aspect of Herakles, the toiling benefactor of civilization. The culture hero falls into another form of excess, that of Prometheus, who appropriated divine fire to human purposes:

> Dann haben des eigenen Rechts
> Und gewiss des himmlischen Feuers
> Gespottet die Trozigen,
> (lines 100–101)

Then, sure of their own right / And of the heavenly fire / Defiant rebels mocked. . . .

Prometheus in turn gives way to two other heroes from Greek tragedy, Oedipus and the mad Herakles of Euripides, who involve those closest to them in the ruin brought on by their failure to observe the boundaries between human and divine (lines 114–20).

At this point the poem withdraws into the contemplation of a hypothetical *Schicksal* that itself culminates in retirement from the preceding forms of active heroic excess, which are left behind as the tormented past of a journey or life that is now recollected in tranquillity:

> Drum wohl ihm, welcher fand
> Ein wohlbeschiedenes Schicksaal,
> Wo noch der Wanderungen
> Und süss der Leiden Erinnerung
> Aufrauscht am sichern Gestade,
> (lines 121–25)

So happy he who has found / A well-allotted fate / Where still of his wanderings / And sweetly of his afflictions / The memory murmurs on banks that are sure. . . .

As the third triad draws to a close, with the hero received into the arms of the divine, which "smiles" on him (line 133) in his retirement, all three agents (divinity, hero, and poet) are drawn together, and the point at which they meet is the end of a *linear* sequence. Here the model of Pindar's *Nemean* 1 reasserts itself, for this vision of the toiling hero's rest in a divine milieu recalls the end of Teiresias's prophecy and the apotheosis of Herakles.

The merging of agents in the closed narrative of an individual life that subsumes all previous forms of heroism into its own past brings with it a shift in the nature of the figure who incarnates this aspect of the demi-god. The hypothetical ("So happy he who") is filled by an historical figure to whom Hölderlin felt particularly close, and that is Rousseau. As the author of the *Confessions* and the *Rêveries*,[40] Rousseau is the hero who creates an internal resolution, through memory (*Erinnerung*), of the alienation that has characterized his past life.[41] However, when Hölderlin recognizes this *Schicksal* as that of one of the "dear ones" whose lives fill him with longing (lines 135–38), he steps back from this all-too-powerful attraction. In the course of this stanza, Rousseau is transformed from one of the "dear ones" to a "stranger" who gives away the language of the gods from his own profusion. The idyll is broken by Hölderlin's consciousness of his own vulnerability to such a priest of immediate revelation. Rousseau himself experiences the same horror at his appropriation of divine language, an act that is cast in the form of one of the labors of Herakles:

> Drum überraschet es auch
> Und schrökt den sterblichen Mann,
> Wenn er den Himmel, den
> Er mit den liebenden Armen
> Sich auf die Schultern gehäufft
> Und die Last der Freud bedenket,
> (lines 153–58)

And therefore it surprises / And startles the mortal man / When he considers the heaven which with loving arms he himself / Has heaped on his shoulders / And the burden of joy, . . .

As the poem is drawn into the continuous linearity of the life of a particular hero, it threatens to enclose the divine source in the *Erinnerung* of Rousseau.[42] But as Rousseau himself shrinks from the "burden of joy" that he has heaped on his shoulders to confine himself to the shade of the forest "where the beam does not sear" (line 161), his situation merges into that of the poet in his midday idyll at the beginning of the poem. The scale of linear time is converted from the life of Rousseau to the day of the poet as the poem takes up its own suspended opening:

> Und herrlich ists, aus heiligem Schlafe dann
> Erstehen und aus Waldes Kühle
> Erwachend, Abends nun
> Dem milderen Licht entgegenzugehen,
> (lines 166–69)

And glorious then it is to arise once more / From holy sleep and awakening / From coolness of the woods, at evening / Walk now toward the softer light. . . .

The various forms of alienation which, in the opening of the poem, had threatened to resolve themselves in a contraction of being are resolved or leveled out (*ausgeglichen*, line 182) in the pervading *Metapher* of the final stanzas of the poem. In his "narrative" of the Rhine's career, Hölderlin has been confronted with the temptation to resolve the alienation of the human from the divine in a contraction that would center on the hero. But it was the *meeting* of heaven and earth that had originated the Rhine's sense of its alienation, for its raging *Schicksal* began as the sun stood above the mountain in the "golden midday." Now the meeting of heaven and earth is represented as the transient moment of evening when the day, "smiling" (line 152), inclines to its "pupil" and "Fate for a while is leveled out" (lines 162–63). The "smiling" relationship between heaven and earth, in which each is extended by the other, is maintained by the transient nature of the union. In a sense, the poem here recreates its own beginning, the "source" which "even song cannot reveal," just as Pindar recreates the original inscription, forgotten by his song, when by an act of naming Herakles establishes the Olympic Games, and Time, moving forward now, reveals the truth. In Hölderlin's midday beginning, the heroic existence is defined by its yearning to rejoin the source, prompted by the alienation in which it becomes conscious of itself. Now the transient moment within heroic *Schicksal*, in which the divine inclines to the human, brings with it a further version of the heroic: the power to survive this moment with a clear consciousness that will maintain its continuity with the rest of time. This form of the heroic is represented by another historical figure important to Hölderlin, Socrates:[43]

> Ein weiser aber vermocht es
> Vom Mittag bis in die Mitternacht,
> Und bis der Morgen erglänzte,
> Beim Gastmahl helle zu bleiben.
> (lines 207–10)

A wise man, though, was able / From noon to midnight, and on / Till morning lit up the sky / To keep wide awake at the banquet.

In this form the relation to the divine can be carried across time, and in the final stanza Hölderlin turns to the most powerful heroic figure in the present, his friend Sinklair. In whatever form the god appears to him, whether immediately or through the turbulence of history, Sinklair recognizes the "smile" of the Ruler, a smile that is connected with the modality of human existence:

> das Lächeln des Herrschers
> Bei Tage, wenn
> Es fieberhaft und angekettet das
> Lebendige scheinet oder auch
> Bei Nacht, wenn alles gemischt
> Ist ordnungslos und wiederkehrt
> Uralte Verwirrung.
>
> (lines 215–21)

the smile of the Ruler / By day, when all / That lives seems febrile and fettered, or also / By night, when all is mingled / Chaotically and back again comes / Primeval confusion.

In form this ending is comparable to Dryden's: the straightening-out of the movement of progress and regress into the linear motion of continuous *Metapher* seems to be retracted in the final alternative (*oder auch*). But where Dryden's complementary and opposite motions arrogate the divine sphere to the human, Hölderlin's alternatives prevent the localization of the divine in any particular earthly moment. The hero's relation to divinity is now established by his very acceptance of modality, in which the smile of the "Ruler" is recognized. The final lines of the poem present the imprisonment of vital forces and the chaotic outbreak of the same, which had earlier been two aspects of the hero's reaction to his alienation from the source, as moments of the temporal dimension (day and night) in which Sinklair recognizes the smile of the god. Sinklair, as the final transformation of the heroic in the *Metapher*, is at once the most immediate and potentially overwhelming presence of the demi-god and the least arrogant (or arrogating) agent of the relation between human and divine. The indifferent alternation of a repressive day and an anarchic night through which the divine smile is apprehended ensures that the evening toward which the end of the poem draws, under the influence of Rousseau, is survived, and that neither the poem nor the relation between god and human is crystallized into an event.

It has been said that the encomiast puts the achievement of the victor in the context of the established values of his class.[44] It cannot be denied that Pindar sees the victory as an exemplification of aristocratic values and as a continuation of the glorious history of aristocratic families reaching back into the mythical past. But the encomium does not simply enshrine the victory in some body of supposedly eternal values. Some time ago Gundert drew attention to the significance of *Kharis*, which he defined as "response" (*Gegenleistung*), in the relation between poet and victor, and, one might add, among all agents involved in the *agōn*.[45] To acknowledge the community of *Kharis* is to acknowledge one's mortal status, which forbids one to make an absolute value out of anything one has, does, or is. In Pindar and Hölderlin and, by implication, in Dryden, the acceptance of the transpersonal status of action and value is also the disclosure of the human to the divine.

6

Order and Violence

Pythian 1, Horace's "Cleopatra Ode," and Marvell's "Horatian Ode"

In these last two chapters I will be concerned with the character of poetic order and texture in the Pindaric and, in the present chapter, more particularly with the function of poetic order as a model of political order. There is a distinct paradox in the fact that the Pindaric has traditionally been regarded as the appropriate form in which to celebrate formal occasions and the political dispensation that supports them, for from the time of Horace the Pindaric has been seen as the type of the irregular, lawless poem. Congreve was the first to confront this problem, insisting, against Cowley and his followers, that "there is nothing more regular than the Odes of *Pindar*"; this statement comes in his "Discourse on the Pindarique Ode," significantly attached to "A Pindarique Ode Humbly Offered to the Queen on the Victorious Progress of Her Majesty's Arms under the Conduct of the Duke of Marlborough."[1] Congreve's apology for the Pindaric anxiously seeks to bypass a genuine paradox. In fact, there are two contradictory aspects to the Pindaric's response to the formal occasion or institution that it celebrates. On the one hand, the metrical pattern and the formalized dance that originally accompanied it celebrate the closed order to which Pindar appeals at the beginning of *Pythian* 1:

> O lyre of gold, Apollo's
> Treasure, shared with the violet-wreathed Muses,
> The light foot hears you, and the brightness begins:
> Your notes compel the singer
> When to lead out the dance
> The prelude is sounded on your trembling strings.
>
> (1–4)

But the unruly leaps of thought and the almost violent dyna-
mism that are equally characteristic of Pindar are also in-
spired by the occasions and institutions he is celebrating:

> If my purpose is set to praise
> Wealth or strength of hands or iron-clad war,
> Dig a long pit for my jump from here;
> I have a light spring in my knees.
> Eagles swoop even across the sea.
>
> (*N*. 5.19–21)

The conjunction of the dance and the leap, of the motion that
encloses a space and the motion that opens it up, is reflected
in phrases such as Boileau's *beau désordre* that traditionally
describe the dynamic formality of the ode.[2] According to
Boileau, Pindar leaves the confines of reason in order to re-
turn to them more securely.[3] This distinction between inside
and outside maintains the closure of a form in relation to
which the leaps reveal an outside that has merely negative or
secondary status. The poems I shall consider in this chapter
are concerned with the relation between outside and inside in
both poetic and political order; they are poems that seem to
derive their own energy from the disruptive presence of the
great opponents of an established political order. In each case
an order founded on the exclusion of a violent opponent is
forced to recognize this opponent as internal to itself, so that
both the poetic and the political order discover a violent en-
ergy within themselves in terms of which they must be re-
defined. This is a reflection of the *agōn* itself, which is both a
gathering and a separating, a conflict and a celebration, and
finally, an articulation of these opposites.

Pythian 1, which celebrates both athletic and military vic-
tory, is one of the most imposing and admired works in the
Pindaric corpus. Its fame depends largely on two passages:
the opening invocation to the lyre as a symbol of the order and
harmony of Zeus's regime, and the description of the erupt-
ing Aetna beneath which lies buried the giant Typhos, enemy
of Zeus.[4] As a poem occasioned by the foundation of a new
city on the site of Aetna by the Sicilian tyrant Hieron, *Pythian*

1 is concerned with the imposition of order, and the victory it celebrates is that of Hieron over the "barbarian" Etruscans and Carthaginians in an important naval battle at Cumae. But after the stately invocation to the lyre, whose prelude "leads the dance," the ode teems with images of violence and conflict that characterize its music far better than the harmonizing effects of the lyre described in the first sentence.[5]

The circumstances of Hieron's foundation of Aetna are relevant here, for this new beginning that is synchronous with the defeat of the barbarians was not as innocent as Hieron might have liked it to be thought. Aetna was founded nearly on top of another city, Katane, whose (Ionian) inhabitants were forced to move into the new city, where they were absorbed into a population of (Doric) mercenaries in the pay of Hieron.[6] This is the aspect of the real situation that corresponds to the persistent confusion of inside and outside, self and other in this ode: the new foundation suppresses and contains an alien element. But the mixture of violence and order is in some ways intrinsic to the Pindaric itself, whose "formality" is anything but static. It is a contradiction that stems from the very essence of the *epinikion*, which celebrates the *agōn* as an instance of, and a recourse against, the chaotic shifting to which human endeavor is subject. Conflict permeates every level of *Pythian* 1, as of all of Pindar's odes; its presence in this particular ode is surprising only because Pindar is celebrating here the institution of political order subsequent to the defeat and (apparent) exclusion of the violent representatives of chaos. In this it is comparable to Horace's "Cleopatra Ode" (*Carm.* 1.37) in which the reinstitution of order by Octavian depends on banishment of the barbarian threat from Rome.[7] The rejoicing at the defeat of the chaotic violence of Cleopatra, with which the ode opens, however, is in the final stanzas channeled into an awed admiration for the Stoic suicide of the noble queen. Cleopatra, far from being excluded as the barbarian opposite of the sober Romans, takes her place *within* Roman tradition and, what is more disturbing, she does so not by abandoning but by maintaining her combative nature in the conflict with Octavian. Both these poems are agonistic in nature as well as in theme, for they conceive of order as an articulation, rather than a resolution, of conflict. If they proffer an easy separation of violence from harmony and a neat distinction between two intrinsically opposite groups (barbarians and Greeks or Romans), they then proceed to bring the excluded term within the one that is privileged. Violence is no longer represented by the barbarians excluded from a legitimately *founded* order; instead, it becomes part of the process by which order is *articulated*.

Marvell's ode on Cromwell, entitled "An Horatian Ode upon Cromwell's Return from Ireland," was clearly written under the influence of Horace's "Cleopatra Ode."[8] In this case, though, the new regime to be celebrated is that of the violent Cromwell who, though he has conquered the barbaric foreigner, has also usurped the "legitimate" power of King Charles I. There can be no question, then, of an appeal to intrinsic status or preestablished foundations in justifying Cromwell's dispensation. His violent career creates its own terms of assessment and forces Marvell to conceive of an order in which Cromwell's violent dynamism is primary. Here again, the "order" of Cromwell manifests and justifies itself in its ability to bring his initially excluded opponent within the world he is in the process of bringing about, to make Charles come into his own in the conflict with Cromwell. The process is the reverse of that of the two ancient poems: instead of the established order finding its excluded Other at its own heart, here the Other recreates what it has supplanted.

The strategy of these poems is agonistic in the sense that it manifests the process by which the Greeks brought the fluctuations of our ephemeral existence into the context of the athletic *agōn,* an order articulated by conflict. For the aristocrats whose victories Pindar celebrated, status must be suspended by the risk of the *agōn* in order to be reinstated within time, for apart from the life-giving soil of time their *phya* (stature/growth) withers.

Pythian 1 begins with a false start, associating the right to rule (*arkhos*) with the control of a beginning (*arkha*) from which an harmonious social order unfolds as the lyre begins to vibrate:

O lyre of gold, Apollo's
Treasure, shared with the violet-wreathed Muses,
The light foot hears you, and the brightness begins:
Your notes compel the singer
When to lead out the dance
The prelude is sounded on your trembling strings.

$$(1-4)$$

Pindar reserves the problematic word for the end of the sentence, where the originating motion of the instrument of Zeus's legitimate dispensation is described as a trembling vibration (*elelizomena, 4*). Much is suggested by this word that ominously evokes a coiling snake and a warcry (*eleleu*),[9] reminding us both of what preceded the institution of order (the snake of chaos) and the means by which it was imposed.[10] The lyre's trembling conceals a more primitive and violent motion that is associated with some very different instruments of order, and the prelude (*ambolas, 4*) of the lyre is revealed to be a suspension (*ambole*) of Zeus's other powers:

You quench the warrior Thunderbolt's everlasting [*aienaou*] flame:
On the scepter [Bowra "eagle," a misprint] of Zeus the eagle sleeps,
Drooping his swift wings on either side,

The king of birds.
You have poured a cloud on his beak and head,
And darkened his face:
His eyelids are shut with a sweet seal.
He sleeps, his lithe back ripples:
Your quivering song has conquered him.
Even Ares the violent
Leaves aside his harsh and pointed spears
And comforts his heart in drowsiness.
Your shafts enchant the souls even of the Gods
Through the wisdom of Lato's son
And the deep-bosomed Muses.

$$(5-12)$$

The eagle and thunderbolt are the true basis of Zeus's rule, for the fire of the thunderbolt flows eternally (*aienaou, 5*) and the very name of the eagle (*aietos, 6*) foregrounds the eternal (*aiei*) presence of these instruments of violence in Zeus's harmonious realm.[11] In what sense, then, can the lyre's music be said to replace or "quench" (5) the thunderbolt? The problem is apparent in the paradoxical nature of this quenching, which is performed not only by a liquid but also *on* a liquid, for the thunderbolt's fire is eternally *flowing* (*aienaou*). This curious effect is repeated in the description of the repression of the eagle, whose lithe back ripples (*aiōrei*, 9) under the quivering ripples (*rhipaisi*, 10) of the music.[12] Here a single rippling motion conceals two agents, or an action with two aspects, for the rippling liquid into which both music and eagle have been resolved manifests both calm and also (latent) violence. This ambiguity was already apparent in the quivering that instituted the order of the dance. Even the lyre itself, the symbolic origin of Zeus's peaceful dispensation, is but one aspect of an entity whose complexity is revealed when the lyre's "*shafts* enchant the souls even of the Gods" (12). The lyre has been conflated with the bow, an instrument related to it by the principle of tension and by its association with Apollo.[13] A further conflation of the martial and the musical is effected by the choice of the word *kēla* for "shafts"; in the context of enchantment (*thelgei*, 12) we cannot help associating it with *kēleō*, another verb meaning "enchant." Language itself seems to revolt against the distinction that is apparently being made between two intrinsically opposed instruments of control.

Three things have happened so far in this ode. First, the lyre is posited as the absolute beginning of an order that unfolded from its initiating motion. Subsequently, this principle of order is revealed to be a *new* beginning that supplants the more primitive and violent instruments of rule, the thunderbolt and the eagle.[14] Finally, the opposition between the two kinds of instruments of order is broken down as one element (water), one motion (quivering/rippling), and even one morpheme (*kēl-*) come to contain both sides of the opposition. Clearly it would be bad faith to claim that the secondary order of the harmonizing lyre makes a clean break with that of its martial "opposites," the thunderbolt and eagle that underlie Zeus's power. That Pindar is aware of this is clear from the suspicious "quenching," by music, of the thunderbolt's ever-flowing fire. What, then, is the nature of music's power, if it is neither an absolute beginning nor an opposite of what it supposedly replaces?

For the answer to this question, we must look ahead to the famous description of the erupting Aetna, where the liquid fire of Zeus's thunderbolt reappears, this time set in motion by Zeus's enemy, the hundred-headed snake Typhos ("whirlwind"):

> The Pillar of Heaven holds him fast,
> White Aitna, which all the year round
> Suckles its biting snows.
>
> Pure founts of unapproachable fire
> Belch from its depths.
> In the day-time its rivers
> Pour forth a glowing stream of smoke:
> But in the darkness red flame rolls
> And into the deep level sea
> Throws the rocks roaring.
> And that huge worm
> Spouts dreadful fountains of flame—
> A marvel and wonder to see it, a marvel even
> To hear, from those that are there,
>
> (19a–26)

To describe the fire that expresses Typhos's continued opposition to Zeus as pure/holy (*hagnotatoi*, 21) seems perverse, until we consider how this opposition manifests itself.[15] Unlike the fire of the thunderbolt, the lava does not flow eternally, but only in the night. During the day Typhos sends up smoke. His opposition, then, serves to show forth the orderly succession of night and day, whose separation out of an original chaos is one of the most important aspects of the ancient cosmogonies. In fact, Aetna, as "the Pillar of Heaven" (19b), is the site of a cosmogony, since it separates heaven from earth and suppresses the worm/snake (*herpeton*, 25) that symbolizes chaos. The ancient cosmogonies represented the emergence of order out of chaos not as a succession from one state to a totally other state, but as a separating out (*krisis*) of opposites which then exist in mutual conflict.[16] These opposites are aspects of the original chaos, which is given a temporal articulation in the permanent conflict between the opposites separated out of it, and this temporal articulation of chaos is order. The fury of Typhos and the eruption of Aetna become a source of holy wonder because they are an intrinsic part of Zeus's order: in the lava pouring from Aetna, the liquid fire of Zeus's thunderbolt reappears within rather than outside time. In fact, the presence of Typhos not only articulates the ever-flowing fire, it also introduces a temporal dimension to that other symbol of Zeus's power, the "Pillar of Heaven," which nurses snow "all the year round" (*panetēs,* 20). Against this unchanging backdrop, Typhos provides a brilliant and articulated display of smoke by day and fire by night.

It is music that takes us from the ever-flowing fire on which the dispensation of Zeus is founded to the display of the erupting Aetna that articulates order. If the violence that underlies all power (and conflates Zeus with his enemies) cannot be laid aside gratuitously in favor of some totally different form of power, if it cannot be left outside the order it founds, then order must be interpreted as a form of violence—and this is where music comes in:

> Your shafts enchant the souls even of the Gods
> Through the wisdom of Lato's son
> And the deep-bosomed Muses.
>
> And things that Zeus loves not
> Hear the voice of the maids of Pieria; they shudder
> On earth and in the furious sea,
> And *he* is afraid who lies in the horrors of Hell,
> The Gods' enemy,
> Typhos the hundred-headed,
>
> (12–16)

The dual power of music, to soothe and to provoke, accounts for the equivocal expression of its power to quench the thunderbolt. It cannot extinguish the fire, but it can transfer it, which is what happens in the transition from antistrophe to epode, for the terror that music inspires in Zeus's enemies will manifest itself in Typhos's firework display on Mount Aetna. The order instituted by music is not the primary order of the harmonious society of singers formed by the performance, nor the secondary order that comes into being when the violence of eagle and thunderbolt is suspended; instead, the order of music consists in the *articulation* of the ambivalent liquid rippling that is the source of all energy. Zeus's dispensation becomes legitimate not when it lays aside fire in favor of music, but when fire appears as the attribute of its enemy, who is in turn absorbed into the dynamics of order. Music's power lies in its ability to bring the eternal, and therefore gratuitous, power of fire into a time that it articulates rather than to quench that fire and found on its ashes an order that will be equally gratuitous.

Of course, music is Pindar's own medium, and toward the end of this ode there is an important passage in which he declares the principle of his art (I substitute my literal translation for Bowra's):

> If your speech hits on the critical point [*kairon*],
> Drawing closely together the limits [*peirata*] of many things,
> Less blame will follow you from men,
> For endless satiety [*koros*] blunts swift hopes.
>
> (81–83)

The precise meaning of this passage is disputed and I cannot pretend to give a complete explanation of it.[17] It is clear, however, that there is a distinction between *kairos* and *koros*, between a critical moment within time and a timeless satiation. The word *aianēs* (endless) qualifies *koros* and links it with the ever-flowing (*aienaou*) fire of Zeus's thunderbolt. Here *koros* is attended by blame (the most negative term in encomiastic poetry) because it blunts the hope that is one of the most important properties of agonistic man.[18] Pindar must use the same strategy as did Zeus's music if his praise is to avoid the charge of falsifying the conditions of the *agōn*; by "drawing together" into close interaction the *peirata* of many things (81–82), Pindar ensures that his praise will claim for the victor a status not outside the human situation but, rather, within the uncertain tensions that govern it.[19] Neither Zeus's rule nor Pindar's praise can be legitimate if it founds an order that is timeless in its monolithic exclusiveness (*aianēs*, 83; *aienaou*, 6).

We get a clearer sense of the procedure Pindar is describing in this passage from what follows, where the metaphor suggested by the expression "*koros blunts* swift hopes" (82–83) is developed in an exhortation to Hieron:

> Guide your host with a rudder of justice,
> And on an anvil of truth
> Forge an iron tongue.
>
> Any small [*phlauron*] spark struck out,
> Being yours, flies with power.
>
> (86–88)

The forging metaphor is another version of the "drawing together" that avoids the blunting effects of *koros*. On the face of it, Pindar appears to be saying that if Hieron forges his tongue on the anvil of truth he will avoid the trivial (*phlauron*, 87) word, and the distinction between positive and negative forms of speech appears to be emphasized by a typical polar movement between strophe and antistrophe. The logic of the metaphor, though, is disrupting, for surely flying sparks (*paraithyssei*, 87) are an inevitable *result* of forging, in which case the unconsidered word is a concomitant of the right kind of speech, not an alternative to it. Insofar as the two opposed values are aspects of the same action, Hieron's control can be at best precarious, and yet the trivial word is now contained in the controlling metaphor rather than lying outside it, where it would present a more dangerous threat to Hieron's leadership. The extraordinary violence of this metaphor reminds us of the punishment of Typhos, for the bed on which Hieron's tongue is forged is hardly more comfortable than the one that provokes Typhos's eruptions:

> The bed he lies on
> Driving furrows up and down his back
> Goads him.
>
> (28)

Zeus's repression of Typhos and Hieron's compression of his own tongue produce brilliant displays of fire that bring the excluded and unruly element *within* the order of these two rulers. Neither of these controlling acts of violence founds a static order where opposition is excluded; instead, each institutes a complex event whose nature depends on the interaction of its various aspects. Hieron's tongue lies between the anvil of truth and the sparks of triviality; the two meet on its cutting edge, the *kairos* that orders conflict without reducing it.

Pindar's situating of order within, rather than before or after, conflict produces a series of actions in which there is a confusion between inside and outside, self and other. Music suspends and provokes fire; Hieron avoids and produces the trivial word, treating his tongue as Zeus treated his enemy Typhos; and the anger of this enemy of Zeus's produces the holy fire that Zeus's subjects wonder at. The same ambiguity functions in the description of Hieron's victory against the barbarians at the naval engagement off Cumae:

> the Lord of Syracuse routed them,
> Who out of their swift-sailing ships
> Cast down their youth in the sea
> —The dragger of Hellas from her weight of slavery.
>
> (73–75)

On the face of it, the naval victory appears to secure the status of the Greeks with a successful act of aggression against the Other. But, like the apparent extinction of the thunderbolt and the suppression of Typhos, this act of exclusion is also an act of inclusion. If the casting of barbarian youth into the sea drags Hellas from her weight of slavery, are not Greeks and barbarians in the same boat?[20] The two distinct actions of casting and dragging, which at first appear to be directed at two separate groups, become aspects of a single action, and Hieron the victorious general becomes Hieron the wise captain who jettisons part of his cargo to save his ship. The metaphor puts Hieron in the same ambiguous relation to the enemy as the forging metaphor put him in relation to the trivial word.

Pythian 1 is an ode preeminently concerned with political order and power and might seem untypical of a corpus whose main theme is athletics. I have argued that this is not so and

that Pindar's conception of political order is essentially ago-
nistic; putting it the other way round, I would argue that the
agōn is itself an attempt to create an order that does not ar-
bitrarily exclude or forget the chaos from which it emerges.
Ostensibly, though, the *epinikion* urges the victor to forget the
suffering and toil from which his victory derives and which it
apparently excludes, much as the music of the lyre apparently
excludes the thunderbolt. How, then, does Pindar's treatment
of the victory compare with his treatment of the dispensations
of Zeus and Hieron? About halfway through this ode, Pindar
makes a prayer for the continued prosperity of Hieron and for
a cessation of his toils:

> Ah! may the rest of time guide him straight
> As now, in prosperous and rich possession,
> And grant him to forget his troubles.
>
> Then will he remember the wars and the battles,
> When his soul endured, and he stood firm,
>
> (46–48)

The prayer for forgetfulness coincides with the end of the
third strophe, as though the accomplishment of the formal
structure itself closed the world of the *epinikion* against the
toil and pain that precede victory. But this proves as illusory
as music's "quenching" of the ever-flowing fire, for the triadic
structure depends on a dynamic opposition, and the anti-
strophe begins by suggesting that Hieron will *remember* what
he had endured. Forgetting and remembering are correlative
actions through which the victory appropriates the toil and
suffering that lie outside it.

Although, strictly speaking, there is no myth in this ode,
there is an important comparison of Hieron to Philoktetes
that follows immediately on the passage I have just quoted,
and this is particularly apposite to the concerns of the poem,
and especially to the pattern of exclusion followed by inclu-
sion that permeates it. Hieron's illness at the time of his victory
provides a point of comparison with Philoktetes, who was
suffering from an incurable snakebite at the time his fellow
Greeks brought him from Lemnos to Troy, where he was

destined to bring the Trojan war to a favorable outcome. Philoktetes had been abandoned on Lemnos because the suffering caused by the snakebite had rendered him unfit for human society but, in response to an oracle announcing that Troy could be taken only by the bow of Philoktetes, an embassy was sent to retrieve him. His story follows the pattern of exclusion followed by inclusion characteristic of this ode, and although Pindar does not specifically mention it, we inevitably call it to mind in relation to the snake Typhos that lives beneath Aetna, where Hieron has founded his new city.[21]

The figure of Philoktetes provides a link with the next poem we are to consider, Horace's "Cleopatra Ode" (1.37). Philoktetes was a citizen excluded from society as a result of a contamination that reduced him to the status of a beast, unapproachable in his violent suffering. But the very society that banished him as the Other was forced to recognize him as its own in order to survive. Horace's ode celebrates Octavian's final victory in a civil war that had put Rome through a severe identity crisis. It is a fascinating poem, which subverts its own apparent program quite as radically as *Pythian* 1. The Cleopatra of official propaganda, drunk in the company of eunuchs in the poem's first half, redeems her Eastern nature, much like Shakespeare's heroine, in the second half, to die a Roman death that earns her Horace's awed respect. One has only to compare his earlier poem celebrating the same event (*Epode* 9) to see how far this poem is from the official cry of triumph that might legitimately have been expected. The key to Horace's treatment of Cleopatra in this poem that ostensibly celebrates victory over a foreign enemy is her partnership with Antony, who is never mentioned, although it is he whom Octavian really defeated at Actium.[22] If the events at Actium allow Octavian to found the Roman order again, they also present the Romans with the phenomenon of their own contamination with the barbarian opposite against which their identity upheld itself. The Romanized Cleopatra with whom this poem ends disguises the barbarianized Antony, who must be taken into account in any true conception of the order that begins at Actium.

Horace starts, like Pindar, with the timeless "now" in which poetic and political order are intertwined. The historical moment in which political order is established is associated with the generic *now* that opens on a preexisting poetic order:

> Nunc est bibendum, nunc pede libero
> pulsanda tellus, nunc Saliaribus
>   ornare pulvinar deorum
>   tempus erat dapibus, sodales.
>
> (1-4)

Now is the time to drink, now the time with free foot to pound the earth, now the time, my friends, to deck the couches of the gods with Salian feasts.[23]

The first two phrases quote the beginning of a famous poem by Alcaeus (332 L.-P.) on the death of the tyrant Myrtilus. Horace appeals to the father of the symposiastic lyric and the authority of the genre to establish a timeless "now" that founds a certain order, much like that emanating from the lyre's prelude in *Pythian* 1. But the symposium as celebration always involves turning away from some dark reality, whether it has been escaped, as is apparently here the case, or still lurks in the wings, as do the more common enemies, mortality and transience. Horace's second stanza introduces the "before" that is the real authority for the opening "now":

> antehac nefas depromere Caecubum
> cellis avitis, dum Capitolio
>   regina dementis ruinas
>   funus et imperio parabat.
>
> (5-8)

before this it would have been high treason to fetch Caecuban wine from family storerooms, while the queen was madly preparing destruction for the Capitol and death for the empire.

The "before" that separates the first stanza from the second founds the world of the symposium in the same sense that music's suspension of the thunderbolt's fire founds the legitimate dispensation of Zeus in *Pythian* 1.

Before Cleopatra had been defeated, it was sacrilege to drink, because of the solemnity of the time, in which Rome was threatened with destruction. More specifically, it was sacrilege to draw on the wine of tradition stored in the ancestral vaults, because that tradition had been tainted by the association of Antony and Cleopatra. As this poem will reveal, there is no intrinsically Roman order to be opposed to the barbarian chaos represented by Cleopatra, for her silent partner, Antony, has confused the distinction between inside and outside vis-à-vis Rome. We might, then, give a further reason for the sacrilegious nature of drinking before Cleopatra's defeat, and that is the possibility of confusion between her drunken recklessness and the rather violent behavior enjoined on the Romans in the first stanza. Looking at the poem as a whole, we see that it moves from a Roman appropriation of barbarian behavior to, in the final lines, a barbarian appropriation of the Stoic suicide, where the noble queen cheats Octavian of his triumph.

Horace raises the question of confusion when he begins the third stanza with the word *contaminato* (tainted):

> contaminato cum grege turpium
> morbo virorum, quidlibet impotens
>   sperare fortunaque dulci
>   ebria.
>
>   (9–12)

with her contaminated pack of shameful men, uncontrollably hoping everything and drunk on sweet fortune.

Since the second stanza is enjambed, we tend to take *contaminato* with the previous *imperio,* which would give us a "tainted empire"; subsequently, *contaminato* is more safely linked with *grege,* Cleopatra's "flock" of eunuchs. The grammatical ambiguity derives its force from the fact that Antony was himself one of that flock—the empire had indeed been tainted. Across the neat separation of "now" from "before," the Romans and the barbarians confront each other as two kinds of revelers; there is no intrinsic difference but, rather, a dangerous continuity between the chaotic revel of Cleopatra and the jubilant abandon of those who have defeated her. As in *Pythian* 1, all difference is but an articulation of one basic element (in that case, liquid fire). If the Romans wish to draw again on the wine of tradition, they must include Cleopatra in that tradition, and this is why Horace devotes the major part of this celebration of Actium to the narrative of Cleopatra's career.

In Pindar, Horace found a model for the kind of poetic order it was necessary for this poem to exhibit, an agonistic order generated by Rome's conflict with a Cleopatra whom it could not claim to have excluded. The poem expands and contracts, separates and conflates, in a thoroughly Pindaric manner, and Horace's use of a pervasive imagery (liquids/ drinking) has the same ambivalent effect as Pindar's.[24] Like Pindar, Horace exhibits poetically the very power he is celebrating, and in much the same way as Typhos's fury is made to show forth the orderly alternation of night and day, Cleopatra's bacchantic power is made to animate the Horatian stanza.

We pick up Cleopatra's career as she threatens the very Capitol of Rome, following an unchanneled hope and drunk on fortune (10–12):

> sed minuit furorem
> vix una sospes navis ab ignibus,
> mentemque lymphatam Mareotico
> redegit in veros timores
>   Caesar ab Italia volantem
>
> remis adurgens, accipiter velut
> mollis columbas aut leporem citus
> venator in campis nivalis
>   Haemoniae,
>
>   (12–20)

But her rage was diminished when scarcely one ship survived the flames, and her mind liquefied by Mareotic wine was brought back to the truth of fear when Caesar's oars pressed her hard in her flight, as a hawk pursues gentle doves or the swift hunter pursues the hare in the fields of snowy Thessaly. . . .

The conflict with Octavian transforms Cleopatra's careering into a career. Her rage is diminished (*minuit*, 12) only in the sense that it is focused and arrives at the fourth stanza concentrated in the narrow compass of "scarcely one ship" (*vix una*, 13). Here the enjambement has the opposite effect of that between the second and third stanzas, as though the preconceived formal unit that had been burst by Cleopatra's random hope ("quidlibet impotens / sperare," 10–11) has been reconceived as an opposing force that channels her energy rather than as a vessel that is meant to contain it. This is borne out by the strikingly Pindaric paradox that Cleopatra's fury (*furorem*, 12) is diminished by being strained through fire (*ignibus*, 13); the opposition to Cleopatra is another form of herself, and this has the effect of focusing rather than eliminating the energy that drives her. Octavian's victorious confrontation with Cleopatra is therefore seen from two perspectives, for while he pursues the fleeing (*volantem*, 16) enemy whom he would exclude from the Roman sphere, he returns (*redegit*, 15) her to reality in the form of true fears. The contrary motions of flight and return in the double perspective of this conflict have the same confusing effect on the distinction between inside and outside as Hieron's casting/jettisoning of the Carthaginian youth. It begins to look as though the two contestants are complementary partners in a single process, a relationship that is further suggested by the metonymy that makes Octavian press the fleeing Cleopatra with *oars* (17): Cleopatra, whose mind is "liquefied" (*lymphatam*, 14) with wine, is not only the object of Octavian's oared pursuit but also the element in which it takes place.

In the conflict of complementaries, the two parties may exchange properties, as did music and war at the beginning of *Pythian* 1. As Horace enters the second half of his poem, the violent and threatening queen becomes a pathetic animal pursued by the savage Roman hunter (17–20). But the victorious Octavian wants to present his vanquished enemy in a rather different guise:

> daret ut catenis
> fatale monstrum; quae generosius
> perire quaerens nec muliebriter
> expavit ensem nec latentis
> classe cita reparavit oras;
> (20–24)

that he might give to chains that deadly prodigy; but she re-
solved to die more nobly, nor did she fear the sword in wom-
anly fashion nor did she seek hidden shores with a swift
fleet. . . .

The power of the victor enables him to deliver his defenseless
prey into the ready-made frame of the sixth stanza as a prod-
igy to be excluded from the natural order. Form, in the hands
of the victor, becomes a frame in which Cleopatra is exhibited
as a *monstrum,* a warning (*monere*), and the two words that fix
her as the victor would show her (*fatale monstrum,* 21) neatly
fill the first half of the line up to the caesura. However, the
caesura immediately becomes a pivot, or *kairos,* of conflict
when the word that follows it (*quae,* 21; "who") introduces
Cleopatra as a subject refusing the significance that Octavian
would assign her.

Curiously, the effect of Cleopatra's resistance to the role in
which Octavian would exhibit her is to make a Roman of her.
Like the unfortunate Typhos, Cleopatra is forced by her very
resistance to Rome to speak its language:

> ausa et iacentem visere regiam
> vultu sereno, fortis et asperas
>   tractare serpentis, ut atrum
>   corpore combiberet venenum,
>
> deliberata morte ferocior,
> saevis Liburnis scilicet invidens
> privata deduci superbo
>   non humilis mulier triumpho.
>   (25–32)

She dared to look on her fallen palace with a calm eye, and was
strong enough to grasp the scaly snakes, so that her body
might gulp down their black poison. In her pondered death
she was fiercer, grudging the savage galleys the cargo, that she
might not be stripped of her position and led in proud tri-
umph—no mean woman.

The stately movement of the last three stanzas is initiated
by the opposition between the two halves of the sixth stanza's
opening line (21). If Cleopatra refuses to be shown in the
stanza's prefabricated frame as a *fatale monstrum,* her reaction

nevertheless articulates that form as a dynamic but controlled oppositional movement. In the sixth stanza, the caesura is articulated by Cleopatra's opposition in each of the first three lines (*quae . . . nec . . . nec*), making it the only stanza in the poem that has a strong caesura in three successive lines. From the sixth stanza, we move to the seventh by an opposition of negative (*nec . . . nec*) to positive (*ausa . . . visere; fortis . . . tractare*). In the seventh stanza, the caesura of the second line is again foregrounded by an opposition between Cleopatra's calm (*sereno*, 26) gaze and her brave (*fortis*, 26) handling of the snake. The three clauses that make up the seventh stanza present Cleopatra progressively outbidding her own ability to master her defeat: she dares to *look* on the ruined palace and bravely *grasps* the snakes in order to *gulp down* their poison. Instead of fitting into the frame that Rome would assign her, Cleopatra creates a Roman identity through her very combativeness and overreaching.

The continuity between the drunken Egyptian and the Roman Stoic who nobly gulps down her poison produces the disturbing paradox that Cleopatra is fiercer (*ferocior*, 29) in her pondered (*deliberata*, 29) death. Her "Roman" suicide emerges as a form of savagery. The comparative, *ferocior*, makes the points that Cleopatra's uncompromising end is no volte-face and that her drinking of the poison has been foreshadowed by the drunkenness of her earlier career. That is the internal significance of the comparative, but Cleopatra's ferocity has been realized in the conflict with Octavian, and when his galleys are described as "savage" (*saevis*, 30) in the following line the comparative is given an external point of reference. The full potential of Cleopatra's wild energy is realized in the confrontation with the enemy who would tame her, an enemy whose opposition is itself a form of savagery that serves to channel her own. Actium had been the scene of a similar event, where Cleopatra's fury had been strained through fire and Octavian's pursuit had returned her to truth.

What emerges from these confrontations, in which the mutual exclusiveness of the contestants is totally undermined, is a triumph that floats between Octavian and Cleopatra. The last line leaves us with "no mean woman" (*non humilis mulier,* 32) in a triumph that almost becomes her own as Octavian loses its most important ornament. The hyperbaton *superbo . . . triumpho,* with the magnificently recalcitrant Cleopatra wedged between, ends the poem with a remarkable combination of pomp and ambiguity. Horace surely intends that the triumph should not properly belong to either contestant; it is, rather, something that they produce between them. After the suspension of tradition caused by the civil wars, the triumph, that most Roman of institutions, returns. But it can no longer be a spectacle in which Rome exhibits the vanquished Other, for the civil war has contaminated difference. Any return to tradition must take account of the experience that had deprived the Romans of their sense of an intrinsic Romanness. At the beginning of this poem, the "now" that marks the return of tradition appears as a *kairos* of Cleopatra's drunken riot, in which the Romans themselves take to their cups, while at the end the Roman suicide appears as a *kairos* of her irrepressible violence. Cleopatra, or what she represents, is now *within* the Roman order. Her victor, Octavian, is as violent as she, and in the hawk (16), the hunter (19), and the savage galleys (30) we recognize the "young butcher" whose victory in the civil wars established peace and order by means of wholesale slaughter.[25] An order that is founded on violence cannot pretend to exclude it in the form of its defeated enemies. In the conflict between Octavian and Cleopatra, the Roman order is born again as a *kairos* of the violence that had dissolved it.

What Horace found in Pindar was a conception of order that gave him a purchase on the political situation after Actium. The triumph with which his poem ends is, like Pindar's Aetna, a scene of conflict that belongs neither to the forces of barbarian expression nor to those of Roman repression. In a sense the Roman order transcends the contestants, its power residing not in its ability to exclude the unruly Other but in its ability to redefine itself so as to include that with which it comes into conflict. Only in this way can it avoid the awkward consequences of the original, gratuitous distinction between

Roman and barbarian. Horace's poem redefines both the Roman order and the poetic order that is its analog, making implicitly the connection that is explicitly made at the beginning of *Pythian* 1. His first stanza is dominated by the generic "now" of the three *nunc*s that mark out the unity of the metrical scheme in the first two lines. But once the presence of Cleopatra has been established by the "before" on which the "now" actually depends, form can no longer be conceived as a prefabricated container. In the sixth stanza, the metrical scheme is articulated by the *nec*s that convey Cleopatra's refusal of Roman frames; form no longer confirms identity. We see the stanzaic form in the process of defining itself as the scene of conflict. Horace's ending must have had a curious effect on the Roman reader, who may have felt satisfaction at seeing Cleopatra speaking the language of Rome in spite of herself, while being at the same time disturbed to see that language become the medium in which violence expresses itself.

Horace had fought at Philippi against Octavian for the losing Republican cause but had accepted pardon, and eventually his Sabine farm, from the victor. He had seen, with whatever reservations, that Octavian was the only hope for the future and had accordingly become a warm, though by no means uncritical, supporter of the new regime. Marvell also gave the new regime his qualified support, having sympathized with the Royalists during the struggle. Like Horace, he saw the victor as a man with history on his side. Clearly, he also saw parallels between the demise of the Republic at Rome and that of the monarchy in England, and his poem is thick with references to Roman authors and with parallels between Roman and English history. He took the occasion of Cromwell's return from his bloody suppression of the Irish to reflect, in a Horatian manner, on what it is that the English are welcoming back, following, and attempting to assess—the career of Cromwell.[26]

Marvell's "Horatian Ode upon Cromwell's Return from Ireland" is perhaps an even more disturbing treatment of the order of violence than its model. It, too, follows a violent career, but this time that of the victor and present ruler, not of the vanquished. Marvell's celebration of the new dispensation, like those of Pindar and Horace, has at its heart an ambiguous representation of the defeat of the (apparently) excluded Other. Pindar's description of Aetna and Horace's representation of Cleopatra in defeat find their counterpart in Marvell's famous description of Charles's execution. Charles, however, is no barbarian but the legitimate king of England, and in celebrating the achievement of an usurper Marvell is tackling the question of intrinsic legitimacy from an even more radical standpoint than that of Pindar and Horace. There can be no appeal to a founding and legitimating principle on the part of a man who emerged from obscurity "to ruine the great Work of Time" (line 34). In the two ancient poems, "the Work of Time" is exposed to the explosive presence of the fire within, out of which it is reborn as a process rather than an artifact. Marvell's phrase "the Work of Time" contains an ambiguity that permeates the language of his poem, and the oscillation between static and dynamic conceptions of time's *work* (product or action?) produces a familiar confusion of outside and inside. Does Cromwell, as an outsider, destroy what time has built or, as an insider, hurry along the work it is engaged in? The two possible ways of understanding "Work" are supported by the possibility of playing off the etymological root of "ruine" (Latin *ruo*, rush) against its vernacular sense of "destroy." This same confusion in the nature of Cromwell's agency is apparent when he is said to have "cast the Kingdome old / Into another Mold." The constructive sense of "cast," which makes Cromwell an agent of time's work, emerges out of the destructive sense ("discard") that we at first give the word in the context of the preceding line, "To ruine the great Work of Time." With this shift we lose any fixed context in which to understand Cromwell as an agent, for he slips into the work of time that he is in the process of bringing to fruition.

Beginning is problematic for all three of these poems. Horace and Pindar both began with a false start, a foundation that depended on the exclusion of an unruly force that proved to be already inside the dispensation to be celebrated. Because he is tackling the same problem from the opposite starting point, Marvell confronts this unruly force directly:

> The forward Youth that would appear
> Must now forsake his *Muses* dear,
>   Nor in the Shadows sing
>   His Numbers languishing.
> 'Tis time to leave the Books in dust,
> And oyl th' unused Armours rust:
>   Removing from the Wall
>   The Corslet of the Hall.
> So restless *Cromwel* could not cease
> In the inglorious Arts of Peace,
>   But through adventrous War
>   Urged his active Star.[27]
>
> (lines 1–12)

The "now" from which this poem takes its start is the essentially incomplete present of ambition, in which the closed world of poetic order appears negatively as a languishing among shadows. Marvell reverses the association, made by the two ancient poets, of a beginning with a poetic order that supersedes war. But what is here laid aside will return at the "tragic" scene of Charles's execution, though redefined and recreated by the "forward" Cromwell. The dispensation of Cromwell may be the opposite of those of Zeus/Hieron and Octavian, but it must legitimize itself in the same way, by proving its ability to include what it initially and gratuitously excludes. From his opposite point of departure, Marvell will be concerned with the same problem as were Pindar and Horace, that is, to conceive of an order based on *kairos* rather than on eternal and intrinsic properties and differences.

Underlying Marvell's approach to Cromwell is the Puritan view of history: that human action looks forward, proving itself in the success that shows it to be in accord with Providence, not by an appeal to established principles.[28] Pindar himself takes a similar view, for the *phya* of the aristocrat is confirmed by success in the *agōn*, and if it is not exposed to risk it is lost. The very word *phya* overlays the conception of essence or birth with that of vegetable growth. In Marvell's poem, Cromwell's star is "active" (line 12) because he urges it;

the proleptic usage is one of the many Latinisms in this poem that impart a dynamic quality.[29] If the relation between Cromwell's star and his action is ambiguous, so is that between his action and the demands of the times. Here again we are not quite sure which derives from which, or what force we are to give to the "So" that connects the second and third stanzas. Is Cromwell compared to the forward youth, as someone who also answers the demands of the times,[30] or is he responsible for the nature of the times, which determines the conditions of the forward youth's appearance? In other words, is the "So" coordinating or resumptive? The ambiguity raises the possibility of deriving action from a prior condition only to suspend it.

Cromwell's political "birth" not only fails to give us a defining origin for his career, it shows that career originating from the very refusal of definition:

> And, like the three-fork'd Lightning, first
> Breaking the Clouds where it was nurst,
>   Did thorough his own Side
>   His fiery way divide.
> For 'tis all one to Courage high
> The Emulous or Enemy;
>   And with such to inclose
>   Is more than to oppose.
>
> (lines 13–20)

After he emerges from his own side (party) in a division that refuses an innate identity, he then escapes acquiring an identity by opposition when he conflates the "Emulous" and the "Enemy." The fluctuation between division within a single entity and conflation of opposites ("For 'tis all one") is familiar from Pindar and Horace; Cromwell takes his place beside the irreducible and irrepressible Typhos and Cleopatra, whose energy challenges an order founded on exclusion, opposition, and intrinsic difference in the two ancient poets. Marvell's poem is itself propelled by Cromwell's resistance to all attempts to "inclose" him, and the tense relation between poetic form and Cromwell's violent force is brought out by the association, made by the enclosing rhyme, between the poet and those who would "inclose" Cromwell.

The simile that compares Cromwell to the "three-fork'd Lightning" assumes a separation of the human and the natural spheres that allow us to compare them in order that one may illuminate the other. But this attempt to acquire a perspective on Cromwell founders when the natural phenomenon in terms of which his career has been anatomized comes to be seen also as the manifestation of God's inscrutable Providence overriding our judgment: "'Tis Madness to resist or blame / The force of angry Heavens flame" (lines 25–26). The nature simile, like the "So" that linked the second and third stanzas, is a bearer of order whose controlling power to establish relations is undermined by the presence of Cromwell. In each case, the same linguistic act conveys both the power and the impotence of the poet's ordering. Cromwell's career, aptly analyzed with the help of natural science, eludes our judgment when seen as the medium of "angry Heavens flame." However, it may still be considered in terms of human ends and means:

> 'Tis Madness to resist or blame
> The force of angry Heavens flame:
>   And, if we would speak true,
>   Much to the Man is due.
> Who, from his private Gardens, where
> He liv'd reserved and austere,
>   As if his highest plot
>   To plant the Bergamot,
> Could by industrious Valour climbe
> To ruine the great Work of Time,
>   And cast the Kingdome old
>   Into another Mold.
> Though Justice against Fate complain,
> And plead the antient Rights in vain:
>   But these do hold or break
>   As Men are strong or weak.
>   (lines 25–40)

The passage moves from the distinction of heaven from man ("Much to the *Man* is due") to the inseparability of Justice and rights from the strength and weakness of men. What is due to Cromwell the *man* eventually depends on the force of Justice's complaint, which in turn appeals to the ancient rights. But the ancient right of the monarchy depends on the relative strength of *men*, and this is not constant, as Cromwell is in the process of demonstrating. The separation, for the purpose of judgment, of Cromwell the man from "the force of angry Heavens flame" leaves us in the same position as did the comparison of Cromwell to lightning: we can neither praise nor blame him, because we have no external perspective on him. The criteria of what is due to this human agent are not prior to the strength that he manifests. Even to describe Cromwell's actions raises the question of whether there is an objectively specifiable and separate world that he acts upon, as the double senses of "cast" and "ruin" remind us.[31] So Marvell's suspensions in this ode are not only a "Horatian" balance of judgment, they are also a Pindaric questioning of the intrinsic by the dynamic.

Since the attempt to see Cromwell from the perspective of what is due to him as a man has raised the question of judgment only to dismiss it in bald contemplation of this primary force, Marvell appeals again to nature:

> Nature that hateth emptiness,
> Allows of penetration less:
>   And therefore must make room
>   Where greater Spirits come.
>   (lines 41–44)

The man who was separated from the angry flame of Heaven has returned to the amoral world of nature. Through Cromwell we experience the neutral force that underlies all particular manifestations of human agency with the same unease that attends the revelation of the liquid rippling and drunken energy underlying the worlds of *Pythian* 1 and the "Cleopatra Ode" respectively. The same contamination of usually distinct categories occurs; a gruesome example of this is Cromwell's own experience of the law he manifests: "What Field of all the Civil Wars, / Where his were not the deepest Scars?" (lines 45–46). These lines follow immediately on the statement of the law that two bodies cannot occupy the same space; Cromwell's scars simultaneously exhibit the brute laws of Nature, who abhors "penetration," and the valor that belongs to the very different sphere of human virtue. The effect is similar to Cleopatra's redefinition of the Roman moral order as a particular form of drunken violence.

It is, of course, in Cromwell's confrontation with Charles that we find the most important upsetting of fixed distinctions:

> And *Hampton* shows what part
> He had of wiser Art.
> Where, twining subtile fears with hope,
> He wove a Net of such a scope,
>   That *Charles* himself might chase
>   To *Caresbrooks* narrow case.
> That thence the *Royal Actor* born
> The *Tragick Scaffold* might adorn:
>   While round the armed Bands
>   Did clap their bloody hands.
> *He* nothing common did or mean
> Upon that memorable Scene:
>   But with his keener Eye
>   The Axes edge did try:
> Nor call'd the *Gods* with vulgar spight
> To vindicate his helpless Right,
>   But bow'd his comely Head,
>   Down as upon a Bed.
>   (lines 47–64)

Cromwell is a hunter, like Octavian, and will also bring his victim through fear to truth. Charles, like Cleopatra, will come into his own in defeat. The tragic scene of Charles's execution is the place where the excluded Muses return as the Royal Actor is prompted into his most authentic role by Cromwell. Marvell's language in this passage is as subtle as Cromwell's net. To begin with, the syntax leaves it unclear whether Cromwell's net is of such a scope that it might chase Charles himself to Carisbroke or that Charles might chase himself.[32] This is a nice way of conveying the subtlety of Cromwell's "wiser Art." But it is more than that, for what is "*Caresbrooks* narrow case" to the king but a second womb from which he is "born" as a "*Royal Actor*" on the tragic stage of history? We have a double perspective on Charles in this passage. On the one hand, Charles *himself* in all his inherited status as the "*Royal Actor* born" is chased by Cromwell and expelled from his position, but on the other hand, responding to the forces of history incarnated by Cromwell, Charles chases himself to "*Caresbrooks* narrow case" to be "thence . . . born" into his true status as the "Royal Actor." In this scene Charles's birth is both a property and an event, and as Cromwell opposes the former he realizes the latter. The possibility of hearing *born* as *borne,* especially in connection with *thence,* adds another layer to the complexity of this passage which, like Horace's description of Actium, presents a double perspective on a single action.[33] Concentrated in the word *born* is the ambiguity between intrinsic and dynamic, or enclosing status and open history, that pervades the times from the moment that the "plot" of Cromwell's garden becomes the scene of a "plot" more ambitious than "to plant the Bergamot."

In a sense, the description of Charles's execution is a replay of this poem's opening, in which any involvement in the times presupposed a desertion of the Muses. As the subsequent attempts to comprehend or judge Cromwell prove, the dynamism of his career not only excludes the Muses' languishing that is its opposite, it also reduces any external standpoint to its own terms. Through Charles the Muses enter the poem again, not as languishing outsiders but as actors in the drama of the times. The "*Royal Actor*" is given his noblest role, perhaps even discovered, by Cromwell, but the role in which the royal actor is born is that of abdication ("but bow'd his comely Head, / Down as upon a Bed").[34] The originally gratuitous exclusion of the Muses presupposed by any attempt to come to terms with Cromwell is now motivated when they are reborn from "*Caresbrooks* narrow case" and discover, along with Charles, their true nature. Cromwell and Charles seem to depend on each other, for if Charles becomes what he is because of Cromwell, Cromwell's destiny is legitimized when Charles realizes himself as tragic victim. As Marvell puts it: "This was that memorable Hour / Which first assur'd the forced Pow'r" (lines 65–66).

If Cromwell and Charles are complementary agents in a single action, they are also two aspects of a single phenomenon, confronting each other like the two forms of liquid rippling at the beginning of *Pythian* 1. As so often in this ode, Marvell uses Latin as an unsettling background to the English language, its presence, like that of Cromwell, suggesting a dynamism that underlies the separation of discrete categories. The word *acies* in Latin means both "sharp edge" and "keenness of vision" (as well as "battle line"), and Marvell draws a connection between the first two meanings of *acies* (aurally present in "axes") when Charles mounts the scaffold, and "with his keener Eye / The Axes edge did try" (lines 57–60).[35] The comparative, *keener*, indicates the interdependence of these two forms of *acies*, concrete and abstract, that represent the two protagonists. Marvell's *acies* corresponds to the triumph that ends Horace's ode, belonging truly to neither contestant but created in the conflict between them. In Horace's ode we waver between seeing the final triumph as the Romanization of the barbarian or the barbarization of the Roman. There is a similar ambiguity here as to whether Charles has judged Cromwell's values with his "keener" eye or whether his values are a parasitically metaphoric version of Cromwell's. Marvell's ode may itself be described as a trial between the "Axes edge," or the Cromwell who divides his fiery way, and the "keener" eye that observes him.[36] The typically Pindaric pattern of expansion and contraction, separation and conflation that characterizes this trial is a product of the oscillation between the two aspects of *acies*, whose conflict determines the poem's movement.

The final attempt to contain or "inclose" Cromwell presents the triumphant general on his return from Ireland as a falcon returning to the arm of the falconer (the English Republic):

> She, having kill'd, no more does search,
> But on the next green Bow to pearch;
>   Where, when he first does lure,
>   The Falckner has her sure.
> What may not then our *Isle* presume
> While Victory his Crest does plume!
>   What may not others fear
>   If thus he crown each Year!
> A *Caesar* he ere long to *Gaul*,

> To *Italy* an *Hannibal,*
> And to all States not free
> Shall *Clymacterick* be.
> The *Pict* no shelter now shall find
> Within his party-colour'd Mind;
> But from this Valour sad
> Shrink underneath the Plad:
>   (lines 93–108)

The "sure" command of the falconer over the falcon that has once killed becomes in the next stanza a *presumption* of future victory that recalls the "forward youth" of the first stanza. Instead of the Republic taking over from Cromwell, become its instrument, Cromwell takes over the consciousness of the Republic. The parallels from Roman history that send Cromwell out as a conqueror of foreign places ("to *Gaul,* / To *Italy*") in fact undermine the implication that this energy has now been harnessed and directed. Caesar and Hannibal, Rome's greatest general and greatest adversary respectively, cancel each other out to distill the pure essence of martial energy, which is impervious to distinctions between "us" and "them." We should note, also, that even the distinction between Caesar and Hannibal is problematic, since it was from Gaul that Caesar himself marched on Rome. It is not only the Pict whose "party-colour'd Mind" is threatened by the neutral valor of Cromwell, but also the English, divided by factions.[37]

Cromwell is the force of history that cannot be confined or contained by an imposed framework, nor divided up within a "party-colour'd Mind," and Marvell's ending recognizes the law of this force:

> And for the last effect
> Still keep thy Sword erect:
> Besides the force it has to fright
> The Spirits of the shady Night,
> The same *Arts* that did *gain*
> A *Pow'r* must it *maintain.*
>   (lines 115–20)

These last lines perform a movement that is by now familiar: the erect sword is first determined in relation to what it con-

fronts ("the Spirits of the shady Night") and to a fixed pur-
pose, but this external perspective on Cromwell's military
progress is overlaid by the more primitive law of its own inter-
nal dynamism, which cannot be justified.[38] Marvell's poem is
the product of a dialectic between the need to *comprehend*
Cromwell through an order of separation, opposition, and
distinction and the need to *realize* the primary dynamism of
history that he incarnates. This dialectic between qualities
and forces pervades all three poems I have examined in this
chapter: the distinction of qualities is continually disturbed
by the presence of a neutral force that underlies them and
threatens the order based on their distinction. The Pindaric
both celebrates and is inspired by a public occasion; hence the
combination of dance and leap. The *beau désordre* that results
does not privilege the *beau* to which Boileau saw it returning
after a refreshing venture into *désordre*. Order is presented as
the articulation of a primary and neutral force that prevents
that order from congealing into stasis.

7

Form and Force

The poetic texture of Pindar's odes is distinguished by a conflict that John Finley has described as typical of the late archaic style: "The immense vitality of the late archaic is in this struggle of impulses, the one simplifying and reducing to form, the other complicating and leading to a thousand responses to the world."[1] In this chapter I will examine the poetic texture of the Pindaric ode, but not in terms of a period style; rather, I will argue that this aspect of the Pindaric can be seen in terms of the distinctive problematics of the mode in general.

Finley is not the first to have remarked on this conflict of impulses, and the formulations of some of Pindar's earlier critics are valuable indications of its essential nature. Cowley's "Resurrection" from the "Pindarique Odes" of 1656 ends with what is known by Pindar scholars as a "break-off formula" in which he describes the "Pindarique Pegasus":

> Stop, stop, my *Muse*, allay thy vig'orous heat,
>   Kindled at a *Hint* so great.
> Hold thy *Pindarique Pegasus* closely in,
>   Which does to *rage* begin,
> And this steep *Hill* would gallop up with violent course,
> 'Tis an unruly, and a *hard-Mouth'd Horse*,
>   Fierce and unbroken yet,
>   Impatient of the *Spur* or *Bit*.
> Now *praunces* stately, and anon *flies* o're the place,
> Disdains the *servile Law* of any settled *pace*,
> Conscious and *proud* of his own *natural force*.
>   'Twill no *unskillful Touch* endure
> But flings the *Writer* and *Reader* too that sits not sure.[2]
>
>   (lines 52–64)

The words "Now praunces stately, and anon flies o're the place" is a characterization familiar to readers of Gray's "Progress of Poesy," where the flood of poetry alternately winds majestically and rolls headlong (lines 7–10). But what is important in these lines by Cowley is the relation between the Pindaric Pegasus and the writer/reader, who must sit sure if he is not to be thrown. Finley's two impulses are here related in a kind of *agōn* in which one elicits the other; as an imitator of Pindar, Cowley has experienced their interdependence. It is interesting to see that Cowley includes the reader as an active participant in the conflict; some five centuries earlier, Eusthathius cast the successful readers of Pindar in the role of the hero Theseus, for these readers "make their way unerringly through the labyrinth of [Pindar's] utterance which baffles most people; and, after passing along the convolutions right to the center, trace their winding course back again and are restored to their homes with intelligence unimpaired."[3] The windings of the labyrinth challenge the unerring reader, forcing him to discover their center in order to preserve his intelligence. Finley's complicating and simplifying impulses are here linked in a form of *agōn* where they mutually provoke each other. Eusthathius has incidentally produced a remarkably accurate description of the movement of the Pindaric ode, and his image of the maze is echoed by one of Pindar's most recent interpreters.[4]

Perhaps the most substantive piece of ancient criticism on Pindar is the description of the "rugged composition" (*austēros harmonia*) by Dionysius of Halicarnassus.[5] Although this style of composition applies to more than one author (Pindar and Demosthenes are the prime examples), it fits Pindar better than anyone else. In the *austēros harmonia* "the words want to stand solidly and adopt strong positions, so that each word can be seen in the round, and the parts (*moria*) want to be distinct from each other separated by distinct intervals (*aisthētois khronois*)."[6] One of the reasons why Dionysius seems to have Pindar particularly in mind is that the architectural metaphor of a row of columns that it suggests recalls Pindar's description of his composition at the beginning of *Olympian 6*, to which I will return. What I would like to stress now is that the rhythm of perceptible intervals is itself constituted by the desire of the parts to maintain their own separate identities and positions, producing the same dialectic as in Cowley and Eustathius. The viewer/reader is able, and perhaps forced, to experience both the individual solidity and integrity of the elements "in the round" (*ek periphaneias*) and the rhythmical succession of elements through their perceptible intervals.

The connection between this aspect of the Pindaric style and the concern with the human experience of divinity that is central to the Pindaric mode can be clearly seen in Hopkins's "Wreck of the Deutschland," a Pindaric whose style is inextricably entwined with its theological vision.[7] This poem is the response of a troubled believer to the wreck of a ship bearing nuns driven from Germany by the Falck laws. Hopkins seeks to experience the presence, or "stress," of God in the brute violence of the storm that drowned these nuns. It is no coincidence that it was this poem in which he perfected the new rhythm that he called "sprung," a word that conveys both violent disintegration and the euphoric bounding of space by an arch; it is a word that fits well into the aesthetics of the Pindaric. At one point in the poem, Hopkins describes the mercy of God with a word taken from his theory of sprung rhythm, "outrides":

> Ground of being, and granite of it: past all
>   Grasp God, throned behind
> Death with a sovereignty that heeds but hides, bodes but
>   abides;
>   With a mercy that *outrides*
>   The all of water. . . .
>   (stanzas 32–33, my italics)

The riding metaphor takes up a passage earlier in the poem where the "stress" of God "rides time like riding a river" (stanza 6); "rides" admits of two different shades of meaning according to whether we give it a strong sense (riding a horse) or a weaker sense (riding out a storm). In the later passage the ambivalence is more pronounced: "outrides" may mean "rides faster than" or, again, "rides out." The relation of God's stress or mercy to the all of water or time (the context of our experience of God) oscillates between mastery and coexistence, external and internal. This same ambiguity attends Hopkins's description of the "outride" that creates sprung rhythm: an outride is "one, two, or three slack syllables added to a foot and not counting in the nominal scanning"; it is "by a sort of contradiction, a recognized extra-metrical effect; it is and is not part of the metre." [8] By straining the meter the outride reveals the meter's tensile strength and, like the "parts" in Dionysius's *austēros harmonia,* insists on its own independent entity while at the same time provoking our sense of the containing rhythm. This contradictory effect is the kernel of Hopkins's experience of God's terror, which is both explosive and cohesive:

> I did say yes
> O at lightning and lashed rod;
> Thou heardst me truer than tongue confess
> Thy terror, O Christ, O God;
> Thou knowest the walls, altar and hour and night:
> The swoon of a heart that the sweep and the hurl of thee
>   trod
> Hard down with a horror of height:
> And the midriff *astrain with leaning of, laced with fire of stress.*
>   (stanza 2, italics mine)

What Hopkins says about the "outride" can be compared to some remarks he made to A. W. M. Baillie apropos of a book he was planning to write on Greek lyric. [9] Hopkins noticed that many choral lyrics (he is thinking primarily of Greek tragedy) contain what he called an "underthought," which is conveyed by a string of metaphors. This underthought is "commonly an echo or shadow of the overthought, something like canons or repetitions in music, treated in a different manner, but . . . sometimes it may be independent of [the overthought]." As an example, he cites a chorus from the *Supplices* of Aeschylus, in which the Danaids call their land *sugkhortos* ("of common feeding ground") with Syria; this has no immediate bearing on the matter at hand, but a series of such bestial images suggest the myth of Io, whose fate bore some resemblance to that of the Danaids: "The item to be compared to the subject of the poem stands quite apart from the text, governing the diction, but nowhere expressed." Pindar scholars will be reminded of Norwood's theory of the unifying "symbols" of the Pindaric ode, and as we shall see, Hopkins's terms may be applied as well to Pindar as to Aeschylus. But Norwood's theory, unfortunately determined by a scholarly tradition of searching for the "key" to the unity of the Pindaric ode,[10] fails to do justice to the *tension* between overthought and underthought that is implied by Hopkins's description. In a given passage, the underthought will stand out, often discordantly, from the overthought, or what is being explicitly conveyed. The part asserts itself against the whole in each individual element of the underthought's metaphorical field, and the underthought's total constellation may clash with the overthought.

To exemplify the stylistic features I have been describing, here is the opening of *Olympian* 6:

> Under the well-made porch of the chamber
> We shall build, as it were, a marvelous hall;
> The face of a work as it begins
> Must be made to shine from afar.
>   If there were an Olympian victor,
> Steward at Pisa of God's oracular shrine,
> And a co-founder of glorious Syracuse,
> What hymn would that man escape
> If he fell in with townsmen
> Unstinting in songs that he loves?
> Let the son of Sostratos know
> He has his blessed [*daimonion*] foot in this sandal.
> Success without risk is not honored
> Among men or in hollow ships.[11]
>
> (1–11)

It is tempting to see in the first three lines the inspiration for Dionysius's description of the *austēros harmonia,* not only because of the architectural metaphor but because in the Greek the rhythm, the colometry, and the word order all contribute to a perfect example of what Dionysius is describing. Unfortunately, this aspect of the passage cannot be conveyed in English. But much of the extraordinarily complex texture of the passage can be grasped even in translation. The first thing to observe is the parallelism between the construction of the architectural picture and the assembling of the victor's career.

Although Pindar is describing the *beginning* (*arkhomenou*, 3) of a work he begins from the outside and works his way inward: the gold of the columns is the first thing we see, and these are in front of the porch (*prothurōi*), which in turn leads to the inner chamber (*thalamou*).¹² Similarly, the construction of the hypothetical man to whom all hymns are owed begins with the most recent *event* (*Olympionikas*, 4), then moves back to the religious *office* he held (*tamias*, 5), and finally reaches his *hereditary* connection with the foundation of Syracuse. Both poem and victor are entities revealed through a dynamic process.

Between the two parallel constructions of temple and man is the gnome "The face (*prosōpon*) of a work as it begins / Must be made to shine from afar (*tēlauges*)." The *prosōpon* is the appearance as it is observed from outside, but *tēlauges* on the next line makes this face a radiant *origin* of light. This play of forces and lines of movement is repeated when Pindar asks of the cofounder of Syracuse, "What hymn would that man *escape/flee* / (*phygoi*, 6) if he *fell in with* (*epikyrsais*, 6) townsmen / unstinting in songs that he loves?" The composition of the poem brings the victor and victory into a kind of force field in which it is impossible to fix the focal point of the energy or to locate an essence.

At the beginning of the antistrophe, Hagesias's motion with respect to the human recognition of his achievement is balanced by a metaphor of stability with respect to the gods: his god-guided (*daimonion*) foot is in its sandal. The movement of Hagesias, fleeing hymns and falling in with townsmen, is halted by this metaphor of stability that recalls Pindar's setting up (*hypostasantes*, 1) of columns in the opening line. That we have a deliberately constructed ring here is confirmed by the fact that this construction of Hagesias's *daimōn* is followed by a gnome supplying an external perspective on his *aretē* (9–10), corresponding to the gnome on the beginning of the work (3–4). But the gnome in the first stanza is tightly connected with the foregoing; this one is tacked on paratactically in such a way that it seems to challenge rather than confirm what has preceded. The stability of Hagesias's foot in the "sandal" of his achievements and status is contrasted with the instability of those in the "hollow ships," which are a symbol of the dangerous arena in which *aretē* wins honor. A précis of the "overthought" of these lines would run something like this: "We will build a hall fronted by golden pillars, for the beginning of a work must shine far and wide. If there were a man, by heredity a founder of Syracuse and by merit an official of Zeus's cult, whose career were capped by an Olympic victory, what acclaim would he not receive from unstinting townsmen? Let Hagesias know that such is his own situation, (which he has attained by the withstanding of risk), for an untried *aretē* receives no honor." This logical unfolding of the overthought is counterpointed by a continual shifting of perspective and of lines of motion. The "underthought" forces itself on the reader's attention with the strange expression "What hymn would he *escape?*" and around this curious choice of vocabulary clusters a group of images that establish a conflict within the notion of fitting: the columns set up as supports (*hypo-stasantes*) and the foot planted in the sandal are undermined by the "hollow" ships of danger, and the praise that Hagesidamos deserves is dependent on the contradictory motions of fleeing and falling in with. The victor is both part of a construction and a man on the move; his foot is in the sandal of greatness and yet the place where greatness is to be achieved is the hollow ship.

Discussions of Pindar's style often draw attention to the associative rather than the logical movement of thought.[13] Norwood's theory of the symbolic unity of the Pindaric ode takes up the second half of a book whose first half describes the poverty of Pindar's thought. Bundy's great service was to show us that a perfectly logical (or rhetorico-logical) "overthought" can be traced in the linear sequence of the ode, and that this derives its coherence from the demands of the encomiastic genre.[14] Unfortunately some of his followers have done us the disservice of making this "overthought" into the raison d'être of the Pindaric ode. By contrast, a number of the most important post-Bundyan studies of Pindar have focused on the "underthought" as the main vehicle of significance (one thinks of

Young and Segal).[15] Here I am less concerned with the location of a given ode's meaning than with the nature of the verbal texture as a mode of experience and a field in which the distinctive problematics of the Pindaric are worked out. In order to appreciate this, we need to see the tensions that account for this texture—specifically, as in the opening of *Olympian* 6, the play between the linear unfolding or construction of an "overthought" and the shifting perspectives, lines of motion, and ambivalences that constitute what we may call the "underthought." But what is the significance of these tensions in terms of the Pindaric mode? Let us again return to Pindar by way of a modern Pindarist.

The conflict of structural intentions that I have been describing also has been attributed to the late hymns of Hölderlin, of which Renate Böschenstein-Schäfer writes: "behind the dissociation, behind the associative logic which presents itself to us as the characteristic of hymnic poetry, a more exacting scrutiny frequently reveals the classical sentence's traditional tendency to a composition intellectually determined in its unity and regulated in the smallest detail. The resistance that the autonomy of the image must afford to the old logic works to increase its intensity."[16] She attributes this conflict to Hölderlin's attempt to integrate Christ into a pantheistic vision for which the phenomena of nature are manifestations of divinity. "The Wreck of the Deutschland" confronts a similar problem,[17] and one might apply to Hopkins's poem these further words of Böschenstein-Schäfer on Hölderlin's use of the image of fire: this image aims to grasp "God together with chaos, to express the ambivalence, recognized both in the structure of the world and in that of the human soul, by virtue of which divine exaltation and the savage propulsion of death manifest one and the same powerful impetus."[18] We must now consider if there is a comparable tension in the religious experience of Pindar's *epinikia*.

In the opening passage of *Olympian* 6, there is only one rather discreet reference to the part played by divinity in the victor's achievement: Hagesias's foot in the sandal of his career is described as "god-guided" (*daimonios*). As we have seen, this metaphorical fitting of a man into his career is imme-diately counterbalanced by the "hollow ships" symbolizing the risk that is the prerequisite of honor from one's peers. The juxtaposition presents two perspectives on human achieve-ment: one a bird's-eye view of the ease that attends those fa-vored by the gods, and the other a ground-level perspective on the uncertainty and danger that attend the *agōn*. The *epi-nikion* must combine these two perspectives, seeking to grasp "at the same time" the ease of divinity and the unease of the competitor. Here we may recall the words of Pelops to Apollo in *Olympian* 1: "For me this ordeal [*athlos*] waits: and you, / Give me the issue I desire" (84–85). It is the uncertainty and risk of the *agōn* that provoke the grace of divinity, and the hope of the latter that underwrites the danger the athlete must undergo. In the proem to *Olympian* 3, which I have already analyzed in detail, Pindar uses the same metaphor of the san-dal (*pedilon*) to describe the predetermined aspects of his poem:

> the Muse has taken her stand at my side,
> And I have found a new and glittering way
> To fit to a Dorian sandal the voice
> Of the choir's praises. [*aglaokōmon*]. . . .
> (4–6)

The "new and glittering way" that Pindar *finds* draws our at-tention to the inventive powers of the poet, which at first ex-tend to the creation of the musical mode itself (*tropos*; cf. *O.* 14.17). But the following line reveals that what Pindar finds is merely a new *way* (*tropos*) of fitting this voice to the sandal. The fact that both Pindar and Hagesias fit into a sandal does not preclude trial and initiative, and that the divinity stands by Pindar's side is not incompatible with the poet's invention. Within the chariot metaphor that conveys the activity of com-position in these lines, there is a tension between invention and predetermination, or a double perspective on human ac-tivity. Here is the Pindaric equivalent of those tense ambiva-lences that characterize the religious experiences of Hölderlin and Hopkins, for whom human experience is both contained within and distinguished from the divine order.

If we turn from the opening of *Olympian* 3 to Milton's highly Pindaric "At a Solemn Music," we can see a Christian version of Pindar's double perspective on the relation between human music and its divine inspiration.[19] The characteristically Pindaric texture of this poem derives from the fact that Milton sees human music as both partaking of and exemplifying our separation from the music that is perpetually sung before the throne of God:

> Blest pair of *Sirens*, pledges of Heav'n's joy,
> Sphere-born harmonious Sisters, Voice and Verse,
> Wed your divine sounds, and mixt power employ
> Dead things with inbreath'd sense able to pierce,
> And to our high-rais'd fantasy present
> That undisturbed Song of pure concent,
> Aye sung before the sapphire-color'd throne
> To him that sits thereon,
> With Saintly shout and solemn Jubilee,
> Where the bright Seraphim in burning row
> Their loud uplifted Angel-trumpets blow,
> And the Cherubic host in thousand choirs
> Touch their immortal Harps of golden wires,
> With those just Spirits that wear victorious Palms,
> Hymns devout and holy Psalms
> Singing everlastingly;
> That we on Earth with undiscording voice
> May rightly answer that melodious noise;
> As once we did, till disproportion'd sin
> Jarr'd against nature's chime, and with harsh din
> Broke the fair music that all creatures made
> To their great Lord, whose love their motion sway'd
> In perfect Diapason, whilst they stood
> In first obedience and their state of good.
> O may we soon again renew that Song,
> And keep in tune with Heav'n, till God ere long
> To his celestial consort us unite,
> To live with him, and sing in endless morn of light.

Milton's poem in its basic outline follows the tripartite Pindaric form revolving about a central myth, which is here represented by the song of the angels to God.[20] Like Pindar's victory, this musical celebration opens the way to a point of stillness in mythical time, and from that point the poem gathers momentum to look toward a desired future. The wedding

of voice and verse presents the heavenly concert to our imagi-
nations *so that* (line 16) we might answer it, keeping in chime
until (line 26) God unites us to his heavenly consort. But this
movement is counterpointed in the latter half by a movement
away from the angels' song that took place in our own distant
past: the story of the Fall is sandwiched between the two parts
of a prayer for redemption.

As I will show, Milton is deeply ambivalent about the sta-
tus of music.[21] The tripartite structure, with its central myth
flanked by the two sections expressing human aspiration to-
ward heaven, presents two conceptions of music that coexist
in the occasion: on the human level, music is an agent of
movement and a product of the mixing of things that are sepa-
rate, whereas on the divine level it is a static harmony created
from the aggregation of units that have no separate identity.
Voice and verse must wed their song and "mixt power em-
ploy" in order to raise us to the divine concert where "the Che-
rubic host in thousand choirs / Touch their immortal Harps of
golden wires."[22] The ranks of the angel choirs are duplicated
by the rows of wires that are their instruments.

Milton's complex grammatical structure interweaves the
purposive progression toward God's concert with the lapse
that not only took place once before but is continually re-
newed in the present. If the heavenly concert in which we
once joined preexists and outlasts the earthly concert which
gives us the hope of reattaining our former state, there still re-
mains the question of whether we can *progress* from one to the
other. In fact, it seems that earthly music is not so much a rec-
tification as a repetition of the Fall. Two passages, approxi-
mately equidistant from the central myth, give this impres-
sion. The Fall is described as sin's interruption of the harmony
in which we once participated:

> till disproportion'd sin
> Jarr'd against nature's chime, and with harsh din
> Broke the fair music that all creatures made
> (lines 19–21)

The clash of stresses in the words "and with harsh din"
breaks the "melodious noise" of the previous line (18). It un-

makes the music that the creatures made, and possibly also unmakes the creatures themselves who are made by this music. But the negative or destructive aspects of music in this passage are creative and life-giving in the opening of the poem where voice and verse are told: "Wed your divine sounds, and mixt power employ / Dead things with inbreath'd sense able to pierce." Here the clash of stress ("and mixt power employ") and the mingling of distinct entities that do not chime *constitute* music and create life. As though to illustrate the mixed power of voice and verse, Milton proceeds to rhyme "present" with "concent": "And to our high-rais'd fantasy present / That undisturbed Song of pure concent." Here the voice affects the verse, for as we read "concent" we hear "consent," and the difference is the distance between the angels, who are assumed into and identified with the pure harmony of God, and we who must consciously (and morally) *react* to that harmony. Because of the Fall, human music has lost the original "chime" and, having discovered the "mixt power" of postlapsarian music, humanity may find the "pure concent" of God's consort less attractive. The rich music created by the rhythm of the double negative "undiscording" on line 17 seduces us from the pallid "melodious" that describes the eternal song in the following line. The function of the words *undiscording* and *content* is to create the "stress" that both yokes and separates the two musics, for while they semantically convey univocity their music arises out of its very lack. Furthermore, the poem as a whole, with its interweaving of times and states into a single sentence, presents us with a structural quandary: does the complex assemblage of temporal planes portray the dissolution of a primal harmony, or does it bind together a variegated cosmos "in perfect Diapason"?

The insistent renewal that is effected in Milton's grammar by the interweaving of the Fall with redemption is the condition of human music itself, and this condition appears in our future transfiguration, in which we will sing "in *endless morn* of light," a perpetually suspended renewal. Because human music is constituted by the tension introduced by the Fall, the music that we will make when God unites us to his "celestial consort" can only be imagined as a continuation of the strain

that pervades this poem. This attitude toward music and po-
etry is expressed in the Latin poem "Ad Patrem,"[23] Milton's
apologia for his vocation:

> Nec tu vatis opus divinum despice carmen,
> Quo nihil aetherios ortus, et semina caeli,
> Nil magis humanam commendat origine mentem,
> Sancta Prometheae retinens vestigia flammae.
>
> (lines 17–20)

> Do not despise the work of the poet, divine song, than which
> nothing more greatly proves our celestial birth and heavenly
> seed and glorifies the human mind in its origin, keeping the
> holy spark of Prometheus's fire.[24]

The syncretism of pagan and Christian here is particularly
uncomfortable, since the figure of Prometheus attributes the
acquisition of music to an act of *defiance* of the gods at the
same time as it proves our heavenly origin. Not only that, but
music seems to stand in the way of redemption since it holds
back (*retinens*, 20) the fire of Prometheus.

Against the divine perspectives of harmony and fitting
conveyed by the containing "overthoughts" of *Olympian* 6 and
"At a Solemn Music," an "underthought" or countermove-
ment is played that carries the perspective of a fallen humanity.
The "stress" that is produced by this interplay maintains the
unity in separation that defines the relation between gods and
men in this mode. But Milton's choice of Prometheus's fire as
the emblem of the divine origin of music indicates the potential
impiety of this stress. Pindar, too, is aware of the dangerous
prometheanism of his poetic style,[25] and this accounts for the
fact that he so often breaks off from his high style into the
more retiring tone of conventional gnomic wisdom. The con-
flict that gives the bulk of Pindar's *epinikia* such a dense tex-
ture is notably missing from other passages where language
becomes the locus of a relinquishing of human initiative in the
face of an unpredictable universe dependent on the dispensa-
tion of an often jealous divinity. The ends of the odes, for in-
stance, are particularly dense with gnomic material and mark-
edly simpler in style.[26] They often shade off into conventional
wisdom and pious caution in much the same fashion as the

endings of Greek tragedies. At this point poet and victor must be particularly on their guard against an overconfident self-assertion. But of course this style is simply the other side of what I have been describing so far, since here too there is an implicit non-coincidence between the language of conventional piety and the subjective impulse that has been reined in. In the typical ending of a Pindaric ode a swift paratactic succession of gnomic statements creates an oscillating rhythm in which human intention seems to have no place. The famous ending to *Pythian* 8 follows the gnomic material with a final list of divinities in whose hand the victor's city, Aegina, lies:

> —But man's pleasure is a short time growing
> And it falls to the ground
> As quickly, when an unlucky twist of thought
> Loosens its roots.
>
> Man's life is a day. What is he?
> What is he not? A shadow in a dream
> Is man: but when God sheds a brightness,
> Shining light [Bowra "life," a misprint] is on earth
> And life is sweet as honey.
>   Aigina, dear mother,
> Keep this city in her voyage of freedom:
> You with Zeus and lord Aiakos,
> Peleus, and noble Telamon, and Achilles.
>   (92–100)

It is from Pindaric passages such as this that the parataxis of Hölderlin's late style is derived, a style whose attitude is well conveyed by the following lines from "Mnemosyne" (third version), which I will later consider in more detail:

> Vorwärts aber und rükwärts wollen wir
> Nicht sehn. Uns wiegen lassen, wie
> Auf schwankem Kahne der See.
>   (lines 15–17)

Forward, however, and back we will / Not look. Be lulled and rocked as / On a swaying skiff of the sea.

Hölderlin's use of parataxis is the subject of a brilliant essay by Theodor Adorno in which he argues that the paratactic dis-ruption of subordinating syntax is a means of denying the unity of subjective intention with language.[27] Hölderlin yields to the objective authority represented by language. The dialectic by which this becomes a form of autonomy and the historical context that provokes this dialectic, both so well described in Adorno's essay, are naturally particular to Hölderlin and hardly applicable to a fifth-century Greek poet. But the fact that the poetic texture is a field in which the relation between human agency, or the subject's self-assertion, and the objective presence of a divine rule is problematized—that is what allows us to consider Pindar and Hölderlin as representatives of the same poetic mode. In the Pindaric endings, the simple juxtapositions, swift polar movement, and commonplace gnomic material, by contrast with the syntactic complexity and saturated imagery of the bulk of the ode, foregrounds the public, ready-made aspects of language and casts the speaker in a more passive role. Take these lines that conclude *Pythian* 12:

> If there is success among men, without toil
> It does not appear. Even today it might be accomplished
> By the god. What is fated one cannot escape.
> But there will be a time that will strike with surprise
> Against a man's expectations,
> To give one thing, withhold another.[28]
>
> (28–32)

The declarative voice of the poet here alternates with a choric voice, or rhythm, that eventually subsumes it. Though the encomiast urges toil as the path to success, that success simply "appears" (*phainetai*, 29). Yet success might be *accomplished* even today; however, the accomplisher turns out to be not the toiling human, but a god. The attempt to grapple with the nature of human endeavor is abandoned in the choric "What is fated one cannot escape"; the prophetic voice then rallies to predict a particular time (*khronos/houtos*, 30–31), but this time quickly becomes general as it is subsumed into the random fluctuation that baffles human calculation. With the polar balance of positive and negative, the poem ends (*to men dōsei to d'oupō*).

Hölderlin's late hymns are influenced stylistically by such passages in Pindar. The lines I quoted above from "Mnemosyne" occur at the end of the first stanza, in which Hölderlin finds mortality precariously situated on an earth that subjects it to conflicting forms of impulse toward transcendence.[29] The resulting tension in the conception of human agency is felt in the poetic texture itself. Hölderlin begins with a vision of the earth as a place of ripening in which, like snakes, all beings cast off their old skin as they transcend the earth. The inversions of grammatical and logical sequence and the accumulative rhythm produce a ripening within language that grows out of the first word:

> Reif sind, in Feuer getaucht, gekochet
> Die Frücht und auf der Erde geprüfet und ein Gesez ist
> Dass alles hineingeht, Schlangen gleich,
> Prophetisch, träumend auf
> Den Hügeln des Himmels.
>
> (lines 1–5)

Ripe are, dipped in fire, cooked / The fruits and tried on the earth and it is law / Prophetic, that all must enter in / Like serpents, dreaming on / The mounds of heaven.

But this coincidence of "law" (*Gesez*) with the organic process of language, this ripening toward the "mounds of heaven," produces a reflex in which the very mounds through which we move upward become a weight on our shoulders, now representing a totality of burdensome particulars bundled like logs:

> Und vieles
> Wie auf den Schultern eine
> Last von Scheitern ist
> Zu behalten.
>
> (lines 5–8)

And much / As on the shoulders a / Load of logs must be / Retained.

A similar passage in "Der Rhein" shows that this burden is the inevitable self-consciousness which "surprises and shocks the mortal when he considers the heaven which with loving hands he has heaped on his shoulders, and the burden of joy."[30] The transformation of the mountains on which we dream to the burden we must retain is a shift in the subject's situation: instead of being the medium of a union with nature, the mountain now represents the burden of a conscious totalizing that demands a conscious retaining on our part. The effect of the enjambements in these lines is to retard the movement with arbitrary caesuras, providing a counterweight to the exuberance of the previous lines. This alternation is now repeated as the sense of burden provokes in reaction the death wish of the "imprisoned elements of the earth," a yearning toward the "unbound":

> Aber bös sind
> Die Pfade. Nemlich unrecht,
> Wie Rosse gehn die gefangenen
> Element' und alten
> Geseze der Erd. Und immer
> Ins Ungebundene gehet eine Sehnsucht. Vieles aber ist
> Zu behalten. Und Noth die Treue.
>
> (lines 8–14)

But evil are / The paths, for crookedly / Like horses go the imprisoned / Elements and ancient laws / Of the earth. And always / There is yearning that seeks the unbound. But much / Must be retained. And loyalty is needed.

Here it is the medium itself (the paths and ancient laws) that exhibits a destructive will which we must resist. The choric refrain of "Vieles . . . ist / Zu behalten" resists identification with the bacchanalian riot of the imprisoned elements. A rhythm of impulse and check abstracts itself from the drama of the subject's relation to the medium, and in the final lines of the stanza this becomes a rocking motion to which the subjective will submits itself:

> Vorwärts aber und rükwärts wollen wir
> Nicht sehn. Uns wiegen lassen, wie
> Auf schwankem Kahne der See.
>
> (lines 15–17)

Foward, however, and back we will / Not look. Be lulled and rocked as / On a swaying skiff of the sea.

The paratactic juxtaposition of the two sentences effects the abstraction of human will from the oscillating rhythm, and so transforms the nostalgic (*rükwärts*) and utopian (*vorwärts*) urges toward identification with totality into a passive receptivity.[31] The willingness to be reconstituted by this oscillating motion, to abandon the will to identify any part of it with a subjective impulse, is for Hölderlin the prerequisite to a choric community that will become song:

> Viel hat von Morgen an,
> Seit ein Gesprach wir sind und hören voneinander
> Erfahren der Mensch; bald sind wir aber Gesang.
> ("Friedensfeier," lines 91–93)

Much, from the morning onwards, / Since we have been a discourse and have heard from one another, / Has humankind learnt; but soon we shall be song.

If Hölderlin is the only poet to absorb the style of Pindar's endings into his own analogous consideration of human agency, we nevertheless find equivalents in other poets. Keats's "Ode on a Grecian Urn" should be included in this context, because the movement of this poem, from its competitive opening to its deferential close, exhibits the same double perspective on human agency that I have been discussing in this chapter. The insistent questioning and provocation of the "foster-child of silence" by which Keats seeks to realize in human experience the scenes contained on the urn through a form of competition with it produces a relation between human and divine artifacts that recalls Milton's "At a Solemn Music." But in the famous ending, this attempt to swell the silence of the urn's medium is relinquished, and the urn is allowed to speak for itself: " 'Beauty is truth, truth beauty,'— that is all / Ye know on earth, and all ye need to know." Here the urn speaks, but without breaking its silence, or even responding *to* the questioner, for these lines simply display the circularity of its medium, inasmuch as the narrative of this "sylvan historian" always returns to the same point to repeat itself. It is the self-contained turning of the urn that ends this poem, not a philosophical message about the urn. In these lines the previously violent rhythm of ecstatic union with, followed by disillusioned falling away from, the scene on the urn is absorbed into the circular motion that is intrinsic to the urn as medium. As the vibrant life of the bacchic rout and the "why" of the pious morn that has left the town desolate can never be recovered from the urn's silent form, Keats's words become an ode *on* this Grecian urn that can only offer to our questioning its own revolving surface. For all the differences between Hölderlin and Keats, there is a common utopian element in the relinquishing of subjective impulses toward identification: the urn is cold, but it is a "cold *Pastoral*" that will remain "in midst of other woe / Than ours, a friend to man." The community that Keats envisages through the mediation of the urn is by no means as optimistic as Hölderlin's "soon we shall be song," but the notion of being a conversation or a song is choric in the same way as Keats's ending to "Grecian Urn."

Pindar's conception of the *agōn* as a meeting of human toil with divine ease finds its modern equivalent in Keats's confrontation with the urn. Here too we find the problem of human agency projected onto the relation between subject and medium: Pindar's setting of a self-assertive "underthought" against a generic "overthought" corresponds to Keats's attempt to swell the silent form of the urn into life, but both poets end by deferring to a medium that can speak for itself. For Pindar as for Keats, the human and the divine are interrelated in a joint action and at the same time tragically distinct, and much the same could be said about Milton's "At a Solemn Music." The mechanism of this paradox can be seen clearly if we compare the beginning of Pindar's *Nemean* 6 to a passage from Keats's "Ode to a Nightingale."

The Pindaric passage is not only one of the most important and well known in the corpus, it is also notoriously elusive in meaning:

> Single is the race, single
> Of men and of gods;
> From a single mother we both draw breath.
> But a difference of power in everything
> Keeps us apart;

> For the one is as Nothing, but the brazen sky
> Stays a fixed habitation for ever.
>
> $(1-4)$

The first statement (*hen andrōn / hen theōn genos*) may be read in two contradictory ways: either "the race of men and gods is one" or "the race of men is one and the race of gods is (another, separate) one."[32] According to which of these alternatives one chooses, the fact that we draw breath from the same mother (Earth) is a comforting corollary for a poignant contradiction. Both this and the next statement are linked to the preceding by the flexible particle *de*, which may be adversative or coordinative. If we have the same mother, nevertheless our powers distinguish us utterly. The last sentence is phrased with typical Pindaric asymmetry, for if "one is as Nothing" (*to men ouden*) clearly refers to the race (*genos*) of men, the other part of the contrast, which the particles (*to men . . . ho de*) would lead us to expect to be symmetrical, describes the permanence of a dwelling-place (of the gods). The effect of this is to mute the terrible separation of human from divine life with a comforting balance (*if* one is as nothing, *yet* the brazen sky stays) that transcends the partial and mutually exclusive perspectives of men and gods. Throughout the passage, the races of men and gods are seen as both separate and one. The contradiction is not as glaring as it seems, for the cosmogonists had described the origin of the *kosmos* as an act of separation (*krisis*), and Pindar's word for the "distinguished" power that separates men and gods, *kekrimena* (2), recalls this cosmogonic act. In this context the notion of a totality constituted by separation is less paradoxical.

Keats's "Ode to a Nightingale," like the "Ode on a Grecian Urn," concerns the relation between two modes of being. Human song can merge with the "full-throated ease" of the nightingale only as the self-consciousness constitutive of humanity is sloughed off in death:

> To cease upon the midnight with no pain,
>   While thou art pouring forth thy soul abroad
>   In such an ecstasy!

> Still wouldst thou sing and I have ears in vain—
> To thy high requiem become a sod.
>
> (lines 56–60)

The moment after the ecstatic union is one of complete separation, for the nightingale's song continues over a deaf (and dead) poet. But although the nightingale's song now becomes a requiem, the poet is, surprisingly, not the corpse for which it is sung. True, the poet is now an inanimate thing, but the nightingale as the singer of a requiem and the poet as the sod of a grave become equally essential aspects of a ceremony that unites them: "*To* thy high requiem become a sod" both makes a comparison between two absolutely separate beings and describes their conjunction in a ceremony that transcends the individual agents.

The central religious experience of the Pindaric is the meeting of God and man *in action,* and the stylistic features that I have been describing in this chapter derive from the poet's need to create a form of poetic action that will be adequate to that meeting. I have described the poetic texture as the result of a non-coincidence between objective and subjective dimensions of the language, but a non-coincidence that produces a "stress" between them. This takes two opposite forms, for the Pindaric athlete both asserts himself in an uncertain world, hoping thereby to fit into his divinely appointed *daimōn,* and also retires from his moment of triumph by deferring to a cosmic rhythm over which he has no control. In the first case, the divine presence is realized as a *strain* within human experience between a predetermined, closed, and embracing pattern and an explosive impulsion; in the second case, it is the absolute separating within experience of subjective from objective moment that constitutes this presence.

Conclusion

My starting point in describing an agonistic mode of poetry was the antithetical senses of the word *agōn* itself (gathering/ contest), and I have ended with a discussion of the manifestation of the antithetical forces it denotes in the poetic texture.[1] Sarpedon's rationale for combat as the communal preservation of *eukhos* in a situation of precarious individual mortality was the text with which I started; I would like to end with a text of Hölderlin's:

> Gott rein und mit Unterscheidung
> Bewahren, das ist uns vertrauet,[2]

> To preserve God pure and with distinction, that is entrusted to us. . . .

Hölderlin encapsulates in these words the tense paradoxes of our relation to divinity, which has *entrusted* to us the maintaining of a *separation* and whose purity is itself produced by this separation. Homer's Sarpedon and Hölderlin are both concerned with the mode in which a humanity that is separated from the gods might yet maintain a divine presence without enclosing it. We could say that the words of Sarpedon present the *agōn* as a mechanism through which the *limitations* of humans with respect to gods conjure up what Pindar refers to as the "god-given ray" of victory. Pindar and Hölderlin are concerned with the other side of the question: how is divinity to be received, given the conditions of its appearance?

It is from the standpoint of this concern that I have examined the kinds of challenges that the Pindaric mode offers to a subjective, possessive notion of lyric, a challenge that is usually alluded to by the word *choral*. Naturally, Pindar was not himself writing against modern notions of the lyric (though

Hölderlin certainly was).[3] However, my analysis of Pindar's understanding of the epinician activity has shown that the poet's task begins as a resistance to the forms of closure and isolation that would prevent the proper reception of victor, victory, and divinity. The accommodation of divinity, or the Absolute, to a humanity that cannot contain it is what prompts the various forms of distributed presence, communal action, and dynamic order that are characteristic of this form of poetry.

By taking as central the resistances and challenges against which the encomiast establishes his poetic calling, I hope to have described a form of poetry that is also agonistic in the modern, Bloomian sense of being engaged in a struggle with anteriority, while being quite different in its intentions and procedures from the Romantic type that he describes. In the absence of the kind of material that might lead us to reconstruct with any confidence the experience of choral poetry, I have chosen to describe the distinctive nature of the poet's role in the *agōn* and the problematic relations between poet, victor, community, and divinity that the *agōn* involves. By comparing poems by Pindar with modern poems, I have tried to define a framework that will allow us to understand the thematic, rhetorical, and stylistic features whose interrelation might define a Pindaric mode of poetry. In other words, given that the figure of Pindar presents a challenge to the conventional idea of the lyric as subjective, inward, and asocial, I have asked myself how we might place him on the lyric map and what kinds of rearrangement of this map his presence might provoke.

Appendix: The Text of *Olympians* 3
and 10 and *Pythian* 1

Olympia III

Θήρωνι Ἀκραγαντίνῳ Ἅρματι εἰς Θεοξένια

στρ. α′   Τυνδαρίδαις τε φιλοξείνοις ἁδεῖν καλλιπλοκάμῳ θ᾽
          Ἑλένᾳ
          κλεινὰν Ἀκράγαντα γεραίρων εὔχομαι,
          Θήρωνος Ὀλυμπιονίκαν ὕμνον ὀρθώσαις,
          ἀκαμαντοπόδων
          ἵππων ἄωτον. Μοῖσα δ᾽ οὕτω ποι παρέστα μοι
          νεοσίγαλον εὑρόντι τρόπον
   5   Δωρίῳ φωνὰν ἐναρμόξαι πεδίλῳ

ἀντ. α′   ἀγλαόκωμον· ἐπεὶ χαίταισι μὲν ζευχθέντες ἔπι
          στέφανοι
          πράσσοντί με τοῦτο θεόδματον χρέος,
          φόρμιγγά τε ποικιλόγαρυν καὶ βοὰν αὐλῶν ἐπέων τε
          θέσιν
          Αἰνησιδάμου παιδὶ συμμεῖξαι πρεπόντως, ἅ τε Πίσα
          με γεγωνεῖν· τᾶς ἄπο
  10   θεόμοροι νίσοντ᾽ ἐπ᾽ ἀνθρώπους ἀοιδαί,

ἐπ. α′   ᾧ τινι κραίνων ἐφετμὰς Ἡρακλέος προτέρας
          ἀτρεκὴς Ἑλλανοδίκας γλεφάρων Αἰτωλὸς ἀνὴρ
          ὑψόθεν
  13   ἀμφὶ κόμαισι βάλῃ γλαυκόχροα κόσμον ἐλαίας, τάν
          ποτε
  14   Ἴστρου ἀπὸ σκιαρᾶν παγᾶν ἔνεικεν Ἀμφιτρυωνιάδας,
  15   μνᾶμα τῶν Ὀλυμπίᾳ κάλλιστον ἀέθλων,

στρ. β′   δᾶμον Ὑπερβορέων πείσαις Ἀπόλλωνος θεράποντα
          λόγῳ·
          πιστὰ φρονέων Διὸς αἴτει πανδόκῳ
          ἄλσει σκιαρόν τε φύτευμα ξυνὸν ἀνθρώποις στέφανόν
          τ᾽ ἀρετᾶν.

193

ἤδη γὰρ αὐτῷ, πατρὶ μὲν βωμῶν ἁγισθέντων,
δεχόμηνις ὅλον χρυσάρματος
20   ἑσπέρας ὀφθαλμὸν ἀντέφλεξε Μήνα,

ἀντ. β' καὶ μεγάλων ἀέθλων ἁγνὰν κρίσιν καὶ πενταετηρίδ'
ἁμᾷ
θῆκε ζαθέοις ἐπὶ κρημνοῖς Ἀλφεοῦ·
ἀλλ' οὐ καλὰ δένδρε' ἔθαλλεν χῶρος ἐν βάσσαις
Κρονίου Πέλοπος.
τούτων ἔδοξεν γυμνὸς αὐτῷ κᾶπος ὀξείαις ὑπακουέμεν
αὐγαῖς ἁλίου.
25   δὴ τότ' ἐς γαῖαν πορεύεν θυμὸς ὥρμα

ἐπ. β' Ἰστρίαν νιν· ἔνθα Λατοῦς ἱπποσόα θυγάτηρ
δέξατ' ἐλθόντ' Ἀρκαδίας ἀπὸ δειρᾶν καὶ
πολυγνάμπτων μυχῶν,
28   εὖτέ νιν ἀγγελίαις Εὐρυσθέος ἔντυ' ἀνάγκα πατρόθεν
29   χρυσόκερων ἔλαφον θήλειαν ἄξονθ', ἄν ποτε Ταϋγέτα
30   ἀντιθεῖσ' Ὀρθωσίας ἔγραψεν ἱεράν.

στρ. γ' τὰν μεθέπων ἴδε καὶ κείναν χθόνα πνοιαῖς ὄπιθεν
Βορέα
ψυχροῦ· τόθι δένδρεα θάμβαινε σταθείς.
τῶν νιν γλυκὺς ἵμερος ἔσχεν δωδεκάγναμπτον περὶ
τέρμα δρόμου
ἵππων φυτεῦσαι. καί νυν ἐς ταύταν ἑορτὰν ἵλαος
ἀντιθέοισιν νίσεται
35   σὺν βαθυζώνου διδύμοις παισὶ Λήδας.

ἀντ. γ' τοῖς γὰρ ἐπέτραπεν Οὔλυμπόνδ' ἰὼν θαητὸν ἀγῶνα
νέμειν
ἀνδρῶν τ' ἀρετᾶς πέρι καὶ ῥιμφαρμάτου
διφρηλασίας. ἐμὲ δ' ὦν πᾳ θυμὸς ὀτρύνει φάμεν
Ἐμμενίδαις
Θήρωνί τ' ἐλθεῖν κῦδος εὐίππων διδόντων Τυνδαριδᾶν,
ὅτι πλείσταισι βροτῶν
40   ξεινίαις αὐτοὺς ἐποίχονται τραπέζαις,

ἐπ. γ' εὐσεβεῖ γνώμᾳ φυλάσσοντες μακάρων τελετάς.
εἰ δ' ἀριστεύει μὲν ὕδωρ, κτεάνων δὲ χρυσὸς
αἰδοιέστατος,
43   νῦν δὲ πρὸς ἐσχατιὰν Θήρων ἀρεταῖσιν ἱκάνων
ἅπτεται
44   οἴκοθεν Ἡρακλέος σταλᾶν. τὸ πόρσω δ' ἐστὶ σοφοῖς
ἄβατον
45   κἀσόφοις. οὔ νιν διώξω. κεινὸς εἴην.

Olympia X

Ἀγησιδάμῳ Λοκρῷ Ἐπιζεφυρίῳ Παιδὶ Πύκτηι

στρ. α′   Τὸν Ὀλυμπιονίκαν ἀνάγνωτέ μοι
Ἀρχεστράτου παῖδα, πόθι φρενὸς
ἐμᾶς γέγραπται· γλυκὺ γὰρ αὐτῷ μέλος ὀφείλων
ἐπιλέλαθ'· ὦ Μοῖσ', ἀλλὰ σὺ καὶ θυγάτηρ
Ἀλάθεια Διός, ὀρθᾷ χερὶ
5   ἐρύκετον ψευδέων
ἐνιπὰν ἀλιτόξενον.

ἀντ. α′   ἔκαθεν γὰρ ἐπελθὼν ὁ μέλλων χρόνος
ἐμὸν καταίσχυνε βαθὺ χρέος.
ὅμως δὲ λῦσαι δυνατὸς ὀξεῖαν ἐπιμομφὰν τόκος· ὁρᾶτ'
ὧν νῦν ψᾶφον ἑλισσομέναν
10   ὁπᾷ κῦμα κατακλύσσει ῥέον,
ὁπᾷ τε κοινὸν λόγον
φίλαν τείσομεν ἐς χάριν.

ἐπ. α′   νέμει γὰρ Ἀτρέκεια πόλιν Λοκρῶν Ζεφυρίων,
μέλει τέ σφισι Καλλιόπα
15   καὶ χάλκεος Ἄρης. τράπε δὲ Κύκνεια μάχα καὶ
ὑπέρβιον
Ἡρακλέα· πύκτας δ' ἐν Ὀλυμπιάδι νικῶν
Ἴλᾳ φερέτω χάριν
Ἀγησίδαμος, ὡς
Ἀχιλεῖ Πάτροκλος.
20   θάξαις δέ κε φύντ' ἀρετᾷ ποτὶ
πελώριον ὁρμάσαι κλέος ἀνὴρ θεοῦ σὺν παλάμᾳ.

στρ. β′   ἄπονον δ' ἔλαβον χάρμα παῦροί τινες,
ἔργων πρὸ πάντων βιότῳ φάος.
ἀγῶνα δ' ἐξαίρετον ἀεῖσαι θέμιτες ὦρσαν Διός, ὃν
ἀρχαίῳ σάματι πὰρ Πέλοπος
25   πόνων ἐξάριθμον ἐκτίσσατο,
ἐπεὶ Ποσειδάνιον
πέφνε Κτέατον ἀμύμονα,

ἀντ. β′   πέφνε δ' Εὔρυτον, ὡς Αὐγέαν λάτριον
ἀέκονθ' ἑκὼν μισθὸν ὑπέρβιον
30   πράσσοιτο, λόχμαισι δὲ δοκεύσαις ὑπὸ Κλεωνᾶν
δάμασε καὶ κείνους Ἡρακλέης ἐφ' ὁδῷ,
ὅτι πρόσθε ποτὲ Τιρύνθιον
ἔπερσαν αὐτῷ στρατὸν
μυχοῖς ἥμενον Ἄλιδος

ἐπ. β' Μολίονες ὑπερφίαλοι. καὶ μὰν ξεναπάτας
35   Ἐπειῶν βασιλεὺς ὄπιθεν
      οὐ πολλὸν ἴδε πατρίδα πολυκτέανον ὑπὸ στερεῷ πυρὶ
      πλαγαῖς τε σιδάρου βαθὺν εἰς ὀχετὸν ἄτας
      ἵζοισαν ἑὰν πόλιν.
      νεῖκος δὲ κρεσσόνων
40   ἀποθέσθ᾽ ἄπορον.
      καὶ κεῖνος ἀβουλίᾳ ὕστατος
      ἀλώσιος ἀντάσαις θάνατον αἰπὺν οὐκ ἐξέφυγεν.

στρ. γ' ὁ δ᾽ ἄρ᾽ ἐν Πίσᾳ ἔλσαις ὅλον τε στρατὸν
         λᾴαν τε πᾶσαν Διὸς ἄλκιμος
45   υἱὸς σταθμᾶτο ζάθεον ἄλσος πατρὶ μεγίστῳ· περὶ δὲ
           πάξαις Ἄλτιν μὲν ὅγ᾽ ἐν καθαρῷ
         διέκρινε, τὸ δὲ κύκλῳ πέδον
         ἔθηκε δόρπου λύσιν,
         τιμάσαις πόρον Ἀλφεοῦ

ἀντ. γ' μετὰ δώδεκ᾽ ἀνάκτων θεῶν· καὶ πάγον
50   Κρόνου προσεφθέγξατο· πρόσθε γὰρ
         νώνυμνος, ἇς Οἰνόμαος ἇρχε, βρέχετο πολλᾷ νιφάδι.
           ταύτᾳ δ᾽ ἐν πρωτογόνῳ τελετᾷ
         παρέσταν μὲν ἄρα Μοῖραι σχεδὸν
         ὅ τ᾽ ἐξελέγχων μόνος
         ἀλάθειαν ἐτήτυμον

ἐπ. γ' Χρόνος. τὸ δὲ σαφανὲς ἰὼν πόρσω κατέφρασεν,
56   ὁπᾷ τὰν πολέμοιο δόσιν
        ἀκρόθινα διελὼν ἔθυε καὶ πενταετηρίδ᾽ ὅπως ἄρα
        ἔστασεν ἑορτὰν σὺν Ὀλυμπιάδι πρώτᾳ
        νικαφορίαισί τε.
60   τίς δὴ ποταίνιον
        ἔλαχε στέφανον
        χείρεσσι ποσίν τε καὶ ἅρματι,
        ἀγώνιον ἐν δόξᾳ θέμενος εὖχος, ἔργῳ καθελών;

στρ. δ' στάδιον μὲν ἀρίστευσεν, εὐθὺν τόνον
65   ποσσὶ τρέχων, παῖς ὁ Λικυμνίου
         Οἰωνός· ἷκεν δὲ Μιδέαθεν στρατὸν ἐλαύνων· ὁ δὲ
           πάλᾳ κυδαίνων Ἔχεμος Τεγέαν·
         Δόρυκλος δ᾽ ἔφερε πυγμᾶς τέλος,
         Τίρυνθα ναίων πόλιν·
         ἀν᾽ ἵπποισι δὲ τέτρασιν

ἀντ. δ' ἀπὸ Μαντινέας Σᾶμος ὡλιροθίου·
71   ἄκοντι Φράστωρ ἔλασε σκοπόν·
         μᾶκος δὲ Νικεὺς ἔδικε πέτρῳ χέρα κυκλώσαις ὑπὲρ
           ἁπάντων, καὶ συμμαχία θόρυβον
         παραίθυξε μέγαν. ἐν δ᾽ ἕσπερον

<pre>
75   ἔφλεξεν εὐώπιδος
        σελάνας ἐρατὸν φάος.
ἐπ. δ′ ἀείδετο δὲ πὰν τέμενος τερπναῖσι θαλίαις
        τὸν ἐγκώμιον ἀμφὶ τρόπον.
        ἀρχαῖς δὲ προτέραις ἑπόμενοι καί νυν ἐπωνυμίαν
            χάριν
        νίκας ἀγερώχου κελαδησόμεθα βροντὰν
80   καὶ πυρπάλαμον βέλος
        ὀρσικτύπου Διός,
        ἐν ἅπαντι κράτει
        αἴθωνα κεραυνὸν ἀραρότα·
        χλιδῶσα δὲ μολπὰ πρὸς κάλαμον ἀντιάξει μελέων,
στρ. ε′ τὰ παρ᾽ εὐκλέϊ Δίρκᾳ χρόνῳ μὲν φάνεν·
86   ἀλλ᾽ ὧτε παῖς ἐξ ἀλόχου πατρὶ
        ποθεινὸς ἵκοντι νεότατος τὸ πάλιν ἤδη, μάλα δέ οἱ
            θερμαίνει φιλότατι νόον·
        ἐπεὶ πλοῦτος ὁ λαχὼν ποιμένα
        ἐπακτὸν ἀλλότριον
90   θνᾴσκοντι στυγερώτατος·
ἀντ. ε′ καὶ ὅταν καλὰ ἔρξαις ἀοιδᾶς ἄτερ,
        Ἁγησίδαμ᾽, εἰς Ἀΐδα σταθμὸν
        ἀνὴρ ἵκηται, κενεὰ πνεύσαις ἔπορε μόχθῳ βραχύ τι
            τερπνόν. τὶν δ᾽ ἁδυεπής τε λύρα
        γλυκύς τ᾽ αὐλὸς ἀναπάσσει χάριν·
95   τρέφοντι δ᾽ εὐρὺ κλέος
        κόραι Πιερίδες Διός.

ἐπ. ε′ ἐγὼ δὲ συνεφαπτόμενος σπουδᾷ κλυτὸν ἔθνος
        Λοκρῶν ἀμφέπεσον, μέλιτι
        εὐάνορα πόλιν καταβρέχων· παῖδ᾽ ἐρατὸν ⟨δ᾽⟩
            Ἀρχεστράτου
100   αἴνησα, τὸν εἶδον κρατέοντα χερὸς ἀλκᾷ
        βωμὸν παρ᾽ Ὀλύμπιον
        κεῖνον κατὰ χρόνον
        ἰδέᾳ τε καλὸν
        ὥρᾳ τε κεκραμένον, ἅ ποτε
105   ἀναιδέα Γανυμήδει θάνατον ἄλκε σὺν Κυπρογενεῖ.
</pre>

Pythia I

Ἱέρωνι Αἰτναίῳ Ἅρματι

<pre>
στρ. α′ Χρυσέα φόρμιγξ, Ἀπόλλωνος καὶ ἰοπλοκάμων
         σύνδικον Μοισᾶν κτέανον· τᾶς ἀκούει μὲν βάσις
             ἀγλαΐας ἀρχά,
</pre>

πείθονται δ᾽ ἀοιδοὶ σάμασιν
ἀγησιχόρων ὁπόταν προοιμίων ἀμβολὰς τεύχῃς
ἐλελιζομένα.
5   καὶ τὸν αἰχματὰν κεραυνὸν σβεννύεις
αἰενάου πυρός. εὕδει δ᾽ ἀνὰ σκάπτῳ Διὸς αἰετός,
ὠκεῖαν πτέρυγ᾽ ἀμφοτέρωθεν χαλάξαις,

ἀντ. α'   ἀρχὸς οἰωνῶν, κελαινῶπιν δ᾽ ἐπί οἱ νεφέλαν
ἀγκύλῳ κρατί, γλεφάρων ἁδὺ κλάϊθρον, κατέχευας· ὁ
δὲ κνώσσων
ὑγρὸν νῶτον αἰωρεῖ, τεαῖς
10 ῥιπαῖσι κατασχόμενος. καὶ γὰρ βιατὰς Ἄρης,
τραχεῖαν ἄνευθε λιπὼν
ἐγχέων ἀκμάν, ἰαίνει καρδίαν
κώματι, κῆλα δὲ καὶ δαιμόνων θέλγει φρένας, ἀμφί
τε Λατοίδα σοφίᾳ βαθυκόλπων τε Μοισᾶν.

ἐπ. α'   ὅσσα δὲ μὴ πεφίληκε Ζεύς, ἀτύζονται βοὰν
Πιερίδων ἀΐοντα, γᾶν τε καὶ πόντον κατ᾽
ἀμαιμάκετον,
15 ὅς τ᾽ ἐν αἰνᾷ Ταρτάρῳ κεῖται, θεῶν πολέμιος,
Τυφὼς ἑκατοντακάρανος· τόν ποτε
Κιλίκιον θρέψεν πολυώνυμον ἄντρον· νῦν γε μὰν
ταί θ᾽ ὑπὲρ Κύμας ἁλιερκέες ὄχθαι
Σικελία τ᾽ αὐτοῦ πιέζει
19ᵇ στέρνα λαχνάεντα· κίων δ᾽ οὐρανία συνέχει,
20   νιφόεσσ᾽ Αἴτνα, πανέτης
20ᵇ χιόνος ὀξείας τιθήνα·

στρ. β'   τᾶς ἐρεύγονται μὲν ἀπλάτου πυρὸς ἁγνόταται
ἐκ μυχῶν παγαί· ποταμοὶ δ᾽ ἀμέραισιν μὲν προχέοντι
ῥόον καπνοῦ
αἴθων᾽· ἀλλ᾽ ἐν ὄρφναισιν πέτρας
φοίνισσα κυλινδομένα φλὸξ ἐς βαθεῖαν φέρει πόντου
πλάκα σὺν πατάγῳ.
25 κεῖνο δ᾽ Ἀφαίστοιο κρουνοὺς ἑρπετὸν
δεινοτάτους ἀναπέμπει· τέρας μὲν θαυμάσιον
προσιδέσθαι,
θαῦμα δὲ καὶ παρεόντων ἀκοῦσαι,

ἀντ. β'   οἷον Αἴτνας ἐν μελαμφύλλοις δέδεται κορυφαῖς
καὶ πέδῳ, στρωμνὰ δὲ χαράσσοισ᾽ ἅπαν νῶτον
ποτικεκλιμένον κεντεῖ.
εἴη, Ζεῦ, τὶν εἴη ἀνδάνειν,
30 ὃς τοῦτ᾽ ἐφέπεις ὄρος, εὐκάρποιο γαίας μέτωπον, τοῦ
μὲν ἐπωνυμίαν
κλεινὸς οἰκιστὴρ ἐκύδανεν πόλιν

γείτονα, Πυθιάδος δ᾽ ἐν δρόμῳ κάρυξ ἀνέειπέ νιν
ἀγγέλλων Ἱέρωνος ὑπὲρ καλλινίκου

ἐπ. β′   ἅρμασι· ναυσιφορήτοις δ᾽ ἀνδράσι πρῶτα χάρις
ἐς πλόον ἀρχομένοις πομπαῖον ἐλθεῖν οὖρον· ἐοικότα
γὰρ
35   κἂν τελευτᾷ φερτέρου νόστου τυχεῖν. ὁ δὲ λόγος
ταύταις ἐπὶ συντυχίαις δόξαν φέρει
λοιπὸν ἔσσεσθαι στεφάνοισί ⟨νιν⟩ ἵπποις τε κλυτὰν
καὶ σὺν εὐφώνοις θαλίαις ὀνυμαστάν.

Λύκιε καὶ Δάλοι᾽ ἀνάσσων
39ᵇ   Φοῖβε, Παρνασσοῦ τε κράναν Κασταλίαν φιλέων,
40   ἐθελήσαις ταῦτα νόῳ
40ᵇ   τιθέμεν εὔανδρόν τε χώραν.

στρ. γ′   ἐκ θεῶν γὰρ μαχαναὶ πᾶσαι βροτέαις ἀρεταῖς,
καὶ σοφοὶ καὶ χερσὶ βιαταὶ περίγλωσσοί τ᾽ ἔφυν.

ἄνδρα δ᾽ ἐγὼ κεῖνον
αἰνῆσαι μενοινῶν ἔλπομαι
μὴ χαλκοπάραον ἄκονθ᾽ ὡσείτ᾽ ἀγῶνος βαλεῖν ἔξω
παλάμᾳ δονέων,
45   μακρὰ δὲ ῥίψαις ἀμεύσασθ᾽ ἀντίους.
εἰ γὰρ ὁ πᾶς χρόνος ὄλβον μὲν οὕτω καὶ κτεάνων
δόσιν εὐθύνοι, καμάτων δ᾽ ἐπίλασιν παράσχοι.

ἀντ. γ′   ἦ κεν ἀμνάσειεν οἵαις ἐν πολέμοιο μάχαις
τλάμονι ψυχᾷ παρέμειν᾽, ἀνίχ᾽ εὑρίσκοντο θεῶν
παλάμαις τιμὰν
οἵαν οὔτις Ἑλλάνων δρέπει
50   πλούτου στεφάνωμ᾽ ἀγέρωχον. νῦν γε μὰν τὰν
Φιλοκτήταο δίκαν ἐφέπων
ἐστρατεύθη· σὺν δ᾽ ἀνάγκᾳ νιν φίλον
καί τις ἐὼν μεγαλάνωρ ἔσανεν. φαντὶ δὲ Λαμνόθεν
ἕλκει τειρόμενον μεταβάσοντας ἐλθεῖν

ἐπ. γ′   ἥροας ἀντιθέους Ποίαντος υἱὸν τοξόταν·
ὃς Πριάμοιο πόλιν πέρσεν, τελεύτασέν τε πόνους
Δαναοῖς,
55   ἀσθενεῖ μὲν χρωτὶ βαίνων, ἀλλὰ μοιρίδιον ἦν·
οὕτω δ᾽ Ἱέρωνι θεὸς ὀρθωτὴρ πέλοι
τὸν προσέρποντα χρόνον, ὧν ἔραται καιρὸν διδούς.
Μοῖσα, καὶ πὰρ Δεινομένει κελαδῆσαι
πίθεό μοι ποινὰν τεθρίππων·
59ᵇ   χάρμα δ᾽ οὐκ ἀλλότριον νικαφορίᾳ πατέρος.
60   ἄγ᾽ ἔπειτ᾽ Αἴτνας βασιλεῖ
60ᵇ   φίλιον ἐξεύρωμεν ὕμνον·

στρ. δ′   τῷ πόλιν κείναν θεοδμάτῳ σὺν ἐλευθερίᾳ

Ὑλλίδος στάθμας Ἱέρων ἐν νόμοις ἔκτισσε· θέλοντι
 δὲ Παμφύλου
καὶ μὰν Ἡρακλειδᾶν ἔκγονοι
ὄχθαις ὕπο Ταϋγέτου ναίοντες αἰεὶ μένειν τεθμοῖσιν
 ἐν Αἰγιμιοῦ
65 Δωριεῖς. ἔσχον δ' Ἀμύκλας ὄλβιοι
Πινδόθεν ὀρνύμενοι, λευκοπώλων Τυνδαριδᾶν
βαθύδοξοι γείτονες, ὧν κλέος ἄνθησεν αἰχμᾶς.

ἀντ. δ'   Ζεῦ τέλει', αἰεὶ δὲ τοιαύταν Ἀμένα παρ' ὕδωρ
αἶσαν ἀστοῖς καὶ βασιλεῦσιν διακρίνειν ἔτυμον λόγον
 ἀνθρώπων.
σύν τοι τίν κεν ἀγητὴρ ἀνήρ,
70 υἱῷ τ' ἐπιτελλόμενος, δᾶμον γεραίρων τράποι
σύμφωνον ἐς ἡσυχίαν.
λίσσομαι νεῦσον, Κρονίων, ἅμερον
ὄφρα κατ' οἶκον ὁ Φοίνιξ ὁ Τυρσανῶν τ' ἀλαλατὸς
ἔχῃ, ναυσίστονον ὕβριν ἰδὼν τὰν πρὸ Κύμας,

ἐπ. δ'   οἷα Συρακοσίων ἀρχῷ δαμασθέντες πάθον,
ὠκυπόρων ἀπὸ ναῶν ὅ σφιν ἐν πόντῳ βάλεθ' ἁλικίαν,
75 Ἑλλάδ' ἐξέλκων βαρείας δουλίας. ἀρέομαι
πὰρ μὲν Σαλαμῖνος Ἀθαναίων χάριν
μισθόν, ἐν Σπάρτᾳ δ' ἄρα τᾶν πρὸ Κιθαιρῶνος μαχᾶν,
ταῖσι Μήδειοι κάμον ἀγκυλότοξοι,
παρὰ δὲ τὰν εὔυδρον ἀκτὰν
79ᵇ Ἱμέρα παίδεσσιν ὕμνον Δεινομένεος τελέσαις,
80 τὸν ἐδέξαντ' ἀμφ' ἀρετᾷ
80ᵇ πολεμίων ἀνδρῶν καμόντων.

στρ. ε'   καιρὸν εἰ φθέγξαιο, πολλῶν πείρατα συντανύσαις
ἐν βραχεῖ, μείων ἔπεται μῶμος ἀνθρώπων, ἀπὸ γὰρ
 κόρος ἀμβλύνει
αἰανὴς ταχείας ἐλπίδας·
ἀστῶν δ' ἀκοὰ κρύφιον θυμὸν βαρύνει μάλιστ'
ἐσλοῖσιν ἐπ' ἀλλοτρίοις.
85 ἀλλ' ὅμως, κρέσσων γὰρ οἰκτιρμοῦ φθόνος,
μὴ παρίει καλά. νώμα δικαίῳ πηδαλίῳ στρατόν·
ἀψευδεῖ δὲ πρὸς ἄκμονι χάλκευε γλῶσσαν.

ἀντ. ε'   εἴ τι καὶ φλαῦρον παραιθύσσει, μέγα τοι φέρεται
πὰρ σέθεν. πολλῶν ταμίας ἐσσί· πολλοὶ μάρτυρες
ἀμφοτέροις πιστοί.
εὐανθεῖ δ' ἐν ὀργᾷ παρμένων,
90 εἴπερ τι φιλεῖς ἀκοὰν ἀδεῖαν αἰεὶ κλύειν, μὴ κάμνε
λίαν δαπάναις·
ἐξίει δ' ὥσπερ κυβερνάτας ἀνὴρ

ἱστίον ἀνεμόεν. μὴ δολωθῇς, ὦ φίλε, κέρδεσιν
εὐτράπλοις· ὀπιθόμβροτον αὔχημα δόξας

ἐπ. ε′ οἷον ἀποιχομένων ἀνδρῶν δίαιταν μανύει
καὶ λογίοις καὶ ἀοιδοῖς. οὐ φθίνει Κροίσου φιλόφρων
ἀρετά.
95   τὸν δὲ ταύρῳ χαλκέῳ καυτῆρα νηλέα νόον
ἐχθρὰ Φάλαριν κατέχει παντᾷ φάτις.
οὐδέ νιν φόρμιγγες ὑπωρόφιαι κοινανίαν
μαλθακὰν παίδων ὀάροισι δέκονται.
τὸ δὲ παθεῖν εὖ πρῶτον ἀέθλων·
99ᵇ εὖ δ᾽ ἀκούειν δευτέρα μοῖρ᾽· ἀμφοτέροισι δ᾽ ἀνὴρ
100   ὃς ἂν ἐγκύρσῃ καὶ ἕλῃ,
100ᵇ στέφανον ὕψιστον δέδεκται.

Notes

1. Curiously enough, the ancient critics did not remark on Pindar's difficulty. Eustathius (twelfth century), in the introduction to his *Commentary on Pindar*, was the first to speak of Pindar's obscurity. Since Eustathius, Pindar's obscurity and the difficulty of his language have been remarked on by almost all his readers.
2. The only other *epinikia* extant are those of Bacchylides, a contemporary of Pindar. Until a papyrus find in Egypt, published in 1897, restored portions of fourteen *epinikia*, only about a hundred lines of this poet were known, all from quotations in other sources.
3. Peter Rühmkorff (1978) probably speaks for many when he says that he finds Pindar interesting precisely because he is the representative of a recurring form of poetic *Hoflieferantentum* that he finds repulsive: "Von Sieg zu Sieg eilend, von Residenz zu Residenz sich durchsingend, von Palast zu Palast sei's weitergereicht, sei es mit hymnischen Gehudel sich selbst in Erinnerung bringend, symbolisiert sich in seiner schwankenden Gestalt der Typ des Allzweckschreibers schlechthin, korrupt genug, jedem Duodez-Tyrannen die göttliche Abkunft anzudichten, jedem erfolgreichen Sportsfreund das Podest anzustocken" (pp. 66–67). The voice of true interest does not sound in these lines. For a less violent and far more subtle analysis of Pindar's relation to the aristocracy, see Rose (1982). Rühmkorff's characterization of Pindar echoes Voltaire's designation of him as the first professional flatterer of literature, in his entry on *Flatterie* in the *Dictionnaire Philosophique* (1878, vol. 19, p. 147).
4. As we know from Eupolis (Athenaeus 1.4), Pindar was not universally appreciated in the fifth century, though this is attributed to the "boorishness" (*aphilokalia*) of the public. Quintilian's rating of Pindar as the "chief" (*princeps*) of the nine lyric poets of the Alexandrian canon (*Inst.* 10.1.61) did much to keep his reputation alive in later times, by virtue of the enormous importance of the *Institutio* in the Middle Ages and Renaissance. During the Middle Ages, Pindar's works, unlike Horace's, were unknown, but his high repute made

the impact of the rediscovery of his works a powerful one. The first modern edition of Pindar was that of the Italian printer Aldus Manutius (1513), and vernacular imitations of Pindar begin in Italy in the 1520s and 1530s. In France, the publication of Ronsard's first book of *Odes* (1550) marks the entrance of Pindar into French literature in a spirit of controversy that will persist around this author in France. English imitations of Pindar begin, under the influence of Ronsard, with Soothern's *Pandora* of 1584 and in Germany with Weckherlin at the beginning of the seventeenth century. For Pindar's influence on the early European ode, see Maddison (1960); for knowledge of Pindar on the continent and in England in the sixteenth century, see Shafer (1918, pp. 56–78); for Pindar in German literature from the beginnings to Gryphius, see Koch (1927) and Gelzer (1981).

Scaliger's (1964, pp. 245–47) criticisms of Pindar in the comparison between his and Vergil's description of the erupting Aetna (*Poetics*, 1561) are the beginning of the modern controversy over Pindar, which is crystallized in the "Querelle des Anciens et des Modernes" in France at the end of the seventeenth century. Out of this quarrel emerges Boileau's defense of Pindar's "beau désordre" against Perrault's attacks on his "galimatias impénétrable." Boileau's formulation was enormously influential for the image of Pindar. The story of Pindar's reputation in the seventeenth and eighteenth centuries in general is told in Lempicki (1930–31), and that of his fame in eighteenth-century Germany in Henkel (1981).

Longinus's canonization of Pindar as a sublime poet (*Subl.* 33.5) whose tremendous flights of inspiration are often followed by a fall endeared Pindar to the Romantics, as did Pindar's own emphasis on the role of genius (*phya*) over art. Modern Pindaric scholarship, from the mid-nineteenth century to the "Bundyan revolution" of the 1960s, has been ambivalent about the value of Pindar as a poet, and a continuous debate about the unity of the Pindaric ode has been the main feature of the scholarship. On Pindaric scholarship see the excellent survey of Young (1964).

5. Pope, Cowley, and Coleridge are among those who have made this comparison; see Wasserman (1967, p. 113).

6. Horace was the first to speak of Pindar as "lawless" (*Carm.* 4.2.11–12), though he is referring specifically (and erroneously) to Pindar's meter. Diderot's entry in the *Encyclopédie* under *Pindarique* shows that the eighteenth century regarded Pindar as an acceptable model for the irregular style of composition. The English critics of the eighteenth century often grouped Pindar with Shakespeare as a sublime, and even "untutored" (!), genius (Monk 1960, p. 102).

7. "More bad poems have been written with the intention of rivalling Pindar than in any other sphere of classical imitation" (Highet 1949, p. 242).

8. Elroy Bundy's *Studia Pindarica* of 1962 began a spate of studies of the encomiastic genre that did much to make Pindar comprehensible, though hardly exciting. However, by making Pindar accessible Bundy paved the way for a number of sensitive literary readings of individual odes of the kind that, had he lived longer, he would have produced himself. Among modern translations, Bowra's of 1969 is recommended for its straightforward dignity, which lets one feel a great writer *behind* it, and it has the advantage of giving brief explanatory notes on each ode. Nisetich (1980) and Lattimore (1976) are more ambitious attempts to capture the experience of reading Pindar, and both are relatively successful. Nisetich's translation contains a long and useful introduction, brief but excellent essays on each ode, and a very full glossary; it is an indispensable tool for the beginner and enlightening for all readers of Pindar. Crotty (1982) is a fine study of Pindar's relation to archaic thought that is accessible to the nonclassicist.

9. See, for instance, the collection of essays on the lyric by Hošek and Parker (1985), where Pindar's name is used, by Frye (pp. 31–32), Patterson (quoting Adorno, p. 151) and Arac (p. 353), to make this point.

10. But see the intelligent and persuasive speculations of Mullen (1982).

11. Johnson (1982, p. 178). Johnson focuses, appropriately enough, on Whitman.

12. On the significance of the *agōn* for Greek civilization, see Burckhardt (1929, vol. 3, pp. 46–108), Nietzsche (1954, pp. 32–39), Gouldner (1965, pp. 41–77), and Slater (1968, pp. 3–49).

13. Bloom (1982).

14. Schlüter restricts himself more or less to a *formal* comparison between the ancient hymn and the English ode.

15. Pindar was a lifelong companion for Hölderlin, who wrote, as early as 1790, "ich möchte beinahe sagen, sein Hymnus sei das Summum der Dichtkunst" (Beissner 1946–77, vol. 4, part 1, p. 202; all references to Hölderlin are from this edition, henceforth referred to as *StA*.) But it is in the later poetry that Hölderlin shows his deepest affinity with the ancient poet. The poem that, as Szondi (1967) has shown, marks the transition into Hölderlin's "late" style is the most Pindaric of all his poems ("Wie wenn am Feiertage. . . ."). Furthermore, it is in the commentaries to the translations of the Pindar fragments (1803) that we find most of the characteristic thinking of the late Hölderlin (see Killy in Schmidt 1970b, pp. 294–319, and Fink 1982).

16. On Pindar and Hölderlin, see the exhaustive, and exhausting, studies of Seifert (1982–83 and 1982) and the books of Benn (1962) and Harrison (1975). Harrison's book is titled *Hölderlin and*

Greek Literature but, surprisingly, devotes only twenty of its three hundred pages to Pindar. The review of Benn by Zernin (1965) also contains much useful material. Hölderlin's translations of Pindar have been studied by Hellingrath (1936), Zuntz (1928), Beissner (1933), and Killy in Schmidt (1970b).

CHAPTER 1: POETRY AND AGŌN

1. *P.* 10.30, 12.24. I quote throughout from the text of Bowra (1935).
2. Newman and Newman (1984, p. 86).
3. Bloom (1982, p. viii).
4. Bloom (1982, p. 29).
5. As Burckhardt (1929, p. 69) points out, apropos of Homeric society: "Wer den Krieg hat bedarf des Turniers nicht."
6. Hegel's (1977) discussion of the "trial by death" in the section on lordship and bondage in the *Phenomenology* (B IV) has some affinities with the speech of Sarpedon.
7. War is a prime example of the "zero-sum game" in which someone can win only if someone else loses, which is the premise of the Greek contest system. See Gouldner (1965, pp. 49ff.).
8. Hamilton (1974, p. 15) distinguishes a group of "peripheral myth odes" that have myths at the beginning and the end of the ode, rather than in the middle, where the myth is situated in about three-quarters of the odes.
9. Although this "loosening" is usually interpreted as a release *from* death, the expression "he loosed the limbs of *x*" is frequently used in Homer to mean "he killed *x*"; compare also Sophocles' *lyei blephara* (*Ant.* 1302). Pindar here uses the compound *analyo*, which in Homer means both "release" (*Od.* 12.200) and "undo" (of Penelope's unweaving of the web: *Od.* 2.105, 109).
10. For the relation between gods and mortals, heaven and earth in this ode, see Stern (1969).
11. The word *Dioscuri* is a latinization of the Greek *Dioskouroi* (children of Zeus).
12. "Wenn aber die Himmlischen," lines 78–80. I quote from the *Grosse Stuttgarter Ausgabe* of Beissner (1946), hereafter referred to as *StA*.
13. Lines 55–60. I quote here, and throughout, from the text of Allott (1970).
14. "Wo nämlich / Die Himmlischen eines Zaunes oder Merkmals, / Das ihren Weg / Anzeige, oder eines Bades / Bedürfen, reget

es wie Feuer / In der Brust der Männer sich" (*StA*. 2.1.223). The gods also need an element in which "to feel warm beside one another" ("Der Ister," line 54). By themselves they cannot do everything, for "mortals reach more easily to the abyss" ("Mnemosyne," 2 Fass. *StA*. 2.1.195).

15. Hegel's Absolute expresses itself as Spirit, or self-consciousness, through the human mind, which, as it were, provides a path for the Absolute back to itself.

16. *P*. 3.86–89.

17. The emphasis on Achilles' terrible carnage here is appropriate to the victory that this ode celebrates, since it was won in that most bloody of contests, the *pankration*.

18. Seifert (1982–83, pp. 80–96) discusses the relation between Hölderlin's *Brautfest* and the wedding of Peleus and Thetis in *Pythian* 3.

19. Here I follow Dickson (1982). In recent years scholars have claimed that the temporal sense of *kairos* (opportune moment) is not operative until after Pindar, and that in Pindar the word should be translated "due measure"; this is the contention of Wilson (1980). Burton (1962, p. 46) argues that in Pindar *kairos* means "the right mark or limit between the too much and the too little, and not the opportune moment in time." Probably the most useful examination of this word in Pindar is that of H. Fraenkel, who pays more attention to its characteristic contexts and functions than to how it should be translated. Fraenkel (1975, p. 448 n. 15) shows that it tends to occur in passages where Pindar confronts an overwhelming multiplicity that he must somehow command, or in contexts where things might go either way (*O*. 8.22 and *P*. 8.6–7). *Kairos* is what gives one a purchase on a confusing and changeable world.

20. H. Fraenkel (1946) established that *ephēmeros* in Pindar means "living from day to day" and not "living only for a day," but see also Dickie (1976). Mähler (1963, p. 50) calls *amēkhania* the *Grundsituation* of archaic lyric.

21. See *P*. 1.81–83 for the relation between *kairos, koros,* and *mōmos* (blame).

22. *StA*. 4.1.282.

23. Kirk and Raven (1957, pp. 119–20, 129–31).

24. See Gundert (1935, pp. 13, 110. *Peira: N*. 3.70, 4.76. *Krisis: P*. 4.253, *O*. 3.21, *N*. 10.23).

25. On the victory ode as debt and healing, see Gundert (1935, pp. 43–45).

26. *Koros: P*. 1.82–83. *Phthonos* (envy): *N*. 8.21.

27. On the Pindaric triad, see Mullen (1982) and Nierhaus (1936). The basic facts of Pindar's meter are succinctly described by Nisetich (1980, pp. 31–39).

28. Mullen (1982) has come up with some convincing specula-
tions on the nature and significance of the dance movements by ob-
serving certain regularities in Pindar's use of the triad.

29. The subject of the "I" in Pindar has been treated at length by
Lefkowitz (1963), and there are important remarks on this subject in
W. J. Slater's article on futures in Pindar (1969). Slater holds that the
"I" in Pindar is "an element that implies in fact a vague combination
of Pindar, chorus and chorus leader" (p. 89).

30. W. J. Slater (1969) concludes that Pindar "formulates his song
by convention roughly for a time, when his chorus is arriving at the
place where they are to sing, but at a moment before the song is to be
sung" (p. 88).

31. As Segal observes (1967, p. 461), apropos of *Nemean* 7.77–79:
"Pindar gives us no word for the finished thing. What he describes is
only the *process* of creation." Cf. *O.* 6.1ff., *O.* 3.8–9, *N.* 4.44–45 for
other metaphors of composition as process.

32. See Lefkowitz (1963, pp. 200ff.).

33. D. E. Sattler's *Frankfurter Ausgabe* of Hölderlin has made this
openness of the text into the principle of the edition, which prints
facsimiles of Hölderlin's drafts in order to rectify the distortion that
Sattler sees in earlier editions guided by a preference for the com-
pleted formal whole. See Sattler (1975, p. 17).

34. W. J. Slater (1969).

35. "Viel hat von Morgen an, / Seit ein Gesprach wir sind und
hören voneinander, / Erfahren der Mensch, bald sind wir aber Ge-
sang" ("Friedensfeier," lines 91–93, from Beissner and Schmidt
[1969], vol. 1, p. 166).

36. "The hymn's variations of tense permit a continuous rhythmic
infusion of the eternal with the temporal, the temporal with the eter-
nal" (Maclaren 1981, p. 185).

37. Fry (1980, pp. 1–14).

38. Twenty-three out of the forty-five *epinikia* begin with an invo-
cation (Hamilton 1974, p. 17).

39. Fry (1980, p. 6). As H. Fraenkel observed (1975, pp. 481–88),
Pindar's invocations are more often than not addressed to "Powers"
rather than to the anthropomorphic deities of Olympus. Fraenkel
describes the ambiguous status of these Powers as follows: "These
realities, as superpersonal powers in life, belong alike to heaven and
to earth. They are so natural that we can grasp them entire, yet they
have a depth that goes beyond the mechanical universe" (p. 482).

40. "In the actions and reactions of life the Pindaric powers some-
times become dynamic to a startling degree" (H. Fraenkel 1975,
p. 483).

41. Goethe was deeply struck by the final words of this strophe,
epikratein dynasthai (to be able to master). He felt, as he read these

words, that his previous work was convicted of triviality and dilettantism. See Zucker (1955, p. 182).

42. Fry (1980, p. 2).

43. Fry (1980, p. 2).

44. Fry (1980, p. 6).

45. One should note that Hegel attributes the uniqueness of the Christian God to the fact that, with Christianity, God is "erscheinende Subjektivität." See Nägele (1982, p. 557), who draws attention to Hölderlin's painful attempt to conjure up, and at the same time to exorcise, the figure of the "Only One" (p. 558).

46. Pindar opens his poem by asking the Muse to read out the name of the victor that is inscribed on his heart, for though he owes him a song he has forgotten his debt. But, he goes on to say, the debt will be repaid *with interest*. Hölderlin's fault is the reverse of Pindar's: he has not forgotten what was inscribed on his heart but has been guided too exclusively by his own heart. This reversal is typical of Hölderlin's understanding of our relation to the Greeks and should be compared with his use of the "chorus on man" from *Antigone* in *Am Quell der Donau* (see pp. 103–6).

47. Fry (1980, p. 7).

48. For an account of the main participants and events in this controversy, which was begun by an article by Pierre Bertaux in the *Hölderlin-Jahrbuch* of 1967–68, see Nägele (1978, pp. 63–64). Helen Fehervary's book on Hölderlin and the Left (1977) is a very interesting history of modern political interpretations of Hölderlin.

49. This contrast between Theognis and Pindar is drawn by Donlan (1980, chap. 3), who gives an excellent account of their respective responses to the "crisis of identity."

50. It may be that Pindar's Panhellenism is to be seen as a reaction against the growth of the Athenian empire, another form in which the power of the *kakoi* was making itself felt. On Pindar and the Athenian empire, see Carne-Ross (1985, pp. 184ff.).

CHAPTER 2: THE POETRY OF RECEPTION

1. See Newman and Newman (1984) for an interesting interpretation of Pindar's odes as "carnival" texts, which stresses their origins in the *kōmos*.

2. For the conditions of performance, as far as they can be reconstructed, see Nisetich (1980, pp. 4–7).

3. See Crotty (1982, chap. 4) for the significance of return in epinician poetry.

4. Redfield (1975) has some excellent words on the Homeric war-

rior that apply equally well to Pindar's athletes: "The hero goes to combat knowing that the honor he claims may be beyond his reach. His excellence is not so much a power he has as an hypothesis on which he stakes his life. Combat is a kind of experiment which falsifies the hypothesis of one party or the other. In combat the hero reaches beyond himself and promises himself greatness; he makes himself by asserting himself. . . . He goes to action in order to prove that he is what he claims to be" (p. 129).

   5. On these metaphors, see Simpson (1969).
   6. *I.* 4.1–3, *O.* 6.22–25, *I.* 2.33–34, 6.22–23.
   7. The connection of the *koros* that may come from success with *hybris* is almost proverbial in archaic Greek literature (Solon 8; Theognis 153); compare *I.* 3.1–3.
   8. This ode is given a subtle analysis by Fry (1980), who has some excellent observations on Jonson's use of the Pindaric triad.
   9. At the end of the ode Jonson recalls Pindar's description of Pythias's earliness ("though his cheeks show not yet the Summer, / The Mother of the grape's soft down") when he describes Cary and Morison as men "Who, ere the first down bloomed on the chin, / Had sowed these fruits and got the harvest in" (127–28). I quote from the text of Parfitt (1975).
   10. See Wayne (1979, p. 92) on Jonson's epigrams: "In order to assert one's self as a subject it is necessary to deny that status to the Other. What constitutes subjectivity is a form of property, or capital; it accrues, it is measurable, it can be acquired only at the expense of others."
   11. "Just 'Ben' may appear over-familiar; with the addition of the enjambed line, the poet, as he would have been known by the living Cary, the late Morison, and the whole 'Tribe of Ben' becomes the public figure, the author of the *Works.* Thus is the poem labeled with the poet's dual name expressing his private and public roles and duties" (Hollander 1975, p. 178).
   12. "From the outset we can expect to find a conflict in this poem between its theme of steadfastness in virtue and the variability of its Pindaric form" (Fry 1980, p. 16). For a similar contrast between arrest and movement in Pindar's *Nemean* 5, see Segal (1974a).
   13. See Lempicki (1930–31) on Pindar's reputation in the seventeenth and eighteenth centuries.
   14. Gundert (1935, pp. 13–14).
   15. *I.* 4.19–29.
   16. Gundert (1935, p. 15).
   17. The possibility of indirect influence is raised by Gordon (1967), who argues that Keats was well acquainted with English Pindarics and that some of his poems were intended to be Pindarics.
   18. Keats's words come from a letter to Benjamin Bailey (13 March

1818) quoted by Bate (1963), who comments: "The theme of much of the greater poetry to come—certainly of the 'Ode on a Grecian Urn' and the 'Ode to a Nightingale'—may be described as the drama of the human spirit's 'greeting' of objects in order 'to make them wholly exist'" (p. 242). Fry (1980) makes a similar point when he says that this ode "pronounces all art that is palpable, visible or melodic to be trapped in its medium and cut off from any realm of signification beyond itself until it is supplied with the sort of hermeneutic commentary that appears in this ode" (p. 249).

19. For an excellent account of the history of Pindar's text, see Nisetich's introduction (1980, pp. 13–21). Nisetich points out that Aristophanes broke with his principle of arrangement for the odes of a particular Games (in accordance with the prestige of the contest involved) by placing *Olympian* 1, celebrating a horse race, before *Olympian* 2, celebrating a chariot race. This he attributes to the majestic opening of the poem (p. 18). I would suggest that this ode, like the poem that opens the Alexandrian edition of Sappho, is to some extent programmatic for the whole collection. Mullen (1982, p. 164) adds that Hieron, the victor of *Olympian* 1, was a more powerful man than Theron, the victor of *Olympian* 2.

20. "Gold mixes with human wealth and is equivalent to fire as it burns (mixes) with night's darkness. Water alone mixes with nothing, possesses no sensible or physical characteristics here; therefore, it is best" (Farenga 1977, p. 200). See Gerber's (1982) commentary on this ode for an account of the scholarship on water's preeminence, which, however, ignores Farenga. His citation of Snell on "monosemantica" is important here (pp. 9–10).

21. The second *Olympian* has a similar tripartite sequence in its opening: "Pisa *belongs to* Zeus, the Olympian feast / Herakles *founded*, the loot of war, / But of Theron *let your voices ring*, / For his victorious four-in-hand" (*O*. 2.3–6). My emphasis shows the progressive contingency in the sequence of verbs.

22. On this ode see Segal (1964).

23. Thummer identifies the cauldron with the bath in which the newborn baby was purified: see Segal (1964, p. 254 n. 16). Some scholars believe that *epei* (26) should be translated "because" rather than "when," giving the reason rather than the time when Poseidon fell in love with Pelops; see Mullen (1982, p. 252 n. 26). The supposed absurdity of Poseidon's falling in love with an infant that this interpretation is meant to obviate is illusory: the gods have a different relation to time than humans do and Poseidon's emotion does not have to wait on the physical development of Pelops. For Poseidon, Pelops is Pelops the moment he is born. Gerber (1982, pp. 55–57) produces a different interpretation of *epei* as temporal.

24. As Mullen points out (1982, p. 176), this "tableau of heroic

solitude" on the strand recalls two scenes from Homer: *Iliad* 1.349–50 and *Odyssey* 2.260–61. See also Gerber (1982, p. 114) for the implications of Pelops's praying by the shore and in the dark, alone.

25. Rose (1982, p. 62) draws our attention to an interesting manifestation of the rivalry between poet and victor: "In *Pythian* X, Pindar celebrates a relatively modest victory in a boy's footrace, but for his own poetic act he chooses as metaphor by far the most prestigious of all contests, the four-horse chariot race."

26. For some pertinent observations on the financial language in this ode, see Kromer (1976) and Norwood (1956, pp. 111–12).

27. There is a version of this passage in the fourth of Claudel's "Cinq Grandes Odes":

> Laisse-moi te [Muse] refouler dans cette strophe, avant que tu ne reviennes sur moi comme une vague avec un cri félin! Va-t-en de moi un peu! laisse-moi faire ce que je veux un peu!

The Muse of ancient poetry is a force antagonistic to the modern poet, who yet writes in an ancient form. In the *refoulement* of the Muse's blood the poet creates his own freedom, and the poem will itself be conceived as a wave; see the analysis by Spitzer (1948).

28. Redfield's (1975, pp. 110–13) discussion of the relation between father and son in Homer is relevant to this passage.

29. On Milton's knowledge of Pindar, see Robinson (1936, pp. 25–29).

30. Lines 22–28. I quote from the text of Merritt Hughes (1957).

31. The typically Pindaric combination of self-assertion and humility has been nicely described by John Broadbent as Milton's "anxiously arrogant art" (Broadbent 1962, p. 30).

32. In *Olympian* 9.1–10, Milton has Pindaric precedent for this contrast between an immediate celebration by those who were present and the later, more complete, reception of the event performed by the ode itself.

33. In Pindar (*N.* 1.35), Herakles, the "son of Zeus," emerges from his mother's womb into the "glittering daylight" (*thaēton es aiglan*); in Milton he *is* that daylight.

34. The dramatic movement of this ode has been described by Maclaren (1981): "Milton is gradually working out the process by which to get the narrator and his reader to the manger as participants, not merely as spectators. This involves harmonizing the omniscient view of the event—God's purpose and his Son's acceptance of that purpose—with the conventional, misguided, human reaction of blind adoration and mere astonishment at the arrival of the redeemer" (p. 188).

35. Gundert (1935, p. 63) stresses that time is not the contingent

space in which an event takes place but *belongs* to the event as the power that realizes it (*telei*).

36. Compare Isaiah 6: 6.

37. See Crotty (1982, chap. 1).

38. On *Pythian* 3, see D. Young (1968, pp. 27–68).

39. Pindar recounts, at *I. 8.63–66* and *N. 5.22–25*, that mortals heard the singing of the Muses at the wedding of Peleus and Kadmos; in both cases this singing is a respite from, or cure for, human troubles.

40. In what follows I am much indebted to the brilliant treatment of this poem by Peter Szondi (1967). Szondi refers briefly to Pindar's influence, but most relevant to my concerns here is his description of Hölderlin's late style as a paradoxical mixture "von Entschlossenheit zum Äussersten und von Zaghaftigkeit, von Kühnheit und von Demut, Kraft und Schwäche" (p. 35). Seifert (1982, pp. 93–349) and Waisinger (1976) deal specifically with the Pindaric influence on this poem, and Beissner (1933, pp. 101–3) with the Pindaric meter.

41. On Dionysus, or Bacchus, in Hölderlin's poetry, see Bäumer (1973–74).

42. *StA.* 2.2.669–70. The interpretation of this poem, and particularly of the relation between Semele and the poet, through the prose draft has been challenged by O'Brien (1979), who argues that a change takes place between the prose draft and the poem. O'Brien denies that the blasting of Semele is to be understood as representing the punishment of a sin that could have been avoided on the part of Semele or the poet. Instead, it is to be understood as an inevitable result of the ineradicable *Ich*'s interruption: the poet's individuality is both the condition for the incarnation of divinity and the reason why this incarnation will necessarily involve a miscarriage. While this is an important correction of earlier critics' exclusive emphasis on the question of the poet's *Frevel*, it seems to me to pay too little attention to the words "da sie sichtbar / Den Gott zu sehen begehrte."

43. In a famous letter to his friend Böhlendorff, written two years after this hymn, Hölderlin explicitly compares himself to Tantalos: "jetzt fürcht'ich, dass es mir nicht geh'am Ende wie dem alten Tantalos, dem es mehr von den Göttern ward, als er verdauen konnte" (quoted by Szondi 1967, p. 46).

44. Hölderlin imagines himself thrown down into the dark "to sing for those who have ears to hear, the warning song" (lines 72–73). Pindar's Ixion is another figure who abused divine favor (he attempted to seduce Hera) and, bound to his flaming wheel in the underworld, he utters the words "Thou shalt be zealous for him that does thee service / And pay him gentle return" (*P.* 2.24). On the importance of Pindar's Ixion for Hölderlin, see Seifert (1982, pp. 514–36).

45. Both Waisinger (1976, pp. 258–59) and Seifert (1982, pp. 122–76) see the influence of the beginning of *O*. 7 on Hölderlin's opening stanza, though Waisinger goes, I think, too far in seeing Pindar's ode as the model of Hölderlin's poem.

46. *I.* 8.1–2.

47. One might compare the shift in focus between the first strophe and antistrophe of *Nemean* 8, where the invocation of *Hōra* (Season) leads to a gnome that concludes the strophe: "In every action the heart / Desires not to stray from the right moment [*kairou*] / But to have power to win the nobler loves [*erōtōn*]" (4–5). The antistrophe begins by making the *Erōtes* (now to be understood as Cupids) into a new subject: "Such [viz. *Erōtes*] as waited upon the bed of Zeus and Aigina, / And brought the Cyprian's gifts to the fold. A son was born" (6–7).

48. Seifert (1982, pp. 216–22) makes some important distinctions between Hölderlin's more historical conception of Nature and Pindar's *phya*, and he points out that Hölderlin did not share the interpretation of Pindar's stress on his natural (as opposed to acquired) poetic ability made by the contemporary writers of the *Geniezeit*.

49. On the Pindaric precedent for a sleeping but *ahnende* Nature, see Seifert (1982, pp. 257–69).

50. Illig (1932).

51. Seifert (1982) is probably right to see in the gesture of the poets the influence of the beginning of *Olympian* 7: "As a man takes in his rich hand a bowl / Bubbling inside with the wine's dew, / And shall give it / To his daughter's young bridegroom to pledge him / From one home to another" (*O.* 7.1–4).

52. Szondi (1967) explicates this purity of heart as follows: "Verlangt wird eine Offenheit die vom eigenen Ich absieht. . . . Rein, schuldlos ist der Kind weil es sich nicht auf sich selbst bezieht, weil es sich noch nicht, als in sich erstarrtes Ich, aus dem kosmisch-göttlichen Zusammenhang ausgeschlossen ist." This receptivity leads to "sharing his sufferings who is stronger than we are": "Und so ist auch das Mitleiden nicht als Mitleid-Haben zu deuten, sondern als Mitvollzug der Erschütterung, die in Gottes zornigen Nahen das Weltall wecken und zu neuer Göttergegenwart führen soll" (p. 44). Szondi connects the "self-inflicted wound" specifically with Hölderlin's suffering as a result of his parting from Susette Gontard. Seifert (1982) would prefer to take it more generally as Hölderlin's potentially gratuitous initiative with regard to the gods (compare "Patmos," line 167), his failure to wait for them to come to him.

53. See Fink (1982, pp. 35–37).

54. "Heaven's youngest-teemed star" that attends the sleeping Lord in the last stanza of the hymn is surely Milton himself.

55. Horace adopts the Pindaric manner in the six so-called Ro-

man odes that open the third book of odes, and in some of the poems of the separately published fourth book. These odes tackle the vital question of the poet's role in the new Augustan dispensation and cast an oblique glance at the epic that this decidedly lyric poet felt was demanded of him. Ronsard opened his literary career with his odes of 1550 in a blare of Pindaric pride and self-importance. Cowley's "Pindariques" were produced by the thirty-three-year-old poet after encountering Pindar in a place "where he had no other books to direct him" (Sprat 1957, p. 16), and they made his fame. Hopkins's "Wreck of the Deutschland" (1875) was the first work that the thirty-one-year-old poet wrote after burning his previous poetry on entering the Jesuit novitiate in 1868.

56. Crotty (1982) shows how the values of the *epinikion* and symposium are derived from the knowledge that the Golden Age is past; see especially chap. 3.

57. Compare Pindar's description of the undertaking of Jason and the Argonauts: "And Hera kindled an all-persuading sweet desire in these demi-gods for the ship Argo, so that no one should remain by his mother nursing [*pessont'*] a life without danger, but even at the risk of death should find the best remedy for his valour [*pharmakon aretas*] with his youthful companions" (*P.* 4.184–87; my translation).

CHAPTER 3: VERTICAL AND HORIZONTAL

1. On *Olympian 3*, see Segal (1964). On *Patmos*, see Binder (1970, pp. 362–402), Warminski (1976), Unger (1975, pp. 180–205), Stierle (1980–81), and Nägele (1982).

2. Finley (1955, p. 119) observes that "as an earthly institution the games are shielded from the full glare of divinity."

3. It is worth noting that Hölderlin translated the beginning of *Olympian 3*.

4. Quoted by Hamburger (1980, p. 13).

5. *StA.* 2.1.180.

6. On the mountaintop in Romantic poetry, see Randel (1981).

7. On the "summits of time," see Unger (1975, p. 183) and Binder (1970, pp. 372–73).

8. In "Der Rhein" (lines 135ff.) the "dear ones" (*die Theuern*) are the demi-gods and include Rousseau, who lawlessly gives away the language of the purest (lines 144–46).

9. *StA.* 2.1.179.

10. Rose (1982, pp. 64–65) sees the myth of the Hyperboreans here as a "*promesse de bonheur.*" See also Köhnken (1971, p. 181).

11. For the significance of the mid-month, see Segal (1964, p. 238).

12. The controversy over whether there is only one journey or two is surveyed by Segal (1964, p. 238 n. 97); see also Carne-Ross (1985, pp. 52–55).

13. There is possibly an ambiguity in the word *received* (*dexat'*, 27), which admits of a hostile, as well as a benevolent, sense. There are versions of this story in which the relations between Herakles and Artemis are less friendly: see Devereux (1966, pp. 289–98).

14. Snell (1953, p. 33).

15. Gildersleeve (1893, p. 160).

16. Pindar uses the pillars of Herakles in a similar way in other odes: see Segal (1964, p. 264).

17. Dornseiff (1921, p. 103).

18. *StA*. 2.1.179.

19. The following words from Hölderlin's essay *Über Religion* are relevant to his conception of divinity as a communal sphere: "wenn es ein Sphäre gibt, in der alle zugleich leben, und mit der sie in mehr als notdürftiger Beziehung sich fühlen, dann, aber auch nur insoferne, haben sie alle eine gemeinschaftliche Gottheit" (*StA*. 4.1.278).

20. See Nägele (1982).

21. Nägele (1982, p. 560).

22. Compare "Der Rhein," lines 96–104.

23. Hölderlin may well be thinking here of Herakles' visit to the Ister in *Olympian* 3. The word *Gastfreundlich* (line 61) suggests the lines from "Der Ister" that refer to Pindar's poem: "So wundert / Mich nicht, das er [Ister] / Den Herakles zu Gaste geladen / Fernglänzend, am Olympos drunten, / Da der, sich schatten zu suchen / Vom heissen Isthmos kam" (lines 26–31).

24. Binder (1970, pp. 363–64) points out that here in "Patmos," as in other poems, Hölderlin presents us with a "Christ without Passion and Redemption" and that these elements of Christian belief give way to an emphasis on the *parousia*. Hölderlin's Christ is "nicht der Stifter eines Bundes, sondern der Öffner des Menschensinnes."

25. Beissner and Schmidt (1969, vol. 1, p. 115) quote Matthew 28:20: "Wo zwei oder drei versammelt sind in meinem Namen, da bin ich mitten unter ihnen."

26. See Warminski (1976, pp. 486–89).

27. Warminski (1976, p. 491).

28. Binder (1970, p. 400) documents both senses from Hölderlin's works, but he believes that the meaning "shared" is inappropriate to this passage.

29. Warminski (1976, pp. 481–83) sees an ambiguity in the final lines of the poem with regard to the service of the *veste Buchstab*. The fact that Hölderlin uses the two non-synonymous terms *gepflegt* and *gedeutet* shows that there is a danger both of excessive submission to the letter and also of positing an excessively individual or subjective

interpretation. Similarly, the word *folgt* in the final line may imply belatedness with respect to the letter or, more figuratively, a "contemporaneity in spirit."

30. I quote the text of W. H. Gardner (1953).

CHAPTER 4: PROGRESS AND FALL

1. On the English Progress poem, see Griffith (1919–20), Swayne (1936), and Hartman (1970).

2. "[Ein] Ausleger, ja ein Schöpfer der Zeiten"; Herder (1967–68, vol. xxiv, p. 338).

3. Zucker (1955, p. 184). On Goethe and Pindar, see also Henkel (1981, pp. 186ff.).

4. Mullen (1982, p. 116).

5. On the form of the Pindaric narrative, see Illig (1932). Herder's appreciation of Pindar as an "Ausleger der Zeiten" stemmed from his observation of the Pindaric ode's movement back to an origin from which the future was projected, an important process for him and his teacher, Hamann (Henkel 1981, p. 184). The lines of his Pindaric "Der Genius der Zukunft" that express this notion contain a reference to Pindar (*O.* 9.5–11):

> Mit Flammenzügen glänzt
> in der Seelen Abgründen der Vorwelt Bild
> und Schiesst weit über weissagend starkes Geschoss
> in das Herz der Zukunft.
>
> (lines 19–22)

6. Köhnken (1971, p. 175) stresses the fact that though Perseus (a mortal) did reach the land of the Hyperboreans, he was not able to enjoy the *immortal* happiness that distinguishes the existence of the Hyperboreans.

7. The term *Abbruchsformel* was coined by Schadewalt (1928) in his study of the structure of the Pindaric ode.

8. Fitzgerald (1983).

9. As Earl has pointed out (1967, chap. 3), the Republican ideal of *gloria* was no longer appropriate to the new order.

10. The notion of the poet as *vates* was resuscitated by the Augustan poets to claim a new seriousness for the poet in the context of the Augustan revolution; see Newman (1967). On the great gap between the institutional role of Pindar's poetry and that of Horace, a gap recognized by Horace himself, see the excellent remarks of Edward Fraenkel (1957, pp. 283–85).

11. On the "focusing priamel," see Bundy (1962). The movement

of this poem is well described by Williams (1969, p. 32): "Thus what happens in this poem is that the poet begins with the most elevated of relationships (that between kings and Juppiter) and then he transposes the contrasted elements in a series of movements that have two effects: first, they reduce the terms on both sides so that finally the poet himself can appear on one side; secondly, they modify the controlling relationship between the contrasted elements so that though it starts as a fundamental ordinance of the universe (the hierarchy of kings and Zeus, then Death) it comes to be a psychological factor identifiable with ambition on one side and contentment on the other."

12. I quote from the Oxford Classical Text of Wickham (1963); the translations are those of Shepherd (1983).

13. Commager (1962, p. 112) draws attention to what Nietzsche would have called the "Pathos der Distanz" in his perceptive remarks on the poem's ending.

14. Collinge (1961, chap. 2) shows that Horace paid considerable attention to the positioning of odes within the books.

15. "Stimme des Volks," (*StA.* 2.1.51–53).

16. In the final poem of book two, Horace proudly claims that his poetry will make him "more famous than Daedalus' Icarus" ("Daedaleo notior Icaro," *Carm.* 2.20.13).

17. Boileau probably conflates the bees of Horace and of Pindar when he says of the ode: "Tantost comme une abeille ardente à son ouvrage / Elle s'en va de fleurs dépouiller le rivage" (Boileau 1966, p. 164). Pindar often compares his poetry to honey (*N.* 3.77, 7.53, *I.* 5.54).

18. Cf. *O.* 1.105, 6.21, *N.* 11.18. *Poikilos* (variegated) and its cognates are also commonly applied by Pindar to his own poetry (*O.* 3.8, 4.3, *N.* 5.42, 8.15, etc.). The significance of this semantic field in Greek thought has been brilliantly studied by Vernant and Detienne (1974).

19. Bloom takes this term from St. Paul's account of Christ's humbling of himself from God to man. "In strong poets, the *kenosis* is a revisionary act in which an 'emptying' or 'ebbing' takes place *in relation to the precursor.* This 'emptying' is a liberating discontinuity and makes possible a kind of poem that a simple repetition of the precursor's afflatus or godhead could not allow. 'Undoing' the precursor's strength *in oneself* serves also to 'isolate' the self from the precursor's stance and saves the latecomer-poet from becoming taboo in and to himself" (Bloom 1973, pp. 87–88).

20. Cf. Huxley (1975, pp. 14–21).

21. Bate (1970, p. 12).

22. Bate (1970, p. 45).

23. "A miracle of compression condenses the vast and compre-

hensive plan of epic into the flashing power of creative phrases and insights" (Eli Mandel, quoted by Fry 1980, p. 111). The shift of emphasis in eighteenth-century aesthetic theory from action to image and the role of the ode in this shift are described in the important study by Maclean (1952).

24. Lonsdale (1969, p. 160).

25. Spacks (1966) takes Gray to task for his reliance on imagery in this poem; as Griffith (1919–20, p. 226) has pointed out, "the eighteenth century liked its poems constructed after the pattern of a cameo necklace . . . the plot is the thin golden chain, and the portraits, situations, topics are the cameos." The tension between narrative and picture is here connected by Griffith to the transition from chronicle to history.

26. I quote the poems of Gray and Collins from Lonsdale (1969).

27. Cf. Fry (1980, pp. 88 and 297 n. 38).

28. Lonsdale (1969, p. 162) quotes the following lines from Young ("To the King"):

> The Roman ode
> Majestic flowed;
> Its stream divinely clear, and strong;
> In sense, and sound,
> Thebes rolled profound;
> The torrent roared, and foamed along.

29. Fry (1980, p. 80).

30. Wickham (1963) reads *Apulo* here.

31. Cf. *Paradise Lost,* book 4, line 936 and *De Rerum Natura* 1.72–74. On Collins's relation to Milton, see Sherwin (1977).

32. Broadbent (1972, p. 46).

33. Compare Horace's Achilles in *Carm.* 4.6, whose direct action (*palam,* 17) would have been both awe-inspiring and horrible and would similarly have cut off the connection between past and present.

34. On Collins's use of Spenser in this poem, see Fry (1980, p. 103).

35. A point made by Fry (1980, p. 106) when he observes that "the object is constituted as a representation by this subject and so, with that Idea in mind, brought into existence. Just so, the maker of odes constitutes an other for his invocation." On the theological and philosophical background of this controversial mesode, see Wasserman (1967).

36. *Paradise Lost,* book 4, line 172. As Lonsdale (1969) points out, the word *embrown* (line 60) comes from Milton's "the unpierc't shade / Imbround the noontide Bowrs" (book 4, lines 245–46).

37. Weiskel (1976, p. 23) best describes this mechanism in defining the sublime object: "We call an object sublime if the attempt to

represent it determines the mind to regard its inability to grasp wholly the object as a symbol of the mind's relation to a transcendent order."
   38. Schiller (1966, vol. 2, p. 676). My translation.
   39. In his essay "Blake and the Progress of Poesy," Hartman (1970, p. 196n.6) relates Hölderlin to the English Progress tradition: "It is significant that Hölderlin, who inherited the same mythology of history (see e.g., his description of the flight of the eagle in '*Germania*,' which is a Progress of Poesy from East to West), will also become involved, as a prophetic poet, in a so-called *Abendländische Wendung* which exactly parallels the turn ('Look homeward') attempted by Milton and Blake."
   40. Cf. Butler (1958). Lacoue-Labarthe (1979) is a brilliant explication of Hölderlin's thought on this subject in relation to contemporary German thought.
   41. Winckelmann (1808–20, vol. 1, p. 31).
   42. *StA*. 4.1.221.
   43. On this, see Lacoue-Labarthe (1979, pp. 470–71).
   44. Cf. Guardini (1955, pp. 23–117).
   45. *StA*. 2.2.687: "Nun aber ruhest du, und wartest, ob vielleicht dir aus lebendiger Brust ein Wiederklang der Liebe dir begegne."
   46. *I*. 4.25, 7.16–17.
   47. Hölderlin seems to have been at work on the translation of *Oedipus the King* and *Antigone* from 1796 to 1804, when they were published. "Am Quell der Donau" was probably written in 1801. On Hölderlin's translations from Sophocles, see Beissner (1933, pp. 65–185).
   48. My translation.
   49. "Brod und Wein," stanza 7 (*StA*. 2.1.93–94).
   50. Cf. Szondi (1967, p. 54).
   51. Bloom (1973, p. 66).

CHAPTER 5: THE HERO'S EXTENSION

   1. From the innumerable examples of this *topos*, one might take Horace *Carm*. 4.8.20–34 and 4.9 passim (cf. Pindar *N*. 7.12–13) as the classic statements.
   2. On this ode see Segal (1974b), Rosenmeyer (1969), and Rose (1974).
   3. Segal (1974b, p. 35).
   4. Here Bowra translates "and his grip," reading *brokhos* (noose) for the *Khronos* (time) of the mss. The manuscript reading has been most convincingly defended by Gerber (1962).

5. On the epinincian motif of rest from toil, see Rose (1974, p. 163).

6. I quote from the text of Kinsley (1962).

7. By a fortunate coincidence, the words that become *mood* and *mode* respectively were identical in spelling and pronunciation in the fourteenth century, and this helped to promote the ancient doctrine of the ethos of the musical modes in English poetry; see Hollander (1970, pp. 208ff.).

8. For Hölderlin's theory of modes, see Ryan (1960, passim; on *Metapher*, see p. 41).

9. Hölderlin's essay "Das Werden im Vergehen" describes the dependence of the appearing of "the living Whole" on moments of transition (*StA.* 4.1.282).

10. The relation of Dryden's St. Cecilia odes to metaphysical theories of music is described by Hollander (1970).

11. "Stimme des Volks," line 13 (*StA.* 2.1.51). Hölderlin's Rhine is clearly related to the river that represents Pindar in Horace *Carm.* 4.2, as well as to the river that represents the hero of Goethe's "Mahomets Gesang," itself Pindaric in inspiration; see Henkel (1981, p. 189), who quotes a very interesting passage from Herder comparing Pindar to a river. Hölderlin seems to be recalling, and revising, "Mahomets Gesang," which has the river's course moving like a snake (*Schlangenwandelnd*) to the level ground where it is joined by friendly streams ("Bäche schmiegen / Sich gesellig an ihn"). As we shall see, in Hölderlin it is the banks that are like snakes, and their relation to the river (derived from Pindar's myth of the baby Herakles) is more aggressive than that of Goethe's compliant streams.

12. The poem was originally addressed to Wilhelm Heinse and had a different concluding strophe. Heinse's death in June of 1803 led Hölderlin to change the addressee.

13. *StA.* 2.1.41–42.

14. The connection in Hölderlin's mind between the river and the mythical figure of Ganymede is shown by his recasting of the poem "Der Gefesselte Strom" as "Ganymed" (*StA.* 2.1.67–68).

15. *StA.* 1.1.239.

16. Pp. 29–31.

17. Mullen (1982, p. 202) suggests that the rule of strict justice in Lokris is to be referred to the famous lawgiver Zaleukos and that the mention of the Lokrians' care of the Muses refers to their poet Stesichoros.

18. Kromer (1976, p. 435) argues that Pindar contrasts two kinds of truth in this poem, *Alatheia* and *Atrekeia*. *Alatheia*, who is invoked by the poet at the beginning of the ode, is identified with subjective personal experience, with vitality and continuity. *Atrekeia*, on the other hand, implies precision and accuracy and is associated with

the world of business and finance. While *Alatheia* has a particular relation to time, *Atrekeia* is connected with *nomos*. It is the poet's task to compose a song that will satisfy the demands of both types of truth.

19. Frisk (1972–73, vol. 1, p. 181).

20. Kromer (1976, p. 431) has this to say on the narrative, which moves from general to explicit: "the order of events is B-A-B'-A'-C, with two references to the killing of the Moliones, B and B', each followed by a past event giving a reason for it, then the death of Augeas, which is related to the first reason, A. The first two accounts of Herakles' actions are in reverse chronological sequence; first effect, then cause; while the third is in its correct position chronologically. The disordering of the chronological sequence complements the description of disorderly human relationships."

21. Cf. *Iliad* 18.262 and *Odyssey* 1.368.

22. "Throughout the ode there is an implied contrast between reading a name and naming" (Kromer 1976, p. 423).

23. "The snow in which the hill was steeped as long as Oinomaos ruled is like the other forms of natural accumulation Herakles had to clear, beginning with the dung of Augeas' stables and continuing through the thick grove and the scrub on the Alpheus bank" (Mullen 1982, p. 205).

24. Compare Vivante (1972, p. 120): "The Homeric action is seen *sub specie aeternitatis;* while in Pindar any act is a term of reference to something else, a gesture that invites or deters."

25. On Pindar's frequent use of verbs of mixing or mingling, see Hoey (1965).

26. Buck (1975–76) sees the Timotheus myth as an indictment of the corruption to which Dryden's times have brought the arts. Miner, on the other hand, claims that the poem asserts the dignity of Dryden's art (1967, p. 273).

27. Shuster (1940, p. 134).

28. Hollander (1970, p. 410).

29. The reciprocal, mirroring relationship between Alexander and Timotheus is interpreted by Fry (1980, p. 55) as a division of the Miltonic Satan between them: "Bard and hero together span the whole of Satan's nature, as sycophantic seducer and seduced prince."

30. Fry (1980, p. 57).

31. "The 'narrow Bounds' which Cecilia 'enlarged' were not merely the technical limitations of music; they were also the fetters of a fallen world. Dryden's use of the word 'enlarg'd' poses a serious problem. We are forced to ask if music can set men free from the fetters of corruption or, on the other hand, if that music merely makes the fetters more comprehensive" (Buck 1975–76, p. 586).

32. Quoted by Buck (1975–76, p. 582).

33. Schaerer (1958, p. 142).

34. For different versions of the application of Hölderlin's *Gesetz* to this poem, see Böschenstein (1968, pp. 135–38), de Man (1967–68, p. 196), Ryan (1960, pp. 249–77), and Seifert (1982–83, pp. 104–24).

35. De Man 1966.

36. Böschenstein (1968, pp. 63–64).

37. De Man (1967–68, p. 194) describes the demi-god as the "Sturz des Heiligen in der Zeit." Killy (1970, p. 298) has some valuable remarks on passages where Hölderlin treats the river as the provider of a "path" for divinity. One might compare to Hölderlin's opening the first stanza of Klopstock's "Unsere Sprache":

> An der Höhe, wo der Quell der Barden in das Tal
> Sein fliegendes Getöne, mit Silber bewölkt,
> Stürzet, da erblickt'ich, zeug'es Hain!
> Die Göttin! Sie kam zu den Sterblichen herab!

38. Cf. Böschenstein (1968, pp. 31–36) for the parallels between the poet and the Rhine in this connection.

39. De Man (1967, p. 194).

40. Hölderlin is thinking of Rousseau's "Cinquième Promenade" in this passage; cf. Böschenstein (1968, pp. 90ff.). On Hölderlin and Rousseau, see de Man (1967).

41. "Diese Problematik, die die Innerlichkeit als dialektisches Moment in der Zusammenhang der Geschichte einfügt, ihr dabei aber doch einen ontologischen Primat vorbehält, sich für Hölderlin weiterhin mit Person und Werk Rousseaus verbindet" (de Man 1967, p. 190).

42. The experience that Rousseau describes in the "Cinquième Promenade" involves a feeling of divinity that accounts for Hölderlin's sense of impiety here: "tant que cet état dure, on se suffit à soi-même comme dieu" (quoted in Böschenstein 1968, p. 91).

43. The reference in this passage is to Socrates' sobriety at the banquet described in Plato's *Symposium*. On Hölderlin and Plato, see Harrison (1975, pp. 43–84).

44. H. Fraenkel (1975, p. 488).

45. Gundert (1935, pp. 30–32).

CHAPTER 6: ORDER AND VIOLENCE

1. Congreve (1964, p. 82) describes the modish irregular Pindarics of his day as "a Bundle of rambling and incoherent thoughts express'd in a like Parcel of irregular Stanzas, which also consist in such another Complication of disproportion'd, uncertain and perplex'd Verses and Rhimes." He insists on the regularity of Pindar's

meter and the coherence of his thoughts. Unfortunately, he does not say much about the coherence of thought beyond alluding to "some secret connection" (p. 83) that always underlies the digressions and transitions. Gilbert West, whose translations of 1749 are accompanied by commentary and notes, makes a real attempt to spell out the coherence of the odes he translates and to reconstruct their original context. For other protest that, contrary to popular opinion, Pindar has his own logic and order, see E. Young (1854, vol. 1, p. 416), Schlegel (1961, p. 32), Saint-John Perse (1972, p. 743), Warton (1782, vol. 1, pp. 389–90), and Herder (1886, vol. 24, p. 337). To these one might add Bundy's (1962, p. 91) insistence that the "linear development" of the ode is "perfectly lucid" if analyzed according to the rhetorical principles of the genre.

2. Boileau, "L'Art Poétique" (1966, p. 164).

3. "Discours sur l'Ode" (1966, p. 227).

4. The invocation to the lyre is the most imitated passage in Pindar; in English poetry the beginning of Gray's "Progress of Poesy" is probably the most famous imitation. More recently, Robert Duncan took a line from this opening ("The light foot hears you, and the brightness begins") for his "Poem Beginning with a Line from Pindar." Pierre-Jean Jouve, in his *Ode*, has an interesting adaptation of the Aetna passage, making the poetic word itself the monster that thunders in "L'Etna de Mémoire"; see Brunel (1977, p. 268).

5. See Norwood (1956, pp. 101–5) on the poem's symbolic use of lyre, music, and harmony.

6. Diodorus Siculus 11.49.

7. Horace actually *imitates Pythian* 1 in another poem, *Carm.* 3.4 (cf. Williams 1969, pp. 53–54).

8. Cf. Coolidge (1968, pp. 85–100). Although Marvell is not usually regarded as a Pindarist, Finley says that, of the English poets, "Only Milton, Marvell and Gray greatly reflect him [Pindar]" (Finley 1955, p. 4).

9. For the suggestion of a snake, cf. *Iliad* 2.316 and 11.39.

10. On the representation of chaos as a snake, see Fontenrose (1959).

11. As H. Fraenkel (1975, p. 477) remarks in another context, "divine rule and amoral force can neither be separated nor united."

12. Skulsky (1975, pp. 11–12) notes the paradoxes but attributes them simply to Pindar's "delight" in stimulating his audience with paradoxes. Gantz (1974 passim) also remarks on the pervasive ambiguity in the conflict between Zeus and his enemies.

13. For the association of the bow with the lyre, see *Odyssey* 21.404–10.

14. Pindar here reverses the historical movement that Vernant (1982) has demonstrated, from mythical to philosophical cosmogo-

nies. The "monarchical" cosmogonies of myth distinguished "between the principle that exists chronologically at the beginning of the world and the prince who presides over its present arrangement." By using *arkhē* "to refer indiscriminately to the first in a temporal series and to primacy in a social hierarchy," the philosophical cosmogonies "abolished the distance on which myth was based" (p. 114). As I have demonstrated, Pindar next proceeds to abolish the "monarchical" distance that he has set up.

15. Skulsky (1975, p. 13) comments on *hagnotatoi*: "The word must be explained in the light of the dual role of Aetna as the symbol of Typhon's rage and of his punishment."

16. Cf. Cornford (1965, pp. 158–86).

17. The problem is really the phrase *pollōn peirata suntanusais* and, especially, the meaning of the problematic *peirar*. See Bergren (1975).

18. *Elpis* (hope) is the necessary spur to great deeds, but it is an ambiguous quality, tinged with *hybris*, in view of the uncertainty and lack of foresight that attends humanity (cf. *N.* 11.44–46).

19. See Crotty (1982, chap. 2).

20. Pindar's use of the middle voice in the phrase *baleth' halikian* ("cast down their youth," 74) suggested to Gildersleeve (1893, p. 250) that Pindar is thinking of the youth as an anchor (cf. *I.* 6.13). Skulsky (1975) takes up this suggestion and, pointing out that Aetna is compared to a ship at 33–35, argues that by hurling the enemy into the sea Hieron has in fact anchored his new ship securely (p. 22). Here again, there is a confusion of self and other insofar as the same word (*baleth'*) expresses both the destruction of the enemy and the safeguarding of Aetna.

21. Gantz (1974, p. 145) observes that Typhos stretches from the northern (Cumae) to the southern (Aetna) limit of Hieron's power and that he may therefore represent the repressed violence and hatred inherent in that kingdom. This would be compatible with the comparison of Hieron to Philoktetes.

22. The relation between the official Roman version of the cause of the war of Actium and the facts is described by Syme (1939, p. 270).

23. Translations of Horace throughout this chapter are mine.

24. See Commager's remarks on the poem's structure and imagery (1962, pp. 88–98). Syndikus (1972, p. 333) points out "Pindaric" elements of this poem's style, which it shares with the more obviously Pindaric imitations, *Carm.* 4.2 and 4.

25. The words *adulescentulus carnifex*, applied by Helvius Mancia to Pompey, could equally well apply to the young Octavian, whom Syme describes as a "chill and mature terrorist" (Syme 1939, p. 191).

26. Wallace (1968, pp. 91ff.) cites contemporary evidence of fears that Cromwell might return from Scotland as dictator or king.

27. I follow the text of Margoliouth (1971).

28. The Puritan conception of the relation between human action and God is described by Hill (1970, chap. 9). Hill stresses the Puritan demand that one cooperate *actively* with God's destiny, which is almost equivalent to the Hegelian force of historical development, rather than passively obey divinely constituted authority.

29. Margoliouth (1971, p. 237) cites Lucan's *successus urgere suos* (*Pharsalia* 1.149) as the inspiration for this phrase.

30. Wallace (1968, p. 74) points out that "Cromwell had taken his sword and succeeded, unlike the youths at Ariminium, in opposing Caesar's tyranny."

31. Lerner (1972, p. 63) describes Cromwell as "a force disruptive of nature which is nonetheless natural," and again "disruptive of society but nonetheless the product of inevitable social forces."

32. There is a third possibility: that *chase* may here be intransitive. See Donno (1972, p. 240).

33. Some editors print "borne." See H. Gardner (1972).

34. For contemporary arguments that Charles had, in effect, abdicated, see Wallace (1968, pp. 80–81).

35. Empson (quoted by Lerner 1972, p. 68) was the first to notice this translingual wordplay.

36. Lerner (1972) is particularly acute on the "keener eye" of the observer: "And in the scene of Charles on the scaffold, the poem is behaving like the Royal Actor; Marvell's keen eye hesitates over the puns and nuances; the language nothing common does or mean. In this assumption that to assess the brave new world one has to use an insight that is part of the old, Marvell adds, not satirically, but with complete grace, an extra dimension to his view of Cromwell that by the later, state poems has gone" (pp. 73–74).

37. Wallace (1968, p. 105) rightly connects the "party-colour'd Mind" that puns on the word "Pict" to the situation in England.

38. This proverb was, as Wallace notes (1968, pp. 96ff.), used both for and against Cromwell.

CHAPTER 7: FORM AND FORCE

1. Finley (1955, p. 45).

2. Cowley (1949).

3. Quoted and translated by Norwood (1956, p. 91).

4. Mullen (1982, p. 221).

5. Dionysius's *austēros harmonia* has been applied to the style of Hölderlin, under the translation *harte Fügung*. See Hellingrath (1936, pp. 20ff.).

6. *De Compositione Verborum* 22.

7. On Hopkins and Pindar, see Hines (1963), Bender (1966), and Anderson (1976).

8. W. H. Gardner (1953, pp. 10, 222).

9. The remarks occur in a letter dated 14 January 1883. See Bender (1966, p. 74).

10. See D. Young (1964).

11. My translation.

12. Fowler (1983, pp. 164–66) has some interesting speculations on the relation between Pindar's compositional style and the "cutting back" technique of archaic sculptors.

13. Van Groningen (1958) sees a loose but continuous construction as typical of archaic literature in general; cf. Fowler (1983, p. 164) and H. Fraenkel (1975, p. 505). Bernard (1963) stresses the role of associative imagery in the movement of Pindar's thought.

14. Bundy (1962, pp. 91–92).

15. "I am not concerned in this paper with the kind of rhetorical structure of encomiastic motifs studied by these authors [Bundy and Thummer] but rather with the latent, secondary structure created by contrasts and parallels between different sections of the ode" (Segal 1974a, p. 397). See also D. Young (1968).

16. Böschenstein-Schäfer (1971, p. 224).

17. Bender (1966, p. 94) points out that water in the "Wreck" manifests at once God's power and mercy. Hopkins must see in the same event and the same element manifestations both of natural power and divine mercy.

18. Böschenstein-Schäfer (1971, p. 232).

19. On this poem, see Hollander (1970, pp. 323–31) and Schlüter (1964, pp. 59–66).

20. Schlüter (1964, p. 59) casts the poem in tripartite prayer form, with apostrophe, myth, and closing prayer.

21. Notice that Milton refers to voice and verse as "Sirens." Schlüter insists upon the fact that the Sirens in Greek mythology were not always the dangerous seductresses of the *Odyssey* (compare Plato *Republic* 617b), but surely Milton cannot entirely neutralize the implications of this most famous appearance of the Sirens, as Schlüter would have us believe (1964, p. 60). Milton's attitude toward music is well described by Finney (1962, pp. 168ff.).

22. "Prayer, since the Fall, must needs be a consciously continued process, a work, in fact, of poetic art; it cannot be automatic and spontaneous as once it was before 'disproportion'd sin / Jarr'd against nature's chime'" (Hollander 1970, p. 329).

23. Though the date of "Ad Patrem" is disputed, it seems probable that, like "At a Solemn Music," it was written when Milton was in his twenties.

24. My translation.

25. In *Olympian* 9, Pindar states that, by contrast with the humble victory song of Archilochus, his poetry "will sweep with arrows like these / Zeus of the scarlet thunderbolt / And Elis' holy peak" (5–8). This act is associated with Herakles' battle against Hades and Poseidon (29–35), but the story of Herakles fighting with the gods is immediately rejected, since "to revile the gods is bad wisdom, and to boast beyond measure is an accompaniment to madness" (35–39).

26. Both Dornseiff (1921, p. 135) and Norwood (1956, pp. 78–79) draw attention to what they regard as the anticlimax of Pindar's endings.

27. Adorno's essay, "Parataxis zur späten Lyrik Hölderlins," appears in Schmidt (1970b, pp. 339–78).

28. My translation.

29. On "Mnemosyne," see Schmidt (1970a, pp. 50–80) and Unger (1975, pp. 206–20).

30. "Drum überraschet es auch / Und schrökt den sterblichen Mann / Wenn er er den Himmel, den / Er mit liebenden Armen / Sich auf die Schultern gehäufft, / Und die Last der Freude bedenkt."

31. See Adorno in Schmidt (1970b, pp. 371–72); de Man (1967–68, pp. 207–8) notes the inspiration of Rousseau's "Cinquième Promenade" on these lines.

32. H. Fraenkel (1975, p. 473) emphatically rejects the translation of *hen . . . hen* as "one . . . another."

CONCLUSION

1. In the context of the last chapter we should note that the verb *eukhomai* means both "boast" and "pray," producing the same dichotomy between assertion and deference that I have been examining in the relation between form and force.

2. *StA.* 2.252. My translation.

3. McLean (1981).

Bibliography

Allott, Miriam. 1970. *Keats: The Complete Poems.* London: Longmans.

Anderson, Warren. 1976. "'Never-Eldering Revel': The Wreck and the Ode Tradition." Pp. 128–41 in Peter Milward, S.J., ed., *Readings of the Wreck: Essays in Commemoration of the Centenary of G. M. Hopkins's The Wreck of the Deutschland.* Chicago: Loyola University Press.

Bate, Walter Jackson. 1963. *John Keats.* Cambridge, Mass.: Harvard University Press.

———. 1970. *The Burden of the Past and the English Poet.* New York: Belknap Press.

Bäumer, Max. 1973–74. "Dionysos und das Dionysische bei Hölderlin." *Hölderlin-Jahrbuch* 18, pp. 105–11.

Beissner, Friedrich, ed. 1946–77. *Friedrich Hölderlin. Sämtliche Werke.* 7 vols. Stuttgart: Kohlhammer.

———. 1933. *Hölderlins Übersetzungen aus dem Griechischen.* Stuttgart: Metzlersche.

Beissner, Friedrich, and Jochen Schmidt, eds. 1969. *Hölderlin: Werke und Briefe.* 2 vols. Frankfurt: Insel.

Bender, Todd. 1966. *Gerard Manley Hopkins: The Classical Background and Critical Reception of His Work.* Baltimore: Johns Hopkins University Press.

Benn, M. B. 1962. *Hölderlin and Pindar.* Mouton: 's-Gravenhage.

Bergren, Anne. 1975. *The Etymology and Use of Peirar in Early Greek Poetry.* (=American Classical Studies 2). Philadelphia: American Philological Association.

Bernard, M. 1963. *Pindars Denken in Bildern.* Pfullingen: Neske.

Binder, Wolfgang. 1970. *Hölderlin-Aufsätze.* Frankfurt: Insel.

Bloom, Harold. 1973. *The Anxiety of Influence.* Oxford: Oxford University Press.

———. 1982. *Agon: Towards a Theory of Revisionism.* Oxford: Oxford University Press.

Böschenstein, Bernhard. 1968. *Hölderlins Rheinhymne.* Zurich: Atlantis.

Böschenstein-Schäfer, Renate. 1971. "La Théologie du Signe dans les

Fragments Hymniques de Hölderlin." *Revue de Théologie et de Philosophie* Ser. 3, 21, pp. 221–39.

Boileau, Nicolas. 1966. *Oeuvres Complètes*. Paris: Gallimard.

Bowra, C. M. 1935. *Pindari Carmina cum Fragmentis*. Oxford: Oxford University Press.

Bowra, C. M., trans. 1969. *The Odes of Pindar*. Harmondsworth: Penguin.

Broadbent, John. 1960. "The Nativity Ode." Pp. 12–31 in Frank Kermode, ed., *The Living Milton: Essays by Various Hands*. London: Routledge and Kegan Paul.

————. 1972. *Paradise Lost, Books 1–2*. Cambridge: Cambridge University Press.

Brunel, P. 1977. "L'Ode Pindarique au XVIᵉ Siècle et au XXᵉ Siècle." *Revue de Littérature Comparée* 51, pp. 264–71.

Buck, J. 1975–76. "The Ascetic's Banquet: The Morality of *Alexander's Feast*." *Texas Studies in Language and Literature* 17, pp. 573–89.

Bundy, Elroy. 1962. *Studia Pindarica I and II*. Berkeley and Los Angeles: University of California Press.

Burckhardt, Jacob. 1929. *Griechische Kulturgeschichte*, vol. 2. Leipzig: Kröner.

Burton, R. W. B. 1962. *Pindar's Pythian Odes*. Oxford: Oxford University Press.

Butler, E. M. 1958. *The Tyranny of Greece over Germany*. Cambridge: Cambridge University Press.

Carne-Ross, D. S. 1985. *Pindar*. New Haven: Yale University Press.

Collinge, N. 1961. *The Structure of Horace's Odes*. London: Oxford University Press.

Commager, Steele. 1962. *The Odes of Horace: A Critical Study*. New Haven: Yale University Press.

Congreve, William. 1964. *The Works of William Congreve*, vol. 4. New York: Russell and Russell.

Coolidge, John. 1968. "Marvell and Horace." Pp. 85–100 in George Lord, ed., *Andrew Marvell*. Englewood Cliffs, N.J.: Prentice-Hall.

Cornford, Francis. 1965. *Principium Sapientiae*. New York: Harper and Row.

Cowley, Abraham. 1949. *Poetry and Prose*, ed. L. C. Martin. Oxford: Clarendon Press.

Crotty, Kevin. 1982. *Song and Action: The Victory Odes of Pindar*. Baltimore: Johns Hopkins University Press.

Culler, Jonathan. 1977. "Apostrophe," *Diacritics* 7, pp. 56–69.

de Man, Paul. 1966. "Wordsworth und Hölderlin." *Schweizer Monatshefte* 45 (2), pp. 1411–55.

————. 1967–68. "Hölderlin's Rousseaubild." *Hölderlin-Jahrbuch* 15, pp. 180–208.

Devereux, G. 1966. "The Exploitation of Ambiguity in Pindar's 0.3.27." *Rheinisches Museum* 109, pp. 289–98.
Dickie, M. W. 1976. "On the Meaning of *Ephēmeros.*" *Illinois Classical Studies* 1, pp. 7–14.
Dickson, Keith. 1982. "*Kairos* and the Anatomy of Praxis in Pindar." Diss., S.U.N.Y., Buffalo.
Donlan, Walter. 1980. *The Aristocratic Ideal in Ancient Greece.* Lawrence, Ks.: Coronado Press.
Donno, Elizabeth. 1972. *Andrew Marvell: The Complete Poems.* Harmondsworth: Penguin.
Dornseiff, Franz. 1921. *Pindars Stil.* Berlin: Weidmann.
Earl, Donald. 1967. *The Moral and Political Tradition of Rome.* London: Thames and Hudson.
Farenga, Vincent. 1977. "Violent Structure: The Writing of Pindar's Olympian 1." *Arethusa* 10, pp. 197–217.
Fehervary, Helen. 1977. *Hölderlin and the Left.* Heidelberg: Winter.
Fink, Markus. 1982. *Pindarfragmente: Neun Hölderlin Deutungen.* Tübingen: Niemeyer.
Finley, John. 1955. *Pindar and Aeschylus.* Cambridge, Mass.: Harvard University Press.
Finney, Gretchen. 1962. *Musical Backgrounds for English Literature, 1580–1650.* New Brunswick, N.J.: Rutgers University Press.
Fitzgerald, William. 1983. "Pindar's Second Olympian." *Helios* 10, pp. 49–70.
Fontenrose, Joseph. 1959. *Python: A Study of Delphic Myth and Its Origins.* Berkeley and Los Angeles: University of California Press.
Fowler, Barbara. 1983. "The Centaur's Smile: Pindar and the Archaic Aesthetic." Pp. 159–70 in Warren Moon, ed., *Ancient Greek Art and Iconography.* Madison: University of Wisconsin Press.
Fraenkel, Eduard. 1957. *Horace.* Oxford: Clarendon Press.
Fraenkel, Hermann. 1946. "Man's '*Ephemeros*' Nature according to Pindar and Others." *Transactions of the American Philological Association* 77, pp. 131–45.
———. 1975. *Early Greek Poetry and Philosophy,* trans. Moses Hadas and James Willis. Oxford: Basil Blackwell.
Frisk, Hjalmar. 1972–73. *Griechisches etymologisches Wörterbuch.* 2 vols. Heidelberg: Winter.
Fry, Paul. 1980. *The Poet's Calling in the English Ode.* New Haven: Yale University Press.
Gantz, Timothy. 1974. "Pindar's First Pythian: The Fire Within." *Ramus* 3, pp. 143–51.
Gardner, Helen, ed. 1972. *The New Oxford Book of English Verse.* Oxford: Clarendon Press.
Gardner, W. H. 1953. *Gerard Manley Hopkins: Poems and Prose.* Harmondsworth: Penguin.

Gelzer, T. 1981. "Pindarverständnis und Pindarübersetzung im deutschen Sprachbereich vom 16. bis zum 17. Jahrhundert." Pp. 81–115 in Walther Killy, ed., *Geschichte des Textverständnis am Beispiel von Pindar und Horaz.* Munich: Wolfenbüttler.

Gerber, Douglas. 1962. "What Time Can Do (Pindar, *Nemean* 1.46–47)." *Transactions of the American Philological Association* 93, pp. 30–33.

———. 1982. *Pindar's Olympian One: A Commentary.* Toronto: University of Toronto Press.

Gildersleeve, Basil. 1893. *Pindar: The Olympian and Pythian Odes.* London: Macmillan.

Gordon, Ian. 1967. "Keats and the English Pindaric." *Review of English Literature* 8, 2, pp. 9–23.

Gouldner, Alvin. 1965. *Enter Plato: Classical Greece and the Origins of Social Theory.* New York: Basic Books.

Griffith, R. H. 1919–20. "The Progress Pieces of the Eighteenth Century." *Texas Review* 5, pp. 218–33.

Guardini, Romano. 1955. *Hölderlin: Weltbild und Frommigkeit.* Munich: Kosel.

Gundert, Hermann. 1935. *Pindar und sein Dichterberuf.* Frankfurt: Klosterman.

Hamburger, Michael, trans. 1980. *Hölderlin: Poems and Fragments.* Cambridge: Cambridge University Press.

Hamilton, Richard. 1974. *Epinikion: General Form in the Odes of Pindar.* The Hague: Mouton.

Harrison, Robin. 1975. *Hölderlin and Greek Literature.* Oxford: Clarendon Press.

Hartman, Geoffrey. 1970. "Blake and the Progress of Poetry." Pp. 193–205 in Hartman, *Beyond Formalism.* New Haven: Yale University Press.

Hegel, G. W. F. 1977. *Phenomenology of Spirit,* trans. A. V. Miller. Oxford: Oxford University Press.

Hellingrath, Norbert von. 1936. *Hölderlin–Vermächtnis, Forschungen und Vorträge.* Munich: Bruckmann.

Henkel, Arthur. 1981. "'Der deutsche Pindar.' Zur Nachahmungsproblematik im 18. Jahrhundert." Pp. 173–93 in Walther Killy, ed., *Geschichte des Textverständnis am Beispiel von Pindar und Horaz.* Munich: Wolfenbüttler.

Herder, J. G. 1967–68. *Sämtliche Werke.* Hildesheim: G. Olms.

Highet, Gilbert. 1949. *The Classical Tradition: Greek and Roman Influences on Western Literature.* Oxford: Oxford University Press.

Hill, Christopher. 1970. *God's Englishman: Oliver Cromwell and the English Revolution.* London: Weidenfeld and Nicolson.

Hines, Leo. 1963. "Pindaric Imagery in G. M. Hopkins." *The Month* 29, pp. 294–307.

Hoey, Thomas. 1965. "Fusion in Pindar." *Harvard Studies in Classical Philology* 70, pp. 235–62.

Hollander, John. 1970. *The Untuning of the Sky: Ideas of Music in English Poetry, 1500–1700*. New York: W. W. Norton.

———. 1975. *Vision and Resonance: Two Senses of Poetic Form*. Oxford: Oxford University Press.

Hošek, Chaviva, and Patricia Parker, eds. 1985. *Lyric Poetry: Beyond New Criticism*. Ithaca, N.Y.: Cornell University Press.

Hughes, Merritt. 1957. *John Milton: Complete Poems and Major Prose*. Indianapolis: Odyssey.

Huxley, George. 1975. *Pindar's Vision of the Past*. Belfast: [The author].

Illig, Leonard. 1932. *Zur Form der Pindarischen Erzählung*. Berlin: Junker und Dünnhaupt.

Johnson, W. R. 1982. *The Idea of Lyric: Lyric Modes in Ancient and Modern Poetry*. Berkeley and Los Angeles: University of California Press.

Killy, Walther. 1970. "Hölderlins Interpretation des Pindarfragments 166." Pp. 294–319 in Jochen Schmidt, ed., *Über Hölderlin*. Frankfurt: Insel.

Kinsley, James. 1962. *The Poems and Fables of John Dryden*. Oxford: Oxford University Press.

Kirk, G. S., and J. E. Raven. 1957. *The Presocratic Philosophers*. Cambridge: Cambridge University Press.

Koch, Wilhelm. 1927. "Das Fortleben Pindars in der deutschen Literatur von den Anfängen bis Andreas Gryphius." *Euphorion* 28, pp. 195–218.

Köhnken, Adolf. 1971. *Die Funktion des Mythos bei Pindar: Interpretationen zu sechs Pindargedichten*. Berlin: de Gruyter.

Kromer, Gretchen. 1976. "The Value of Time in *Olympian Ten*." *Hermes* 104, pp. 420–36.

Lacoue-Labarthe, Philippe. 1979. "Hölderlin et les Grecs." *Poétique* 40, pp. 465–74.

Lattimore, Richmond. 1951. *The Iliad of Homer*. Chicago: University of Chicago Press.

———. 1976. *The Odes of Pindar*. Chicago: University of Chicago Press.

Lefkowitz, Mary. 1963. "*To Kai Ego*: The First Person in Pindar." *Harvard Studies in Classical Philology* 67, pp. 28–39.

Lempicki, Z. 1930–31. "Pindare Jugé par les Gens de Lettres du XVIIᵉ et du XVIIIᵉ Siècle." *Bolletin Nationale de l'Académie des Sciences et des Lettres de Cracovie*, pp. 28–39.

Lerner, L. D. 1972. "Marvell: An Horatian Ode." Pp. 59–74 in John Wain, ed., *Interpretations: Essays on Twelve English Poems*. London: Routledge and Kegan Paul.

Lonsdale, Roger. 1969. *The Poems of Gray, Collins and Goldsmith.* London: Longmans.

Maclaren, I. S. 1981. "Milton's Nativity Ode: The Function of Poetry and Structures of Response in 1629." *Milton Studies* 15, pp. 181–200.

Maclean, Norman. 1952. "From Action to Image: Theories of the Lyric in the Eighteenth Century." Pp. 408–60 in R. S. Crane, ed., *Critics and Criticism, Ancient and Modern.* Chicago: University of Chicago Press.

McLean, William Scott. 1981. "Private Song and the Public Sphere: Some Remarks on the Development of Hölderlin's Later Poetry." Pp. 265–80 in *Goethezeit: Studien zur Erkenntnis und Rezeption Goethes und seiner Zeitgenossen. Festschrift für Stuart Atkins.* Bern: Francke.

Maddison, Carol. 1960. *Apollo and the Nine: A History of the Ode.* Baltimore: Johns Hopkins University Press.

Mähler, Herwig. 1963. *Die Auffassung des Dichterberufs in frühen Griechentum bis zur Zeit Pindars.* Göttingen: Vandenhoeck and Ruprecht.

Margoliouth, H. M. 1971. *Marvell's Poems and Letters,* 2 vols. Oxford: Clarendon Press.

Miner, Earl. 1967. *Dryden's Poetry.* Bloomington: Indiana University Press.

Monk, Samuel. 1960. *The Sublime: A Study of Critical Theories in XVIII Century England.* Ann Arbor: University of Michigan Press.

Mullen, William. 1982. *Choreia: Pindar and Dance.* Princeton, N.J.: Princeton University Press.

Nägele, Rainer. 1978. *Literature und Utopie: Versuche zu Hölderlin.* Heidelberg: Stiehm.

———. 1982. "Fragmentation und Feste Buchstab: Zu Hölderlin's Patmos-Überarbeitungen." *MLN* 97 (3), pp. 556–73.

Newman, J. K. 1967. *The Concept of Vates in Augustan Poetry.* Brussels: Latomus.

Newman, J. K., and F. S. Newman. 1984. *Pindar's Art: Its Traditions and Aims.* Hildesheim: Weidmann.

Nierhaus, Rolf. 1936. *Strophe und Inhalt im Pindarischen Epinikion.* Wurzburg: Triltsch.

Nietzsche, Friedrich. 1954. *The Portable Nietzsche,* ed. Walter Kaufmann. New York: Viking.

Nisetich, Frank. 1980. *Pindar's Victory Songs.* Baltimore: Johns Hopkins University Press.

Norwood, Gilbert. 1956. *Pindar.* Berkeley and Los Angeles: University of California Press.

O'Brien, William. 1979. "Getting Blasted: Hölderlin's 'Wie Wenn am Feiertage. . . .'" *MLN* 94, 3, pp. 569–86.

Parfitt, George. 1975. *Ben Jonson: The Complete Poems.* New Haven: Yale University Press.

Randel, Fred. 1981. "The Mountaintops of English Romanticism." *Texas Studies in Language and Literature* 23, pp. 294–323.

Redfield, James. 1975. *Nature and Culture in the Iliad.* Chicago: University of Chicago Press.

Robinson, David. 1936. *Pindar: A Poet of Eternal Ideas.* Baltimore: Johns Hopkins University Press.

Rose, Peter. 1974. "The Myth of Pindar's First *Nemean:* Sportsmen, Poetry and Paideia." *Harvard Studies in Classical Philology* 78, pp. 147–75.

———. 1982. "Towards a Dialectical Hermeneutic of Pindar's Pythian X." *Helios* 9, 1, pp. 47–76.

Rosenmeyer, Thomas. 1969. "The Rookie: A Reading of Pindar's *Nemean* 1." *California Studies in Classical Antiquity* 2, pp. 233–46.

Rühmkorff, Peter. 1978. *Strömungslehre 1.* Hamburg: Reinbeck.

Ryan, Lawrence. 1960. *Hölderlins Lehre vom Wechsel der Töne.* Stuttgart: Kohlhammer.

Saint-John Perse. 1972. *Oeuvres Complètes.* Paris: Gallimard.

Sattler, D. E. 1975. *Friedrich Hölderlin. Frankfurter Ausgabe. Einleitung.* Frankfurt: Roter Stern.

Scaliger, Julius Caesar. 1964. *Poetices Libri Septem* (facsimile edition of Lyon, 1561). Stuttgart: Frommann.

Schadewalt, Wolfgang. 1928. *Der Aufbau der Pindarischen Epinikion.* Halle: Niemeyer.

Schaerer, René. 1958. *L'Homme Antique et la Structure du Monde Intérieur.* Paris: Payot.

Schiller, Friedrich. 1966. *Werke in drei Bänden.* Munich: Hanser.

Schlegel, Friedrich. 1961. *Geschichte der alten und neuen Literatur.* Munich: Schöningen.

Schlüter, Kurt. 1964. *Die Englische Ode.* Bonn: Bouvier.

Schmidt, Jochen. 1970a. *Hölderlins letzte Hymnen.* Tübingen: Niemeyer.

———, ed. 1970b. *Über Hölderlin.* Frankfurt: Insel.

Segal, Charles. 1964. "Pindar's First and Third *Olympian Odes.*" *Harvard Studies in Classical Philology* 68, pp. 211–67.

———. 1967. "Pindar's Seventh *Nemean.*" *Transactions of the American Philological Association* 98, pp. 431–80.

———. 1974a. "Arrest and Movement: Pindar's Fifth *Nemean.*" *Hermes* 102, pp. 397–411.

———. 1974b. "Time and the Hero: The Myth of *Nemean* 1." *Rheinisches Museum* 117, pp. 29–39.

Seifert, Albrecht. 1982. *Untersuchungen zu Hölderlins Pindar-Rezeption* (=Münchner Germanistischer Beiträge, 32), Munich: Fink.

———. 1982–83. "Die Rheinhymne und ihre Pindarische Modell:

Struktur und Konzeption von Pythian 3 in Hölderlins Aneignung." *Hölderlin-Jahrbuch* 23, pp. 79–133.

Shafer, Robert. 1918. *The English Ode to 1660: An Essay in Literary History*. Princeton, N.J.: Princeton University Press.

Shepherd, W. G., trans. 1983. *Horace: The Complete Odes and Epodes with the Centennial Hymn*. Harmondsworth: Penguin.

Sherwin, Paul. 1977. *Precious Bane: Collins and the Miltonic Legacy*. Austin: University of Texas Press.

Shuster, George. 1940. *The English Ode from Milton to Keats*. New York: Columbia University Press.

Simpson, Michael. 1969. "The Chariot and the Bow as Metaphors for Poetry in Pindar's Odes." *Transactions of the American Philological Association* 100, pp. 437–73.

Skulsky, S. D. 1975. "*Pollōn peirata suntanusais:* Language and Meaning in *Pythian* 1." *Classical Philology* 70, pp. 8–31.

Slater, Philip. 1968. *The Glory of Hera: Greek Mythology and the Greek Family*. Boston: Beacon Press.

Slater, W. J. 1969. "Futures in Pindar." *Classical Quarterly* (n.s.) 19, pp. 86–94.

Snell, Bruno. 1953. *The Discovery of the Mind: The Greek Origins of European Thought*, trans. T. G. Rosenmeyer. Oxford: Blackwell.

Spacks, S. Patricia. 1966. "Artful Strife: Conflicts in Gray's Poetry." *PMLA* 81, 1, pp. 63–69.

Spitzer, Leo. 1948. *Linguistics and Literary History: Essays in Stylistics*. Princeton, N.J.: Princeton University Press.

Sprat, Thomas. 1957. "An Account of the Writings of Mr. Abraham Cowley." Pp. 119–46 in J. E. Springarn, ed., *Critical Essays of the Seventeenth Century*, vol. 2. Bloomington: Indiana University Press.

Stern, Jacob. 1969. "The Myths of Pindar's *Nemean* 10," *Greek, Roman and Byzantine Studies* 10, pp. 125–32.

Stierle, Karlheinz. 1980–81. "Dichtung und Auftrag: Hölderlins Patmos Hymne." *Hölderlin-Jahrbuch* 22, pp. 47–65.

Swayne, Mattie. 1936. "The Progress Pieces of the Seventeenth Century." *University of Texas Bulletin* 16, pp. 84–92.

Syme, Ronald. 1939. *The Roman Revolution*. Oxford: Oxford University Press.

Syndikus, Hans. 1972. *Die Lyrik des Horaz: Eine Interpretation der Oden*. 2 vols. Darmstadt: Wissenschaftliche Buchgesellschaft.

Szondi, Peter. 1967. *Hölderlin-Studien*. Frankfurt: Insel.

Unger, Richard. 1975. *Hölderlin's Major Poetry: The Dialectics of Unity*. Bloomington: Indiana University Press.

Van Groningen, B. A. 1958. *La Composition Littéraire Archaïque Grecque*. Amsterdam: Noord-Hollandsche Uitg.

Vernant, Jean-Pierre. 1982. *The Origins of Greek Thought*. Ithaca, N.Y.: Cornell University Press.

Vernant, Jean-Pierre, and Marcel Detienne. 1974. *Les Ruses de l'Intelligence: La Mètis des Grecs.* Paris: Flammarion.

Vivante, Paolo. 1972. "On Time in Pindar." *Arethusa* 5, pp. 107–31.

Voltaire, François. 1877–85. *Oeuvres Complètes.* Paris: Garnier.

Waisinger, Kenneth. 1976. "Hölderlin's 'Wie Wenn am Feiertage' and Its Pindaric Model." *Monatshefte für deutsche Unterricht, deutsche Sprache und deutsche Literatur* 68, 3, pp. 257–69.

Wallace, John. 1968. *Destiny His Choice: The Loyalism of Andrew Marvell.* London: Cambridge University Press.

Warminski, Andrzjey. 1976. "Patmos: The Senses of Interpretation." *MLN* 19, 3, pp. 488–500.

Warton, Joseph. 1782. *Essay on the Genius and Writings of Pope.* 2 vols. London: J. Dodsley.

Wasserman, Earl. 1967. "Collins's 'Ode on the Poetical Character.'" *ELH* 34, pp. 92–115.

Wayne, Don. 1979. "Poetry and Power in Ben Jonson's *Epigrammes:* The Naming of Facts or the Figuring of Social Relations." *Renaissance and Modern Studies* 23, pp. 79–103.

Weiskel, Thomas. 1976. *The Romantic Sublime.* Baltimore: Johns Hopkins University Press.

West, Gilbert. 1749. *The Odes of Pindar.* London: n.p.

Wickham, Edward. 1963. *Q. Horati Flacci Opera.* Oxford: Clarendon Press.

Williams, Gordon. 1969. *The Third Book of Horace's Odes.* Oxford: Clarendon Press.

Wilson, John R. 1980. "KAIROS ab 'Due Measure'," *Glotta* 58, 3, pp. 177–204.

Winckelmann, Johann. 1808–20. *Werke.* 8 vols. Dresden: Walther.

Young, David. 1964. "Pindaric Criticism." *Minnesota Review* 4, pp. 584–641.

———. 1968. *Three Odes of Pindar.* Leiden: Brill.

Young, Edward. 1854; repr. 1968. *The Complete Works of Edward Young.* 2 vols. Hildesheim: Olms.

Zernin, V. 1965. Review of M. B. Benn, *Hölderlin and Pindar. Comparative Literature* 17, pp. 177–82.

Zucker, Friedrich. 1955. "Die Bedeutung Pindars für Goethes Leben und Dichtung." *Das Altertum* 1, pp. 171–86.

Zuntz, Gunther. 1928. *Über Hölderlins Pindar Ubersetzung.* Marburg: Thiele und Schwarz.

Index

Abbruchsformel (break-off formula), 74, 170
Absolute, 7, 44–45, 73, 192
Achilles, 84–86
Actium, 151, 154
Adorno, Theodor, 183–84
Aeneas, 86
Aeschylus, 173
Aetna, 140–47
Agōn, x, 1, 7, 140, 141, 142, 149–50, 188, 191
Alatheia, 221n18
Alcaeus, 152
Alexander, 113, 124–28
Anaximander, 10
Anteriority, xi, 192
Antony, 151, 153
Anxiety of influence, *chapter 4 passim*
Apeiron, 10–11
Apollo, 84–86
Asclepios, 34–36
Augeas, 117–21
Augustus, 76, 78, 80
Austēros harmonia, 171–72, 226n5

Bacchus, 37, 42
Bacchylides, 203n2
Bate, W. J., 86–87
Binder, Wolfgang, 216n24
Bloom, Harold, xi, 1, 84, 109, 192, 218n19
Böschenstein-Schäfer, Renate, 177
Boileau, Nicolas, 140, 169, 204n4, 218n17
Bowra, C. M., xiii
Buck, J., 226n26, 226n31
Bundy, Elroy, 176, 205n8
Burckhardt, Jakob, 205n12, 206n5

Caesar, Julius, 168
Cecilia, Saint, 124–25, 127
Charles I, 160–69
Choral, x, 11–17, 184–88, 191
Claudel, Paul, 212n27
Cleopatra, 141, 151–59
Closure, resistance to, x, 21–24, 192
Collins, William ("Ode on the Poetical Character"), 87, 94–99
Community, x, 7, 19–20, 70
Congreve, William, 139, 223n1
Coronis, 34–35, 37
Cosmogony, 10–11, 145–46, 189, 224n14
Cowley, Abraham, 44, 139, 170, 215n55
Cromwell, Oliver, 142, 159–69

Danaids, 173
Daedalus, 81, 83
Deconstruction, xi
De Man, Paul, 130, 223n37, 223n41
Demi-god, 113, 130–32
Diderot, Denis, 204n6
Dionysius of Halicarnassus, 171, 173, 174
Dioscuri syndrome, 3–7, 13
Dryden, John, 93; "Alexander's Feast," 112–13, 114, 124–29; "Song for St. Cecilia's Day" (1687), 125
Duncan, Robert, 224n4

Envy (*Phthonos*), 10, 36
Ephemerality, 10, 207n20
Epicurus, 92
Epinikion, ix, 150, 178
Eukhos, 2–3, 191, 228n1

Eupolis, 203n4
Eustathius, 203n4

Finley, John, 170, 224n8
Flattery, ix, 203n3
Fraenkel, Hermann, 207n19,
    208n39, 208n40, 224n11
Frankfurter Ausgabe (of Hölderlin),
    208n33
Fry, Paul, ix, 13–15, 89, 126, 219n35,
    222n29, 222n30

Ganymede, 123–24, 221n14
Gods and humans, 2–3, 7–10,
    34–44, 48–52, 58–59, 124–38 *pas-
    sim, chapter 7 passim*
Goethe, Johann Wolfgang, 73, 130,
    208n41, 221n11
Gray, Thomas: influence of Horace
    on, 87, 88, 89, 91–92; "Progress of
    Poesy," 84, 87–94
Gundert, Hermann, 138

Hagesidamos, 115–23
Hamburger, Michael, xiii
Hannibal, 168
Hartman, Geoffrey, 220n39
Hegel, G. W. F., 2, 7, 206n6, 207n15,
    209n45
Herakles, 32, 48–49, 54–62, 74,
    111–12, 115, 117–22, 133–34
Herder, J. G., 73, 217n5
Hermes, 17
Hieron, 34–36, 140–41, 148–49
Hill, Christopher, 226n28
Hölderlin, Friedrich: the Athletic in,
    49–50; attitude to the Greeks,
    100–101, 104–5; conception of
    poetry, 13, 69–72; Empedocles in,
    69; *Metaphor* in, 129, 132; Nature
    in, 102; Pindaric influence, xi, 16,
    38, 39–40, 48–49, 102, 103,
    115–16, 205n15, 209n46, 213n44,
    214n45, 214n48, 215n3, 217n23;
    and presocratics, 10–11; religious
    syncretism in, 6, 16–17, 65, 177;
    and revolution, 17, 38, 81, 115;
    river in, 115, 130
—Works: "Am Quell der Donau,"

101–9; "An Eduard," 115; *Anti-
gone* translation, 103–5; "Brod
    and Wein," 45; "Buonaparte," 116;
    "Das Werden im Vergehen,"
    221n9; "Der Einzige," 15; "Der Is-
    ter," 48–49, 207n14; "Der Rhein,"
    7, 9, 113–14, 115–16, 129–38,
    185–86; Letter to Böhlendorff, 49;
    "Mnemosyne," (2nd version)
    207n14, (3rd version) 183, 185–
    87; "Patmos," *chapter 3 passim;*
    Pindar fragments, 44; "Uber reli-
    gion," 216n19; "Wenn aber die
    Himmlischen," 6; "Wie wenn am
    Feiertage," 37–44
Hollander, John, 227n22
Homer, 1–2, 7–8
Hopkins, G. M., 44, 215n55; outride
    in, 172–73; sprung rhythm in,
    172; underthought in, 173; "The
    Wreck of the Deutschland," 72,
    172–73, 177
Hōra, 14
Horace, 44; Pindaric influence, 76,
    77, 78, 79–86, 154, 158, 215n55,
    224n7, 225n24; Republic and Prin-
    cipate in, 76, 78–80
—Works: *C.1.2*, 80–81; *C.1.37*, 141,
    151–59; *C.2.20*, 219n16; *C.3.1*, 77;
    C.3.5, 78; *C.4.2*, 80—83, 101;
    C.4.6, 84, 219n33; *Carmen
    Saeculare*, 84–85; *Epode 9*, 151
Hymn, xi, 13–17
Hyperboreans, 54

Icarus, 81
Influence, xiii. *See also* Gray; Höld-
    erlin; Horace; Milton
Invocation, 13–15
Io, 173
Isaiah, ix, 33, 213n36

Johnson, Samuel, 129
Johnson, W. R., x
Jonson, Ben, 5, 22–24, 44
Jouve, Pierre-Jean, 224n4

Kadmos, 36
Kairos, 10, 147, 158, 207n19

Keats, John, 6–7, 25–26, 187–88, 189–90, 210n17
Klopstock, F. G., xi, 63, 73, 223n37
Kōmos, 19
Koros, 10, 11, 147
Krisis, 10–11
Kromer, Gretchen, 221n18, 221n20, 221n22
Kydos, 2

Lerner, Lawrence, 226n36
Limits (mortal), 54–55, 60–61, 74–75, 118
Longinus, 204n4
Lyric, x, 192

Marvell, Andrew: "Horatian Ode," 142, 159–69
Mediation, 37, 48
Milton, John, 87, 92–93, 98–99; Pindaric influence, 32, 212n29, 212n32, 212n33; "At a Solemn Music," 179–82; "Ad Patrem," 182; "On the Morning of Christ's Nativity," 13, 31–32, 44, 90–91
Miner, Earl, 222n26
Mode, 113, 129
Mousikē, x
Mullen, William, 74, 272n25
Music, 114, 124–25, 144, 146–47, 179–82

Narrative and image, 87, 94
Newmans, J. K. and F. S., 1, 209n1
New Testament, 68–69
Nietzsche, Friedrich, 205n12, 218n13
Niobe, 84, 86
Nisetich, Frank, x
Norwood, Gilbert, 173–74, 176

O'Brien, William, 213n42
Octavian, 151–59 *passim*. *See also* Augustus
Ode, xi, 13–17, 140
Oedipus, 134
Olympia, 126
Openness of text, 13
Orpheus, 133

Peira, 11, 25
Peleus, 8–9, 36
Pelops, 15, 27–28, 38, 46
Perrault, Charles, 204n4
Philippi, 159
Philoktetes, 150–51
Phya, 25, 142, 161
Pindar: and archaic thought, 170; and Athenian empire, 209n50; conception of *agōn*, 11; conception of poetry, 11–12, 20–21, 52–53, 83, 218n18; debt in, 29–31, 117–23; difficulty of, 203n1; endings, 61, 108, 182–83; gnome in, 74–76, 183; influence of, *see* Hölderlin, Horace, Milton; invocations in, 14, 208n39; narrative in, 74–76, 84, 118–19; order of the odes, 211n19; pindarizing, xiii; and political change, 17; reputation of, ix, 203n4, 204n6, 224n1; triad in, 11, 12, 113, 150
—Works: *Olympian 1*, 15, 25, 26–28, 33, 60–61, 178; *Olympian 2*, 75, 211n21; *Olympian 3*, 33–34, *chapter 3 passim*, 74, 178; *Olympian 6*, 74, 174–76, 177; *Olympian 9*, 212n32, 228n25; *Olympian 10*, 29–31, 117–24; *Olympian 14*, 178; *Pythian 1*, 139–51, 207n21; *Pythian 3*, 34–37, 95–96; *Pythian 4*, 215n57; *Pythian 6*, 74; *Pythian 8*, 20, 55, 183; *Pythian 10*, 54, 74–75, 83, 206n1; *Pythian 12*, 184, 206n1; *Nemean 1*, 111–12, 134; *Nemean 5*, 21, 24, 140, 213n39; *Nemean 6*, 3, 188–89; *Nemean 8*, 14, 214n47; *Nemean 10*, 4; *Isthmian 8*, 8, 20, 213n39; *Fr. 12*, 21
Pindaric, 44, 73, 76, 87, 124, 139, 214n55, 223n1
Pindaric mode, 13–17
Plato, 23, 223n43
Praise, 19–33, 110
Praiser as competitor, 19, 28–29, 31–33, *chapter 5 passim*, 212n25
Priamel, 77
Progress poem, 73–74, 87, 100
Prometheus, 133, 182

Quintilian, 87, 203n4

Recusatio, 80
Redfield, James, 209n4
Regulus, 78–79
Return, 20
Ring-composition, 74, 78
River as Pindaric image, 73, 80–81,
    89, 101, 221n11
Ronsard, Pierre, xii, 44, 204n4,
    215n55
Rousseau, Jean-Jacques, 131,
    134–35, 223n40, 223n42, 228n31
Rühmkorff, Peter, 203n3

Sarpedon, 1–2, 17
Scaliger, Julius Caesar, 204n4
Schaerer, René, 129
Schiller, Friedrich, 99
Segal, Charles, 177, 211n23
Semele, 37–38, 41–43, 72
Shakespeare, William, 87, 91–92,
    151
Shlüter, Kurt, xi, 13
Sinklair, Eduard, 15, 131, 137
Socrates, 131, 136
Solon, 210n7
Soothern, John, 204n4
Spenser, Edmund, 94, 98–99
Stesichoros, 87, 221n17
Subjectivity, 1, 12, 16, 62–64,
    69–70, 129, 184–88, 190, 191,
    208n29, 216n29

Sublime, 99, 219n37
Symposium, 152
Szondi, Peter, 43–44, 213n40,
    214n52

Tantalos, 38, 213n43
Themis, 8
Theognis, 17, 210n7
Thetis, 8–9
Time, 112, 114, 121–23
Timotheus, 113, 124–29
Typhos, 145–46

Vates, 77, 79, 217n10
Vernant, Jean-Pierre, 224n14
Vivante, Paolo, 223n24
Voltaire, François, 203n3

War, 1, 206n7
Warminski, Andrzjey, 216n29
Weckherlin, Georg, 204n4
Weiskel, Thomas, 219n37
West, Gilbert, 224n1
Williams, Gordon, 218n11
Winckelmann, Johann, 100–101

Young, Douglas, 219n28

Zaleukos, 221n17
Zeus, 143

Compositor: G & S Typesetters, Inc.
       Text: 10/12 Palatino
   Display: Palatino
   Printer: Braun-Brumfield, Inc.
    Binder: Braun-Brumfield, Inc.